The Secret of Poetry

The Secret of Poetry

Essays by Mark Jarman

Story Line Press | *Pasadena, CA*

The Secret of Poetry

ISBN 978-1-58654-361-7 (tradepaper)
       978-1-58654-359-4 (casebound)

The National Endowment for the Arts, the Los Angeles County Arts Commission, the Ah-
manson Foundation, the Dwight Stuart Youth Fund, the Max Factor Family Foundation,
the Pasadena Tournament of Roses Foundation, the Pasadena Arts & Culture Commission
and the City of Pasadena Cultural Affairs Division, the City of Los Angeles Department
of Cultural Affairs, the Audrey & Sydney Irmas Charitable Foundation, the Kinder Morgan Foundation, the Meta & George Rosenberg Foundation, the Allergan Foundation, the
Riordan Foundation, Amazon Literary Partnership, and the Mara W. Breech Foundation
partially support Red Hen Press.

Second Edition
Published by Story Line Press
an imprint of Red Hen Press
www.redhen.org

Acknowledgments

The essays and reviews collected in this book appeared in the following publications, sometimes in different versions:

"Aspects of Robinson," *AWP Chronicle*, December 1997, V. 30, N. 3

"Br'er Rabbit and Br'er Possum: The Americanness of Ezra Pound and T.S. Eliot," *Forked Tongues?: Comparing Twentieth Century British and American Literature*, eds. Ann Massa and Alistair Stead, Longman, 1994

"Contemporary Mannerism: American Poetry Slips into Something Comfortable," *Kayak*, September 1980, N. 54

"The Curse of Discursiveness," *The Hudson Review*, Spring 1992, V. XLV, N. 1

"The Grammar of Glamour: The Poetry of Jorie Graham," *The New England Review*, Fall 1992, V. 14, N. 4

"In Memory of Orpheus: Three Elegies by Donald Justice," *ELF: Eclectic Literary Forum*, V. 8, N. 2, Summer 1998

"John & Randall, Randall & John: On the Poetry of John Berryman and Randall Jarrell," *The Gettysburg Review*, Autumn 1991, V.14, N.4

"Letter from Leeds," *The Hudson Review*, Autumn 1990, V. XLIII, N. 3

"Narrative Beauty in Booklength Poems," *The Gettysburg Review*, Fall 1989, V. 2, N. 4

"Poetry and Religion," *Poetry After Modernism*, ed. Robert McDowell, Story Line Press, 1991, pp. 134–174

"The Pragmatic Imagination and the Secret of Poetry," *The Gettysburg Review*, Fall 1988, V.1, N.4

"Robinson, Frost, and Jeffers, and the New Narrative Poetry," *Expansive Poetry*, ed. Frederick Feirstein, Story Line Press, 1989

"A Scale of Engagement, from Self to Form Itself," *The Hudson Review*, Summer 1987, V.XL, N.2

"Shifting Sands: *The Columbia History of American Poetry*," *The Hudson Review*, Winter 1995, V. XLVII, N. 4

"Sheathed in Reality: Clare Walker in Robinson Jeffers's 'The Loving Shepherdess'": American Literature Association Convention, Baltimore, MD, May 1993

"Singers and Storytellers," *The Hudson Review*, Summer 1986, V. XXXIX, N. 2

"Solving for X: The Collected Poetry and Prose of Wallace Stevens," *The Hudson Review*, Spring 1998, V. LI, N. 1

I should like to thank these publishers for permission to reprint the following poems:

"A Pact" from *Personae* by Ezra Pound, copyright 1926. Reprinted by permission of New Directions Publishing, Corp.

"Germanicus Leapt" from *Collected Poems 1937–1971* by John Berryman, copyright 1989. "Hook" from *To a Blossoming Pear Tree* by James Wright, copyright 1977. Reprinted by permission of Farrar, Straus & Giroux, Inc.

"On the Death of Friends in Childhood," "In Memory of My Friend, the Bassoonist, John Lenox," "In Memory of the Unknown Poet, Robert Boardman Vaughn," "Invitation to a Ghost" from *New and Selected Poems* by Donald Justice, copyright 1995. Reprinted by permission of Alfred Knopf, Inc.

"Silver Slur" from *The Ghost of Eden* by Chase Twichell, copyright 1995. Reprinted by permission of Ontario Review Press.

"Sleeping in the Forest" from *New and Selected Poems* by Mary Oliver, copyright 1993. Reprinted by permission of Beacon Press, Inc.

"Sorrow Figure" from *The Niobe Poems* by Kate Daniels, copyright 1988. Reprinted by permission of the University of Pittsburgh Press.

"Then Sings My Soul" from *Salvage Operations: New and Selected Poems* by Paul Mariani, copyright 1990.

This book is for Frederick Morgan and Paula Deitz

Contents

Part I
Essays

Part II
Reviews

Part I

Essays

1

Poetry and Religion

Man needs a metaphysics;
he cannot have one.
—Frank Bidart

... logic doesn't stand a chance, a prayer.
—Andrew Hudgins

Just as poetry persists in the face of widespread indifference, so has a sense of the religious in poetry continued to exist despite the indifference of most poets to religion. It might be better to modify the word *indifference* or to refract it into ignorance, nostalgia, and animosity. Nevertheless, the religious impulse in poetry endures; many poems being written today show that urge to be tied to or united with or at one with a supernatural power that exists before, after, and throughout creation. I plan to draw most of my examples from contemporary American poetry, with counterpoint examples from the English past during the greatest period of devotional verse and from modern American poetry wherein the breakdown of an institutional and monolithic religious view began to be clear. Even the more or less devout among religious poets today suspect the institution of religion, and not as Dante and Milton did, because of its corruption, but because of the requirements of orthodoxy.

I do not believe that there is one genre of religious poetry being written in America today, as there was in England in the 17th century, despite the appearance of recent anthologies like *Contemporary Religious Poetry*, edited by Paul Ramsey, and *Odd Angles of Heaven*, edited by David Craig and Janet McCann. In fact, these anthologies include many who profess no religion and might have written their religious verse inadvertently. Still, religion is important to contemporary poetry. For poets who have grown up with strong religious training, it provides a background, usually a violent one. The desire for atonement, secularized by the Romantic movement, takes a characteristic form in American poetry about nature. The imagination, in Wallace Stevens' terms, provides a substitute for God for some poets, and the need for alternative, non-Christian myths fills the gap for others. When alternatives fail, poets may still try to make peace with present circumstances and regard grace or mercy with almost theological reverence. T. S. Eliot's "Ash Wednesday" and "Four Quartets," two of the greatest achievements at uniting religion and poetry in this century, loom over the vestigial modes of the religious poem in our time. Even contemporary readings of Eliot's poems, emphasizing their secular themes, suggest that they embody all the approaches to religion and poetry taken by Eliot's grandchildren and great grandchildren. Finally, there are exceptions—poems written out of genuine religious conviction that do not beg the question of belief but, in fact, call non-belief itself into question.

I

Batter my heart, three-personed God; for You
As yet but knock, breathe, shine, and seek to mend;
That I may rise and stand, o'erthrow me, and bend
Your force to break, blow, burn, and make me new.
I, like an usurped town, to another due,
Labor to admit You, but O, to no end;
Reason, Your viceroy in me, me should defend,
But is captived, and proves weak or untrue.
Yet dearly I love You, and would be loved fain,
But am betrothed unto Your enemy.
Divorce me, untie or break that knot again;
Take me to You, imprison me, for I,
Except You enthrall me, never shall be free,
Nor ever chaste, except You ravish me.

—John Donne

The language of overthrow, assault, abduction, and rape still gives Donne's poem its vigor; for him and his first readers, violence is redemptive; Christ's sacrifice for us is harrowing. Like Saint Theresa, Donne invites a sexual assault; some argue that he meant the poem to shock the readers of his own day. Yet today the language of violence, with some exceptions, still has an impact. The taking and holding and retaking of towns recalls the feudal importance of the city state, but the news today is full of similar battles. The Platonic argument for Reason as a viceroy might seem especially dated, both for the French notion of the king's representative, but also for the belief that reason represents a higher power. What is current still is the mingling of abduction, divorce, chastity, rape; we still see these actions played out in the popular media, even though we have an increasingly complex political response to them. To wit, violence against a spouse or lover is never justifiable. We suspect sexuality that includes violence, even among consenting adults. We can read Donne's poem within its 17th century context as playing with a radical paradox, making the most carnal of metaphors out of God's grace, and see it as the poem of a believer who may even relish the discomfort his final metaphor will give the puritanical. What is striking today, as it was then, is the combination of violence, and especially sexual violence, and religion.

For Donne this combination sprang from the intensity of his religious feeling. For the contemporary American poet steeped in some religious background, the combination of religion and violence springs from the intensity of his feeling *about* religion. More often than not it is an intense feeling about religion's failure to explain or redeem the world. Still, the most highly charged language available to the poet is the language of faith. Sometimes it is the problem of still having a religious bent that hangs the poet up.

In Frank Bidart's "Confessional," the poet confronts the division between a unified religious view of experience and the belief that such a view is impossible. Religion is the problem in the poem; when the speaker's mother has had her conversion experience, she kills her son's pet cat to demonstrate denial of the world. Clearly the speaker's mother is mad. It is less clear if the speaker is conversing with a priest or with an analyst whose job is to show him that "forgiveness," that virtue neither mother nor son could show to each other, "doesn't exist." The speaker contrasts his relationship with his mother and St. Augustine's with his mother, St. Monica. He calls "The scene at the window at Ostia / in Book Nine of the *Confessions*" one "to make non-believers / / sick with envy . . ." The speaker envies the supernatural closeness of Monica and Augustine. After the scene in which they meditate on the lives of the saints, Monica feels her relationship with her son, converted now to Christianity as she had wished him to be, is "complete" as we might say in contemporary psychological terms; thus satisfied, she dies nine days later. But it appears that the poet Bidart, who paraphrases the *Confessions* so beautifully, is sick with envy for another thing—the immediate experience of God without the veil of nature. He must conclude, speaking now as the listener, priest, or analyst, *"Man needs a metaphysics; / he cannot have one."* How violence is manifested may be at the heart of this problem. Killing a pet cat is a far cry from "NO

REMISSION OF SINS / WITHOUT THE SHEDDING OF BLOOD";
the psychological violence between mother and son also yields no salvation.
When he learned that his mother miscarried his stepbrother or sister the
day she saw a man fall from a tree and lie screaming on the ground at a golf
course, the speaker recalls that he was "GLAD." Perhaps, salvation through
violence and the completion of relationships happens only to others, like St.
Augustine and his mother, people in other times and other places, characters
so distant that the idea that forgiveness does not exist or that man cannot
have a metaphysics has no effect on them. The pathos of this supposition is
contemporary and ours alone.

A number of poets share Bidart's nostalgia for faith, especially those who
have recognized its transforming power in others and have some experience of
it in their own lives. But they approach the subject obliquely, as if they would
not be taken seriously otherwise. Bidart contrasts stark denial and its equally
stark irresolution with the richness of resolution and belief, yet concludes that
the latter is impossible. Andrew Hudgins in "Prayer" shows the embedding
of religious experience, most of it Southern fundamentalism, in his life, and
its strongest vestige in him today—prayer, "of all things I've given up to logic / . . . the one I can't / let go . . ." In a two-part poem, he devotes the first
part to ringing changes on ecstatic religious utterance as he recalls hearing a
woman in church holler, *"Hep me, Jesus! Hep me, Jesus!,"* then hearing another in a backwoods Baptist revival cry, *"Hurt me, Jesus! Hurt me, Jesus Lord!,"*
and finally in a cheap motel hearing a woman scream, *"Fuck me, Jesus! / Fuck
me, Jesus!"* To the last he responds drily, "It must have been a prayer." But in
part two of the poem he confesses that having learned his girlfriend had been
raped at seventeen, he cannot convince himself that it doesn't bother him and
that, implicitly, he will not leave her, even though she says she will understand
if he does. He confronts the impotence of prayer, as he employs it, and the fact
that "when I put my hands on friends and say, / *Be healed*, nobody yet has
been healed." Though the analytical, logical voice of Bidart's confessor might
intone, "Prayer is useless," Hudgins compares his urge to pray to "the virtues
of a vicious circle, why / a mother suckles her contagious child, / or why the
victim has to be rebuked." Hudgins does not appeal to Donne's viceroy, Reason, but to its opposite. Against this, "logic doesn't stand a chance, a prayer."
Hudgins describes a persistent faith that is still useless against violence.

In terms of the world, it has always been so. The world's urge toward violence ends, in Christian mythology, in the murder of God Himself. It is an

article of faith, based on the accounts of a few witnesses, that the man who admitted to being God was resurrected from the dead. No amount of belief in Him averted the catastrophe. The orthodoxy of the Christian church, both Catholic and Protestant, maintains that the event was necessary, even while condemning those who brought it about. "NO REMISSION OF SINS / WITHOUT THE SHEDDING OF BLOOD." No chastity without ravishment. Yet how can we see metaphorical redemption in such violence, when we cannot see redemption in literal fact?

Violence within a religious context still shocks us, even when we know that violence is an essential part of religion. Thus, David Dooley's "Revelation" is as disturbing as any of Flannery O'Connor's stories for much the same reason; it drops the catalyst of violence into a world of religious faith and produces a monstrous shape. Dooley's poem narrates the story of a clergyman who takes a boy, probably a young male prostitute, in off the streets and tries to give him a new life, only to learn that he has murdered a little girl in the neighborhood and stowed her body in the basement room where he has been put up. The poem is full of the vocabulary of religion, but when the preacher sees the child's body and remarks, "Precious Jesus, the blood," Dooley demands that we think twice: once about the statement and the literal fact of the victim's blood; once about the precious blood of Jesus which, if we think of it at all, we remember only in figurative terms, even though it, too, was a literal fact. Here, the redemptive blood and the convicting blood have nothing to do with one another. The minister lets the boy escape, giving him his car to get away, then to himself tries "to name all the authorities who must be notified." The violence at the heart of Christianity, which allows Donne to create his great paradox, no longer maintains its metaphorical meaning in the contemporary poem that includes religion. Its literalness is a sign that religious poetry, like Donne's, is impossible.

II

Love bade me welcome: yet my soul drew back,
　　　Guilty of dust and sin.
But quick-eyed Love, observing me grow slack
　　　From my first entrance in,
Drew nearer to me, sweetly questioning
　　　If I lacked anything.

"A guest," I answered, "worthy to be here":
　　　Love said, "You shall be he."
"I, the unkind, ungrateful? Ah, my dear,
　　　I cannot look on thee."
Love took my hand, and smiling did reply,
　　　"Who made the eyes but I?"

"Truth, Lord; but I have marred them; let my shame
　　　God where it doth deserve."
"And know you not," says Love, "who bore the blame?"
　　　"My dear, then I will serve."
"You must sit down," says Love, "and taste my meat."
　　　So I did sit and eat.

—George Herbert

Aggressive violence is not the only metaphor, of course, for the way God calls his own. Herbert's famous "Love (III)" presents an entirely different human milieu, in which God offers his grace courteously, requiring only humble acceptance (rather than humble refusal). By taking the mystery of the Eucharist and turning it into a simple domestic meal, Herbert expresses a desire for a gentler atonement than Donne's. In American poetry, in most poetry since the Romantic era, this desire is clearest in poems about the natural world.

The poet William Matthews has observed humorously that American literature is "thick with forest Christians" and that the theme of many nature poems is "I went out into the woods today and it made me feel, you know, sort of religious." The satire is effective because of its self-evidence. Matthews' lampoon depicts American poetry of the natural world, but it certainly doesn't eradicate it. Perhaps the too fluent poet of nature will be rendered a little more self-conscious. What interests me, however, is how in approaching the mystery with religious respect, American poets anthropomorphize nature, even to the point of domesticating it, as Herbert does Love, in order to make it inviting, and most importantly, inviting to us.

James Dickey does this in "In the Tree House at Night." Having built his ladder up into the tree, he and his brothers, "one dead, / The other asleep from much living," rest above "lakes / Of leaves" and "fields disencumbered of earth / That move with the moves of the spirit." In this case, Dickey makes the spirit of nature one with that of the dead brother; it "touches the tree at the root" and sends "A shudder of joy" up the trunk. As important as the biographical detail is (Dickey has another poem about this brother who died before he was born), the drama of the poem is to invest nature with a believable spirit, e.g. a dead brother's, so that communication with nature can seem human, specific, domestic, and not merely oceanic; Dickey does have poems, of lesser quality, with larger and vaguer aspirations. The idea that his dead brother's spirit, once he has located himself deep and high inside the natural world, may be inhabiting his own body allows him these powerful lines which still may convey the conventional Romantic goal of nature poetry

> My green, graceful bones fill the air
> With sleeping birds. Alone, alone
> And with them I move gently.
> I move at the heart of the world.

The dead brother has been reincarnated in the tree, and Dickey, through an act of Keatsian empathy, knows how that feels, and thus in a complicated interplay makes a metaphor of atonement. It is the religious impulse that leads to such a poem, one of gentle invitation and submission, but the impulse is separate from any recognizable religion.

"Sleeping in the Forest" by Mary Oliver is a quieter, less dramatic, and even clearer expression of the desire for atonement, but the desire is for unification with nature rather than with God.

> I thought the earth
> remembered me, she
> took me back so tenderly, arranging
> her dark skirts, her pockets
> full of lichens and seeds. I slept
> as never before, a stone
> on the riverbed, nothing
> between me and the white fire of the stars

but my thoughts, and they floated
light as moths among the branches
of the perfect trees. All night
I heard the small kingdoms breathing
around me, the insects, and the birds
who do their work in the darkness. All night
I rose and fell, as if in water, grappling
with a luminous doom. By morning
I had vanished at least a dozen times
into something better.

This is a poem of faith just like Donne's or Herbert's, but based on a fundamental belief that we share, at least as American readers, that nature or the earth is better than the world where we actually do our living. Earth, personified as having not only memory but "dark skirts" and "pockets," appears as a classical female deity, Mother Earth. She accepts the speaker, like Herbert's Love, "tenderly." But the actual atonement occurs while the speaker sleeps, like Jacob's vision of the angelic ladder. Now Oliver loses her humanity and becomes "a stone" which presumably has "thoughts" that interpose between it and "the white fire of the stars." I hesitate to look too closely at Oliver's poem, since it is deeply flawed as a poem (for example, how can she hear if she's asleep?), but its flaws are part of its faith. The stone is on a riverbed, but perhaps it is a dry riverbed; the stone's thoughts are compared to moths. And the trees the moths play about are perfect. Dream logic justifies all. Thus, thought and hearing unite the poet with nature: thought, hearing, and sleep. It is a sleep like water, perhaps like the river's water that might move a stone up and down all night (one can't look too closely), in a dream where the speaker grapples with "a luminous doom." The most interesting phrase in the poem, it suggests that literal unification with nature would result in doom for the poet; but dreamed of this way, it takes on an inviting luminosity. The poet dreams of a dozen transformations into something better than what she is on waking and, implicitly, on having to leave this setting. She has gone out into the woods and felt more than "sort of religious." Nevertheless, "Sleeping in the Forest" is a definite example of American forest Christianity.

Robinson Jeffers' late poem "Vulture" offers something a bit sterner than either Dickey's or Oliver's poems, but with the same underlying belief. Jeffers' refusal to anthropomorphize gives the poem is austerity. Yet, in the pantheistic view of nature I have been describing, the idea of reconstitution as reincarnation is strong; certainly it is implicit in the Christian sacrament of communion. Jeffers' poem resonates across religious boundaries, even though he presents his view as an alternative to them all:

I had walked since dawn and lay down to rest on a bare hillside
Above the ocean. I saw through half-shut eyelids a vulture wheeling high up in heaven,
And presently it passed again, but lower and nearer, its orbit narrowing, I understood then
That I was under inspection. I lay death-still, and heard the flight-feathers
Whistle above me and make their circle and come nearer.
I could see the naked red head between the great wings
Bear downward staring. I said, "My dear bird we are wasting time here.
These old bones will still work; they are not for you." But how beautiful he looked, gliding down
On those great sails; how beautiful he looked, veering away in the sea-light over the precipice. I tell you solemnly
That I was sorry to have disappointed him. To be eaten by that beak and become part of him, to share those wings and those eyes—
What a sublime end of one's body, what an enskyment; what a life after death.

Did I say he did no anthropomorphize the bird? But what is an address to an inhuman presence, concrete or abstract, but a recasting of that inhuman other into human terms? Still, the eating here does not involve suffering, but organic recycling. No wonder Jeffers has been claimed, or reclaimed, by the environmentalists. He says mostly the right things about the natural world, the orthodox things. Jeffers could be called a prophet for their movement; he could be called a priest of nature poetry; depending up on how you see the sad development of the wild land around Tor House, his home in Carmel, California, he might even be thought of as a martyr, and partly because of the decline of his reputation. But his reputation did not decline because of his romanticism or his religious faith in the natural world as an expression of God, in fact, as God itself. It declined because of his loathing for humanity, his absolute contempt for humanity's place in the grand scheme of things. Even forest Christians might find this hard to swallow—but Jeffers was one of them.

III

Those—dying then,
Knew where they went—
They went to God's Right Hand—
That Hand is amputated now
And God cannot be found—

The abdication of Belief
Makes the Behavior small—
Better an ignis fatuus—
Than no illume at all—

—Emily Dickinson

We say God and the imagination are one . . .
How high that highest candle lights the dark.

—Wallace Stevens

For poets who make a religion of nature, albeit one rooted in the romantic faith in one's intuitive, singular response to experience without the intercession of orthodoxy or institutionalized ritual, I have tried to show that at least one of the aspirations is the same—atonement or a oneness that implies forgiveness. Just as Love's meal will make one better, so will sleeping in the forest at night. Note that missing from these examples is the desire to be ravished or ravaged by a greater power. There is good reason for this, but I'll go into that later. The subject of this section is how a poet makes an alternative to religion or to a given monolithic belief; that is, here I wish to discuss the role of the imagination and the poet as its priest.

Emily Dickinson's poem of 1882, written four years before her death, makes "The abdication of Belief" a practical ethical problem; to have no belief shrinks the compass of one's "Behavior." The key word is "Belief." Dickinson offers, with true American horse sense, the preferability of a deceptive hope, a fool's fire, to none at all, for it is that which gives illumination. Again, she does not appeal to reason, although she makes a reasonable appeal. She recognizes the necessity of an illumination to live by. Remaking the imagination has been as much an American project as reclaiming the continent.

In contemporary terms, the substitution of the imagination for a traditional belief in God has included the replacement of Christian and Judaic myths with myths reclaimed from the past or from other cultures. Leslie Silko's "Prayer to the Pacific" invokes an ancient native American myth of origin.

> Thirty thousand years ago
>   Indians came riding across the ocean
>   carried by giant sea turtles.
> Waves were high that day
>   great sea turtles waded   slowly out
>   from the gray unknown
>   sea.
> Grandfather Turtle rolled in the sand four times
>   and disappeared
>   swimming into the sun.
>
> And so from that time
>   immemorial,
>   as the old people say,
>   rain clouds drift from the west
>   gift of the ocean.

In "Prayer to the Pacific" Silko refers to the Pacific as being "Big as the myth of origin," then enters into the animistic faith that endows the natural world with spiritual identity. At the same time she identifies herself with her own native American ancestors. Quite apart from the quality of the poem, its religious foundation must enjoy our assent; we must not quarrel with it. Thus, we may read Leslie Silko's revival of an Indian myth with none of the doubt we might experience reading a contemporary poem of equal faith about the birth of Christ, because she has remade the religious imagination without asking us to accept it as part of an orthodoxy or institution. We acknowledge what she has done as an act of imagination.

Quality of the composition, the excellence of the art, is, however, indivisible from authentic religious feeling in poetry. In this way, Robert Pinsky's "The Figured Wheel" is a masterful Ecclesiastical *memento mori*, while at the same time appropriating a symbol and sentiment from the old Peter, Paul, and Mary hit, "The Great Mandala":

> Take your place on the Great Mandala
> As it moves through your brief moment of time.
> Win or lose now, you must choose now.
> And if you lose you're only losing your life.

So went the song, which was also a parable protesting the war in Vietnam. Pinsky's poem achieves a greater semantic thickness, and thus extends the significance of the mandala far beyond the limits of the popular song:

> The figured wheel rolls through shopping malls and prisons,
> Over farms, small and immense, and the rotten little downtowns.
> Covered with symbols, it mills everything alive and grinds
> The remains of the dead in the cemeteries, in unmarked graves and oceans . . .

> . . . the wheel hums and rings as it turns through the births of stars

> And through the dead-world of bomb, fireblast and fallout
> Where only a few doomed races of insects fumble in the smoking grasses.
> It is Jesus oblivious to hurt turning to give words to the unrighteous,
> And is also Gogol's feeding pig that without knowing it eats a baby chick

> And goes on feeding.

As a metaphor for the irresistible force of the cosmos, Pinsky's figured wheel, whereon even his own death and annihilation are "figured and pre-figured," is undeniable, for he combines the old myths of Jesus and the mandala itself with the news myths of science and global unity. The wheel is covered with "Hopi gargoyles and Ibo dryads" as well as "wind-chimes and electronic in-struments." To write a religious poem, a poem in which some binding belief is at work, a poem in which as Philip Wheelright states in the *Princeton Encyclopedia of Poetry and Poetics* there is "an imaginative fusion of the elements of experience and a responsive faith in a reality transcending and potentially sanctifying the experience," the author must possess some grain of faith that the concrete details of his metaphor represent a transcendent reality. Pinsky's poem has to be considered a religious poem, though certainly not a devotion-al one like one of Donne's or Herbert's addresses to a personal, loving, though mysterious God. Pinsky creates a terrifying juggernaut, offering no salvation from ultimate destruction. Yet the wheel's all inclusiveness invites our belief. It offers a kind of mercy, but only to:

> . . . dead masters who have survived by reducing themselves magically

> To tiny organisms, to wisps of matter, crumbs of soil,
> Bits of dry skin, microscopic flakes, which is why they are called "great,"

In their humility that goes on celebrating the turning
of the wheel as it rolls unrelentingly . . .

The adverb "magically" has a whiff of Emily Dickinson's "ignis fatuus" but the relative clause, "which is why they are called great," contains Pinsky's own brand of irony—a necessary cynicism in the face of his monolithic metaphor. If we assent, finally, to the religious view of "The Figured Wheel," then we accept an imaginative substitute for many religious myths, both Western and Eastern. An affirmation of art lurks throughout Pinsky's poem. If "God and the imagination are one," as Stevens says in "Final Soliloquy of the Interior Paramour," then it is through art that we worship them.

Christianity and its traditional icons rarely enter contemporary poetry as a source of devotional attention or religious celebration, but more often as art or as a stimulus to the imagination to make art—its religion. For if the imagination is God, then for poets, poetry is its church. In Jorie Graham's "Pietà" the purpose is to communicate the visual effect of a picture in the belief that, if successfully communicated, it will put one in touch with some transcendent reality, whose nature is relative. After a description of light on the broken body of Jesus, of how Mary holds him, how the soldiers cast lots for his garment, "blazing where the light snags on the delicate / embroidery, and black where the neck-hole gapes," the resurrection is prefigured in the statement that the body, missing from the garment, is "the form / gone." Formal qualities move Graham throughout the poem, because, whether abstract or figurative, form in a piece of art evokes feelings and creates meaning. At the end of the poem, we are asked if we hear "the spirit of / / matter." And "the proof of god" becomes a "cry sinking to where it's / / just sound, part of one sound, one endless sound—maybe a cry maybe a / / countdown, love—" The word "countdown" is charged with its contemporary meaning, for Graham associates the death of Christ with the annihilation of the earth (Graham plays on this analogy throughout her recent work). She asks us to believe in this death as representative of all deaths and not as a divine act in which our sins are forgiven and death is defeated. For Graham, art is the highest good, the transcendent reality that will itself be lost if we destroy ourselves. This recognition has separated the violence in Christianity into another, terrible category, and set apocalypse apart as an end to avoid and not accept as the completion of a divine plan.

Christopher Buckley's "Why I Am in Favor of a Nuclear Freeze" enunciates this division, this belief that nuclear annihilation has nothing to do with a divine scheme, or with the idea of Omega, the end of time, built into Christian myth and other religious systems. Buckley reminisces about being with a friend as teenagers, hunting doves on his friend's father's ranch, and talking about various things, including their days in parochial school.

> We even talked of the nuns
> who terrified us with God and damnation. We both recalled
> that first prize in art, the one pinned to the cork board
> in front of class, was a sweet blond girl's drawing
> of the fires and coals, the tortured souls of Purgatory.

Not to acknowledge the crucifixion as suffered for our sakes leads to condemnation to far worse suffering. This way of scaring people, especially children, repels the two friends. But armed with their 12 gauge shotguns, they shoot doves, and at one point the poet accidentally discharges his gun, narrowly missing his friend's head and his own foot. Then, when they come upon "two tall ears" in the dry grass, he admits "we together blew the ever-loving Jesus out of a jack rabbit / until we couldn't tell fur from dust from blood . . ." One of their nuns would call this gratuitous violence a manifestation of original sin. Yet Buckley's conclusion is much the same and meant to suggest the larger potential for a final violence against ourselves and nature. Recalling that day of hunting with his old friend, now a family man with children, who, like the speaker, doesn't hunt any more, the poet asks about the rabbit, "why the hell had we killed it so cold-heartedly?" The poem's final statement illuminates its title: "it was simply because we had the guns, because we could."

Granted, the poem is a personal statement explaining why the poet is, as he says in the title, in favor of a nuclear freeze. But a Roman Catholic grounding in the agonies of damnation and the essential corruption of man also ties together the elements of the poem. It is a poem with a religious background, and plays with the poet's alienation through phrases like "ever-loving Jesus" and "why the hell." Still, it may also be seen as a religious poem. For though it makes the distinction clear between Omega and annihilation, it implies that with the right, or the wrong, weapons, man will cause destruction, because of his innate depravity, his original sin.

The poem as prayer against nuclear annihilation became a genre unto itself during the Cold War. It is curious to note how often such poems play against the Christian notion of the end of days. Chase Twichell's "When the Rapture Comes, I Will Depart Earth (Sign seen in a car window in Kansas)" takes a secular view of this idea; that is, Twichell offers no particular religious background for her statement, but she uses religious vocabulary when she writes, "What should we pray / to the smoke and bone of the grass? / That its death light our way into otherness?" And she ends with a secular prayer, an appeal more to those of like mind, those who would regard the sign in the car window as silly at best and at worst somewhat frightening:

> When the rapture comes,
> let the car continue through the woods
> unharmed by miracles.
> And if a fierce, atomic heaven falls,
> let it stop us in an ordinary act.

Finally, poems like Buckley's and Twichell's appeal to us to forgo notions of transcendent reality, especially religious ones, for they depend inevitably on the end of *this* reality, the one in which we are at home with our ordinary acts, like the acts of the imagination, "unharmed by miracles."

IV

There is not any haunt of prophecy
Nor any old chimera of the grave...
...that has endured
As April's green endures...

—Wallace Stevens

*The poem is about the majesty of our planetary world, than which no greater
majesty is available to the human senses; no world beyond nor world to come
that perception can find or imagination invent.*

—John Crowe Ransom
on "Sunday Morning"

Poetry that takes the imagination as God and presents atonement as the creation of art or the experience of it also holds the earth as the highest reality. Thus, John Crowe Ransom reads Stevens' "Sunday Morning." Thus, we find the total destruction of nuclear war abhorrent both for its fact and for its fictional part in the myth of the end, of Omega, and in any religious belief that would subvert existence as we have come, finally, to appreciate it, including especially the Christian belief in judgment. And yet spiritual yearning still exists, and being at one with a painting or a landscape or a natural phenomenon, some inhuman force, itself mortal or inorganic (Jeffers' granite, for example), does not satisfy that yearning. Often its expression hearkens back nostalgically to a former assurance. Charles Wright is the master of this sentiment and its language:

Ancient of Days, old friend, no one believes you'll come back
No one believes in his own life anymore.

—"Stone Canyon Nocturne"

In his book *Zone Journals*, Wright reiterates his regret and adds a comment about the limitations of language and therefore of the imagination.

—Words, like all things, are caught in their finitude.
They start here, they finish here

No matter how high they rise—

                               my judgement is that I know this

And never love anything hard enough

That would stamp me

                and sink me suddenly into bliss.

—"Night Journal"

When Wright does recognize and admit to feeling the sort of transcendence or unity a religious poet depicts, it is with natural cycles, in traditional American fashion, though not exactly as in the nature poetry of Dickey or Oliver. "Bays Mountain Covenant" offers an austere, Zenlike resolution, still taking the natural world as the paradigm.

> Sir you will pardon him you will wave if he now turns
> To the leaf to the fire in the swamp log to the rain
> The acorn of crystal at the creek's edge which prove
> Nothing expect nothing and offer nothing
> Desire no entrance and harbor no hope of change
> Foxglove that seeks no answer nightshade that seeks no answer
> Not to arrive at and be part of but to take
> As the water accepts the whirlpool the earth the storm.

Only Jeffers might have taken the imagination and its earthly dominion to this logical end. Wright's spirituality, like his, is austere, even forbidding.

For lesser mortals, those moments when we call on the assistance of a power greater than ourselves or feel that still point in the turning world when we are capable of blessing because we feel blessed, the language of our religion, whatever that religion it might be, comes into play, because it is the language that is most highly charged with feeling. Lest that sound like circular reasoning, let me restate myself to say that religious language, whether it is Christian or Buddhist, exists because it expresses religious feeling most powerfully. It was invented, manmade, to describe states attributed to a divine presence.

Sydney Lea's "Sereno" begins as a poem of the American in the wild, feeling that solitary union the American poet seeks with nature. Then the poem changes to another issue entirely. Hunting duck in December, in the northeast, the poet is suddenly struck by the unusual warmth of the wind, "wafting / forgiveness here." Just as he lets his quarry go, so he lets go a catalog of forgiveness, including himself in the list:

> I forgive all beings in their desperation:
> murdered, murderer; mothers, fathers wanting something
> the children they bring forth can't give;
>
> Myself for my own childhood cruelties—
> the way I taunted Nick Sereno
> (*serene*, a thing that neighbor never was,
>
> Dark hungry victim, bird-boned butt of my deceptions . . .
> the time I decoyed him out onto the raft
> and cut him loose, and jumped.
>
> I cut the frail hemp tether, and off he drifted, quacking fear).
> And I forgive the fact that cruelty can circle:
> grown he paid me back one night in a steaming gin mill.

Lea opposes Bidart's assurance that forgiveness doesn't exist. He knows "There is more to all this than I allow." There is, indeed. The idea of forgiveness is rooted deeply in the belief in a merciful God. To forgive, even if aided by circumstances conducive to feeling good, like a warm wind in December, is still a spiritual discipline. It's not easy.

It's not easy invoking the elements of a faith we have grown to mistrust or grown away from simply because of the pressures of life, especially in a culture that either ignores the religious or offers it up in the crudest, most simplistic, and bigoted forms. Many of Garrett Hongo's poems deal with the deracinated Japanese of Hawaii and the mainland U.S. who have kept traditions alive, sometimes in the face of deliberate persecution. In "O-Bon: *Dance for the Dead*" he recognizes that the most potent way to redeem the memories of his dead father and grandfather, to keep familial feeling alive, is through invocation of Buddhist ritual. Yet he confesses:

> I have no story to tell about lacquer shrines
> or filial ashes, about a small brass bell,
> and incense smoldering in jade bowls, about the silvered
> black face of Miroku gleaming with detachment,
> anthurium crowns in the stoneware vase
> the hearts and wheels of fire behind her.

He has tried to observe rituals:

. . . pitched coins and took my turn
　at the *taiko* drum, folded paper fortunes
　and strung them on the graveyard's *hala* tree . . .

Though he has hewed to the requirements of faith, still "the cold sea chafes the land and swirls over gravestones / and the wind sighs its passionless song through ironwood trees." Rarely does the earth send the warm wind at the right time to inspire us with blessèdness. Our only approach to the divine, to a force powerful enough to forgive us, appears to be a route of ritual and language whose potency is as mysterious as the goal itself. And as unpredictable:

I want the cold stone in my hand to pound the earth,
I want the splash of cool or steaming water to wash my feet,
I want the dead beside me when I dance, to help me
flesh the notes of my song, to tell me it's all right.

Hongo ends his poem with a supplication to spirits out of his reach. Their paradoxical response, if it comes at all, comes without warning and often without invitation. T. S. Eliot represents it as the intersection of the timeless moment and the temporal world. He is the great poet of this experience and I turn now to him.

V

This the time of tension between dying and rebirth.

—"Ash Wednesday"

Who then devised the torment? Love.

—"Little Gidding"

In his essay, "Grace Dissolved in Place: A Reading of *Ash Wednesday*," Ver-een Bell argues that "what happens or fails to happen in 'The Waste Land' produces the experience of 'Ash Wednesday,' and what happens or fails to happen in 'Ash Wednesday' issues eventually in the disconsolate theological affirmations of the plays and the 'Four Quartets.'" Or, in other words, "As 'Ash Wednesday' was latent in 'The Waste Land,' so the 'Four Quartets' is latent in 'Ash Wednesday,' an alternative when the quest in 'Ash Wednesday,' perhaps because the result is foreseen, fails." The quest Bell speaks of is for "redeemed time," for "grace dissolved in place," and "not a transcendence of time altogether," as a religious reading of the poem might seek. Bell's stated intention is to do a secular, psychological reading; by so doing, he helps us better to understand what persists in our poetry and links it to religious poetry. The plea "Ash Wednesday" ends with—"Suffer me not to be separated / / And let my cry come unto Thee"—is, Bell claims, for a union of flesh and spirit in the natural world, *this* world; or, as T. S. Eliot himself writes, "even among these rocks." Certainly that describes the yearning for a greater wholeness or spiritual integrity that marks the poetry I have discussed so far.

But what of the "disconsolate theological affirmations" Bell alludes to in "Four Quartets"? Bell quotes these lines about "the gifts reserved for age" in part II of "Little Gidding."

> . . . the cold friction of expiring sense
> Without enchantment, offering no promise
> But bitter tastelessness of shadow fruit
> As body and soul begin to fall asunder.

These lines are spoken by the "dead master." The poet meets him "In the uncertain hour before morning." The master extends his advice, which is practical as well as theological, from the realm of experience, which Eliot himself has already entered. But not all of the "theological affirmations" of the poem are "disconsolate," unless one refuses to accept redemption on their terms.

"Burnt Norton," the most secular of the four poems because of its avoidance of theological language, presents the "grace dissolved in place" that Bell perceives as the heart of "Ash Wednesday." It is there in the rose garden, where "rises the hidden laughter / Of children in the foliage . . ." In "Burnt Norton" Eliot describes "the still point of the turning world" in a number of paradoxes. Finally, Eliot resorts to Dante's metaphor of the prime mover (drawn from Aquinas).

> Love is itself unmoving,
> Only the cause and end of movement,
> Timeless, and undesiring
> Except in the aspect of time
> Caught in the form of limitation
> Between un-being and being.

"Love," the mover of all things, unmoved by "the tension between dying and birth" in "Ash Wednesday" and all the riot of experience that swirls and hurries over the brown land of "The Waste Land," reveals itself to Eliot in "Burnt Norton," because of his oblique approach, through paradox. Still, his appropriation of the Thomist meaning of Love, and his syntax, which is reminiscent of the beginning of the Gospel of John, testify to the power of religious language, even when approached indirectly and perhaps precisely because of that indirect approach.

"East Coker" continues this approach, maintaining that "To arrive where you are, to get from where you are not, / You must go by a way wherein there is no ecstasy," and proceeds with the famous allegory of redemption as an act of surgery:

> The wounded surgeon plies the steel
> That questions the distempered part;
> Beneath the bleeding hands we feel
> The sharp compassion of the healer's art
> Resolving the enigmas of the fever chart.

Here we learn that "the whole earth is our hospital / Endowed by the ruined millionaire," Adam. Here also, turning bizarrely on the medical metaphor, Eliot introduces his memorable depiction of Purgatory:

> If to be warmed, then I must freeze
> And quake in frigid purgatorial fires
> Of which the flame is roses, and the smoke is briars.

The surgical poet here has exposed the violent heart of Christianity, where suffering is the way to salvation. The paradox works against common sense, as all paradoxes do; but even when we resolve it intellectually and recognize its innate truth, we still must make sense of another paradox—the strange contract or covenant between this God, the wounded surgeon, and his patients:

> The dripping blood our only drink,
> The bloody flesh our only food:
> In spite of which we like to think
> That we are sound, substantial flesh and blood—
> Again, in spite of that, we call this Friday good.

Here is a disconsolate affirmation, indeed.

"The Dry Salvages" adds to it, but not as powerfully (it is the weakest of the four poems), extending a metaphor of seafaring and addressing us, the readers, as "O voyagers, O seamen" who "suffer the trial and judgement of the sea." Eliot brings Krishna in here, too, and alludes to his admonition to Arjuna in the *Upanishads* that there is no death because the killer cannot truly kill, even though the battle must be fought. As with "East Coker," part IV is the lyrical passage containing the Christian element of the poem; it addresses the Queen of Heaven in Dante's terms as "daughter of your son" or "Figlia del tuo figlio" and beseeches her to:

> . . . pray for those who were in ships, and
> Ended their voyage on the sand, in the sea's lips
> Or in the dark throat which will not reject them
> Or wherever cannot reach them the sound of the sea bell's
> Perpetual angelus.

Yet in "The Dry Salvages" Eliot comes closest to describing the attainable goal for the spiritual aspirant:

> For most of us, there is only the unattended
> Moment, the moment in and out of time,
> The distraction fit, lost in a shaft of sunlight,
> The wild thyme unseen, or the winter lightning
> Or the waterfall, or music heard so deeply
> That it is not heard at all, but you are the music
> While the music lasts. These are only hints and guesses,
> Hints followed by guesses; and the rest
> Is prayer, observance, discipline, thought and action.

I think most of the poets I have discussed in this essay would recognize and agree with the above description, especially since the "unattended moment" occurs on earth at its best and in conditions when we are at our best. Many might balk at the monastic overtones of passing the rest of the time in "prayer, observance, discipline, thought and action," but only the word "prayer" keeps these terms from being those of artistic practice.

Eliot's greatest problem in "Four Quartets" is how to make a palatable metaphor out of redemptive suffering or the cleansing pain of Purgatory's "refining fire." He must also justify Love's role in the creation of suffering, since Love is the still point, the godhead, the first cause, from which all effects come. Part IV of "Little Gidding" is the lyrical, hymnal movement of this "Quartet":

> The dove descending breaks the air
> With flame of incandescent terror
> Of which the tongues declare
> The one discharge from sin and error.
> The only hope, or else despair
>   Lies in the choice of pyre or pyre—
>   To be redeemed from fire by fire.
>
>   Who then devised the torment? Love.
> Love is the unfamiliar Name
> Behind the hands that wove
> The intolerable shirt of flame
> Which human power cannot remove.
>   We only live, only suspire
>   Consumed by either fire or fire.

That dove has made an appearance earlier as "the dark dove with the flickering tongue" in the meeting with the dead master in section II of "Little Gidding."

It has been seen as one of the German bombers besieging England during World War II. This lethal dove, associated also with the Holy Spirit, connotes violence; it brings the "flame of incandescent terror" and purgation, "the one discharge from sin and error." As Eliot transforms German bombers into doves, dark or holy, so he takes Purgatory's flames and makes them the petals of a rose, "infolded / Into the crowned knot of fire ..." His poem finds its way back to its beginning, and it bears with it a great weight of wisdom delivered with perfect, even effortless expression, after so much "periphrastic study":

> ... the end of all our exploring
> Will be to arrive where we started
> And know the place for the first time ...
> At the source of the longest river
> The voice of the hidden waterfall
> And the children in the apple-tree
> Not known, because not looked for
> But heard, half-heard, in the stillness
> Between two waves of the sea.
> Quick now, here, now, always—
> A condition of complete simplicity
> (Costing not less than everything) ...

Though Eliot can say that "all shall be well" upon arrival, upon attaining this simple "grace dissolved in place," the absolute cost of this "complete simplicity" is problematic at best.

At the end of this century, is it possible to think of suffering as Christianity has thought of it and as Eliot describes it here, as redemptive? The sufferings of the century include wars and genocide and individual acts of violence against which even the most devout have been helpless. Furthermore, is it possible to believe that the conflagration of the final and greatest suffering will be redemptive at all? The meaning of Omega has been divided from its religious promise for as long as we perceive it as synonymous with holocaust. A cost that would be "not less than everything" would leave nothing to redeem. Is it no longer possible to see history in religious terms, as a function of the personality of God, a God capable of judgment and mercy and expecting obedience? Moments of grace are still moments of grace; we have no other way to describe them except in theological terms. But wariness as to whom we owe them and what might be demanded from us—everything?—has estranged poets to the point that even those who approach the devotional, the religious, in their poetry, do so obliquely, almost in code, afraid to name a God detached from history. Eliot's "Four Quartets" prefigures much that we see of the religious in contemporary poetry. Yet because it portrays suffering—the *sine qua non* of Christian belief—as religiously redemptive, it divides its readers into believers and non-believers.

VI

I know you are there. The sweat is, I am here.

—John Berryman

John Berryman's "Eleven Addresses to the Lord" are remarkable for their power, religious sentiment, and simplicity, a characteristic that Berryman achieved in many of his poems before he ended his life in 1972. In the eleventh of the addresses, the poet asks God that he be an acceptable and ready witness "at the end of time." The poem serves as a believer's eloquent response to many of the reservations stated and implied in this essay so far:

> Germanicus leapt upon the wild lion in Smyrna,
> wishing to pass quickly from a lawless life.
> The crowd shook the stadium.
> The procunsul marvelled.
>
> "Eighty & six years have I been his servant,
> and he has done me no harm.
> How can I blaspheme my King who saved me?"
> Polycarp, John's pupil, facing the fire.
>
> Make too me acceptable at the end of time
> in my degree, which then Thou wilt award.
> Cancer, senility, mania,
> I pray I may be ready with my witness.

Though a contemporary poet may no longer possess the intellectual framework to invest divine meaning in metaphor, as the metaphysical poets did, still he may look to examples of faith. By dramatizing acts of witness he can point to them as examples of Paul's definition of faith in Hebrews 11:1: "Now faith is the substance of things hoped for, the evidence of things not seen." But how is this different from begging the question, when the argument can no longer be logical, reasonable, or even widely disseminated as it was during some previous Age of Faith? In fact, the appeal is emotional, not rational, but the method—witnessing—is till part of our social make-up. From the testimony in the courtroom to the customer's statement of satisfaction with the product, the scale of testifying or witnessing runs from the sublime to the ridiculous. Unlike the metaphysical argument for the existence of a supreme being, this drama in which an individual swears on his own experience persists effectively in our culture. Its most powerful manifestation is steadfastness in the face of suffering and death.

A contemporary religious poet like Berryman must be careful not to assume his suffering will be redemptive. In his eleventh "Address to the Lord" he points to the deaths of other Christians and requests that he, too, will be acceptable, as they presumably were, after death. He proposes three unhappy fates for himself—"Cancer, senility, mania"—and we know that the fate he chose was unhappier still. He prays that he will be a ready witness or, in other words, that his conviction will remain unshaken, that despite suffering he will somehow remain intact. He puns on his own academic career, saying, "Make too me acceptable at the end of time / in my degree, which then Thou wilt award." Thus he regards his own capacity for suffering and belief as something God will acknowledge and award retroactively. In this ambiguous and rich conceit (as close as we can come to Donne and Herbert), we can see the ancient structure of faith as Paul describes it. Since its substance is invisible, we can glimpse evidence of it only in actions. If it is actually present in ourselves, God will recognize it, though others may marvel. The early Christian martyrs Germanicus and Polycarp embody their faith in acts appropriate to their maturity. The wild young man embracing his fate, Germanicus wishes "to pass quickly from a lawless life." Polycarp, the stoic, older scholar, asks a rhetorical question with an obvious answer. Berryman prays only that he "may be ready." He invites our admiration not for secular acts of courage in the face of death but for acts of courage based on faith in God, who will be made manifest "at the end of time." Here the idea of that end is also clarified; since it must come, there will be no escape. How it will come is not the issue (although as I have pointed out it has become an issue in our day). What is important is that because time will have an end, the readiness is all.

Paul Mariani probes the ambiguous nature of modern faith in "Then Sings My Soul," the last poem in his book *Prime Mover*. Like Berryman, he discovers its evidence in the example of another human being, although not a saint, and also in his own surprising emotional response to that example:

> Who can tell a man's real pain
> —or a woman's either—when they learn
> the news at last that they must die? Sure
> we all know none of us is going anywhere

except in some pineslab box or its fine
expensive equal. But don't we put it off
another day, and then another and another,
as I suppose we must to cope? And so

with Lenny, Leonardo Rodriquez, a man
in the old world mold, a Spaniard
of great dignity and fine humility,
telling us on this last retreat for men

that he had finally given up praying
because he didn't want to hear
what God might want to tel him now:
that he wanted Lenny soon in spite

of the hard facts that he had his kids,
his still beautiful wife, and an aged
mother to support. I can tell you now
it hit us hard him telling us because

for me as for the others he'd been
the model, had been a leader, raised
in the old faith of San Juan de la Cruz
and Santa Teresa de Avila, this toreador

waving the red flag at death itself,
horns lowered and hurling down on him.
This story has no ending because there is
still life and life means hope. But

on the third day, in the last Mass, we were
all sitting in one big circle like something
out of Dante—fifty laymen, a priest, a nun—
with Guido DiPietro playing his guitar

and singing an old hymn in that tenor voice
of his, all of us joining in at the refrain,
Then sings my soul, my Savior God to thee,
How great thou art, how great thou art,

and there I was on Lenny's left, listening
to him sing, his voice cracked with resignation,
how great thou art, until angry glad tears
began rolling down my face, surprising me. . . .

Lord, listen to the sound of my voice.
Grant Lenny health and long life. Or,
if not that, whatever strength and peace
he needs. His family likewise, and

his friends. Grant me too the courage
to face death when it shall notice me,
when I shall still not understand why
there is so much sorrow in the world.

Teach me to stare down those lowered horns
on the deadend street that shall have no alleys
and no open doors. And grant me the courage
then to still sing to thee, *how great thou art*.

Mariai gives us a fuller, contemporary, human situation with a larger sense of community than does Berryman. In this case, the example is not a martyr but an ordinary man, Lenny Rodriquez, whom his friends had mistaken for an extraordinary model of faith, like San Juan de la Cruz or Santa Teresa de Avila, and cast in the romantic role of "toreador // waving the red flag at death itself, / horns lowered and hurling down on him." Both Mariani's and Berryman's poems have a homiletic structure, although Mariani's is more narrative and Berryman's more elliptical, and Mariani makes a proposition first and Berryman gives examples. Both end with a prayer, as a preacher's sermon would end, which is both personal and on behalf of their audience, their congregation or community, i.e. their readers. Since Lenny Rodriguez turns out not to be a Germanicus or a Polycarp, but another like the fifty laymen he is on retreat with, the problem of how to face death is more clearly existential in Mariani's poem. Lenny has stopped praying because he does not want to hear God tell him death is coming soon despite all of his obligations. He has chosen not to be ready, in defiance, returning spite for spite. Germanicus made his leap of faith and Polycarp faced his death stoically, with the fortitude of 86 years. But Mariani's question is one of immediate concern: "Who can tell a man's real pain / —or a woman's either—when they learn / the news at last that they must die?" What we put off daily, in order "to cope," is facing the death which has not yet come. Lenny Rodriguez's confession of estrangement throws the speaker, and presumably the others, into a state of introspection. "If Lenny's feeling this way, how must I feel?" might be their sentiment.

This is much closer to the emotion of the common person than to the saint. When the poet hears Lenny beside him singing, "How Great Thou Art," "his voice cracked with resignation," he recognizes also just how the normal sinner submits—broken and "cracked," resigned, before a power he acknowledges as insuperably "great." Of course, the terms of the hymn are in hopeful praise of this power, whose greatness is synonymous with benevolence, and who is called not only "God" but "Savior." The soul, the immortal part, sings to Him, because the mortal part has submitted at last. This response has nothing to do with reason; but as Andrew Hudgins explains it: "logic doesn't stand a chance, a prayer." Rodriguez's estrangement from this all too demanding God is reasonable; its logic distresses his admirers. Mariani describes the emotional breakdown or, rather, the emotional triumph that unites the soul with God. And the poet's own response—"angry glad tears"—surprises him.

Mariani's prayer is different from Berryman's. It makes no mention of final judgment, of "the end of time." It keeps the issue personal, drawing its metaphorical structure from the experience and model of Leonardo Rodriguez, "a Spaniard / of great dignity and fine humility," the romantic "toreador" facing death. The poet asks for courage to face death the bull and hopes that he will still be able to praise God when death shall "notice" him. What is most affecting, however, is the first line of this prayer: "Lord, listen to the sound of my voice." In that line is the Christian belief that a personal God exists to hear one's witness, one's prayer, a God who understands one's suffering, even one's despair, because He suffered and came near despair Himself. When a Christian faces his personal end, he hopes that his death will mean more than physical termination; he hopes that God will take it personally, as he will himself. The cracked resignation of Lenny Rodriguez's voice leads Mariani to say to God, "Listen to me now, too."

Christianity sees suffering as redemptive, because the central event in Christian belief is the triumph over suffering and death—Christ's resurrection. I have alluded to this as the violence at the heart of Christianity and I have also referred to the contemporary use of Christian iconography and art in poems, like Jorie Graham's "Pietà," that make a statement about this violence but for artistic rather than religious purposes. But religious poems themselves may take events, icons, or art as subjects of meditation; though the formal properties of the art move the poet, the end or aim is recognition or re-affirmation of faith. Such a poem is Clare Rossini's "Angelico's 'Crucifixion,' Cell 42, Convent of San Marco."

> Under the sagging gentility of Christ,
> Mary staggers towards the emptiness
> That looms beyond the picture plane, her hands
> Covering her face. Martha turns to follow,
> Her sympathetic hand stalled in space
> Inches from Mary. On the rock that runs
> Across the fresco's foreground like the bared
> Spine of the world, Dominic is kneeling,
> His hands locked in prayer, his eyes fixed on
> The shaded features of his expired god
> As if he were reading a meaning there.
> Only John manages to protest, lifting
> One hand beseechingly towards the soldier
> Who heaves his lance at Christ's sealed, pearl-gray side.
>
> Above them, nothing: no father-God
> Parting clouds, revealing banks of angels
> Singing; beyond them, no hills droning off
> Suggesting places where angelus bells
> Rock slowly in dusk-swathed towers. No,
> This is the world with the fat burned off,
> Honed to rock, a scattering of grievers,
> The muscles rippling through the soldier's arm.
> And now we hear it as the Fra did, the sound
> Of flesh slowly parting before metal—
>
> An almost imperceptible sound,
> Like a curtain in the distance being torn.

One act of religious meditation is to regard the moment of utter hopelessness that the crucifixion was; thus, Fra Angelico painted it in cell 42, in the Convent of San Marco, in Florence. Whoever occupied that cell certainly had a disconsolate image to contemplate, especially when compared to the rainbow-striped wings of the annunciation angel in the cell down the passageway. The line that unites the painting's context in the convent, its situation, the death of Christ, and its meaning is "This is the world with the fat burned off." This amazing line—figurative and colloquial at once—bursts through, uniting self-denial, sacrifice, and American pragmatism, even mixing in a witty play on metabolism, all to emphasize the fact of the body. The attenuated Christ, with his ascetic's flesh, obviously meant to be an example to the Dominicans who studied this picture (they were not known for asceticism), hangs dead above the "bared / Spine of the world," which has been "Honed to rock." This is the foundation for what Bell calls Eliot's "disconsolate theological affirmations." Christ is dead, Mary turns away, Martha reaches to console her, John protests uselessly as the soldier, the one potent character in the picture, "heaves his lance at Christ's sealed, pearl-gray side," his own arm muscles "rippling" with power. Meanwhile, in a touch notable in Renaissance Italian paintings, St. Dominic himself kneels before the event, *in* the even as it were, with Christian piety, fully knowledgeable of all that this means in a way Mary, Martha, and even John presumably are not. Here Rossini interprets, keeping the occasion dark, describing Dominic's "eyes fixed on / The shaded features of his expired god / As if he were reading a meaning there." Her interpretation is due to the oblique approach I have also discussed that poets are likely to take in the religious poem. No consolation can even be suggested until the full desperation of the moment has been recognized.

Again, Rossini points out that no pastoral Italian landscape has been painted in the background of this picture, suggesting the church's manifestation and the resurrection's triumph. However, she makes her own imaginative leap beyond meditation on the picture to a scriptural allusion and thus, lightly, deftly, and exactly, crosses the divide between self and God that the picture dares one to cross. Imagining how the lance blade sounded as it pierced Christ's flesh, she compares it to "An almost imperceptible sound, / Like a curtain in the distance being torn." The synoptic gospels report that at the moment Christ gave up the ghost, the veil in the temple was torn. Matthew adds that the earth shook and the dead were raised, and Luke that the sun was darkened. All are signs of heaven's dismay, the tragic recognition that Man has indeed murdered God. Rossini engages our understanding of this very subtly, for she says we hear this action—the piercing of the lance—as "the Fra did." She assumes that we hear what she hears, in fact: the relation between this human death and its divine consequence, one that Fra Angelico would have recognized. Thus while including all the readers of this poem, her "we" actually draws a smaller circle around Christian believers like herself and Fra Angelico; that is to say, readers who are actually outside the circle of belief may be included without realizing it as they, too, make the connection between the images in the final four lines.

Rossini's critique of the Fra Angelico painting makes her poem, on the surface anyway, more an appeal to reason than the poems by Berryman or Mariani. But her actual subject is the painter's subject, the first example of Christian witness, the sacrifice that set all other Christian sacrifices in motion, made them possible, and gave them meaning. Rossini's final assertion is quiet, not so dramatic as Berryman's and Mariani's closing prayers to their Lord, and yet it is vital to the poem's religious foundation. Without it, the poem would still be a poem, but not necessarily a religious poem, one that expresses the belief of the poet in, to use Philip Wheelright's terms again, "a reality transcending and potentially sanctifying . . . experience." Specifically, without the final lines, the poem would not be a Christian poem and thus part of a tradition that includes much of Western civilization's greatest literature.

It is inconceivable that a religious poem can be written by accident. Yet the religious impulse in poetry today moves many poets who would not call themselves religious. Obviously the need to see one's experience as linked to a transcendent reality and thus sanctified by that connection continues to affect some poets strongly, as I have tried to show. But the religious poem of a believer has a quality of conviction that still resonates with extraordinary power, especially when one considers the risk the poet has taken to witness, in effect, in a poetic mode that has passed out of fashion.

2

Br'er Rabbit and Br'er Possum:

The Americanness of Ezra Pound and T. S. Eliot

How much easier it would be to talk about the Americanness of Robert
Frost or Wallace Stevens, of Marianne Moore or William Carlos Williams.
Though Frost lived in England for three years, from 1912 to 1915, he wrote
there some of his most unmistakably American poems, poems which include
the landscape of New England and the flat accents of its speech. That speech
with its dry inherent understatement is audible in these lines form "Birches,"
a poem composed in England when, Frost says, he was "a little homesick."

> I'd like to get away from earth awhile
> And then come back to it and begin over.
> May no fate willfully misunderstand me
> And half grant what I wish and snatch me away
> Not to return: Earth's the right place for love:
> I don't know where it's likely to go better.

William Carlos Williams, the other master of American speech in poetry, is
also immediately recognizable as an American, from this poem of 1917 (the
year *Prufrock and Other Observations* was published in England). Addressing
his mother at the end of the poem "January Morning," he writes:

> All this—
>   was for you, old woman.
> I wanted to write a poem
> that you would understand.
> For what good is it to me
> if you can't understand it?
>   But you got to try hard—

> But—
> Well, you know how
>   the young girls run giggling
>   on Park Avenue after dark
>   when they ought to be home in bed?

Well,
    that's the way it is with me somehow.

The indulgence in incorrect grammar for its own sake ("you got to try hard"), the facetious disapproval ("when they ought to be home in bed?"), and the adverb "somehow" employed for its relative mystery are all characteristic of an American mixture of the down-to-earth and the fanciful.

    Moore and Stevens are rather more exotic than Frost or Williams and rarely affect an earthy tone in their poems, but their very individuality bespeaks an Americanness. We do see this in Pound and Eliot, as well, a characteristic that often puzzles their British biographers. But Moore sounds especially American, if it is American to say directly, about her own art, in her famous poem, "Poetry,"

    I, too, dislike it: there are things that are important beyond all this fiddle.

To employ a vernacular figure of speech ("all this fiddle") without attributing it to a character's dialect but letting it characterize the poet herself is clearly an American mannerism. As for Stevens, to an American he seems thoroughly American, walking to work with the rhythm of his stretched pentameter line and imagery of the tropics crystallizing in his head. Though isolated from his society on the enchanted, coral lagoon of his imagination, still he located himself in his own country, in the state of Florida.

    A few things for themselves,
    Convolvulus and coral,
    Buzzards and live-moss,
    Tiestas from the keys,
    A few things for themselves,
    Florida, venereal soil,
    Disclose to the lover.

    The dreadful sundry of this world,
    The Cuban, Polodowsky,
    The Mexican women,
    The negro undertaker
    Killing the time between corpses
    Fishing for crayfish . . .

    —"O Florida, Venereal Soil"

Like Whitman, that most American of poets, Stevens in these lines includes the "sundry of this world." It is with something of an aesthete's distaste that he calls them "dreadful," but he's willing to employ a pretty dreadful American pun in the line about the negro undertaker who is "Killing the time between corpses."

Frost, the Californian, adopting New England as his home, Williams with his general practice in Paterson, New Jersey, Moore living with her mother in Brooklyn, and Stevens, the insurance executive, vacationing yearly in Florida—all were contemporaries of Pound and Eliot. All, especially Stevens and Frost, were exposed to the same end of the 19th century ideas, including the aestheticism that drove Pound and Eliot abroad in revulsion from America's vulgarity and from the literal increase in this vulgarity—humanity itself— during the great influx of immigrants from Europe. Yet Frost and Williams, Moore and Stevens, remained (or came home to stay), and their poetry as an American product is, to an American reader, much less problematic than the subject before us.

Why is it harder to locate the American in the poetry of Pound and Eliot? It can and has been done. Probably I am defining the issue too narrowly to the language and the sound of the language, but these are distinguishing factors of poetry. For all their critical pronouncements and the size of their historical presence, Ezra Pound and T. S. Eliot are poets first. To identify their Americanness based solely on their poetry is not easy and critics tend not to do a completely successful job of it, as if listening for that inconsistency of speech whereby the non-native speaker betrays his foreignness. I am going to broaden the issue and describe ideas and conditions that formed them as individuals as well as American poets of their time.

In 1938, when he was in his early thirties, Louis MacNeice commented upon the poets Pound and Eliot in this way, in his book, *Modern Poetry, a Personal Essay*:

> Eliot and his early model, Pound, are both first and foremost American tourists. They wish to shake off the vulgarity of America—of Sweeney, Miss Nancy Ellicott, Mr. Hecatomb Styrax, to become European, cosmopolitan. They take long trips through history and the history of art and literature, eagerly "aware that the mind of Europe . . . is a mind that changes, and that this change is a development which abandons nothing *en route*, which does not superannuate either Shakespeare or Homer, or the rock drawing of the Magdalenian draughtsmen."

This opinion of Pound and Eliot seems to have changed very little, at least in the minds of their most recent biographers, both of whom—Peter Ackroyd, author of *T. S. Eliot, a Life*, and Humphrey Carpenter, author of *A Serious Character: the Life of Ezra Pound*—are English. The opinion is just, though perhaps more trenchant coming from the young poet MacNeice whose intention is to clear ground for himself and others of his generation, particularly his friends, W. H. Auden, C. Day Lewis, and Stephen Spender. Ackroyd and Carpenter include with this belief a reflex response to anything non-English or non-European about their respective subjects. They conclude that it must be an aspect of Pound's or Eliot's Americanness. Thus, for Ackroyd, all signs of self-denial in Eliot are facets of his American puritanism. For Carpenter, Pound's energy and entrepreneurial spirit mark him, at worst, as a P. T. Barnum, an American huckster.

Actually, this contrast might be useful to establish an importance difference between Pound and Eliot, especially to examine generalizations about their Americanness. For it is just as possible that their differences identify them just as well as Americans and perhaps more so. Their strongest similarity was that as young men they came to Europe before World War I, from America, and there began their careers as writers. They brought with them two similar traits that served their modernism and their poetry. One was an iconoclasm, bred in the bone as Monroe Spears has said in his book *American Ambitions* and formed by the habit of revolution in American society. The other was a desire for unity or syncretism, another American paradox founded on the intellectual conundrum of *E Pluribus Unum*, "From the Many, One." The very diversity that Pound and Eliot seem to have fled, they sought to recreate and unify in their own ways.

Their biographers justly take them to task for another aspect of their Americanness—their anti-Semitism, which flourished in England. Its roots were in the growth of the immigrant population in America at the turn of the century. This anti-Semitism was met and nurtured by the English sort, which regarded any attempt to assimilate, to become English, with raised eyebrows, and the more virulent European variety, which sent many Jews in flight from Europe and led eventually to the Holocaust. Eliot managed to suppress or disguise his. Pound, as we all know, gave his free rein, and it stampeded through his poetry, marring much of his magnum opus, *The Cantos*.

Finally, an essential feature of both men is that they were American natives and grew up in the United States. To use Monroe Spears' useful phrase again, they had bred in the bone not only indigenous American qualities, like Eliot's puritanism and Pound's pragmatism, but individually each possessed a set of experiences that marked him from childhood. These experiences are much clearer in Eliot's poetry whose late work returns to the scenes of his boyhood. His story of reading *Huckleberry Finn*, a book forbidden to him as boy in St. Louis, the city on the great river of the novel, is poignant; implicit in the opening lines of "The Dry Salvages" is his own feeling for Huck's Mississippi River. Pound's childhood is harder to tease out of his poetry, though one significant biographical event—his visit to his boyhood home after his release from St. Elizabeth's in 1958—is told romantically by Hugh Kenner at the end of *The Pound Era* and also by Carpenter in his biography with equally characteristic matter-of-factness. Pound is really best at recalling his American apprenticeship and journeyman status in England. His less-than-minor poem "L'Homme Moyen Sensual" and his famous farewell to England "Hugh Selwyn Mauberly" tell us much about Pound, the young American, in England. Eliot's Americanness can be traced through poems in his first two books, and also in part of "Four Quartets," and in the childhood scenes recaptured in two of his so-called minor poems, "New Hampshire" and "Cape Ann," from the group entitled "Landscapes." Eric Sigg in his book *The American T. S. Eliot* has also identified a self-portrait of Eliot as a child in his poem "Animula" from *The Ariel Poems*.

Iconoclasm, the desire for unity, anti-Semitism, and the influence of childhood—these are the ideas and conditions I will examine in order to describe the Americanness of Pound and Eliot and its effect on their poetry.

An iconoclast needs an icon to destroy, and for Pound and Eliot these were actually different images. Though a convincing argument has been made for their reaction against American vulgarity and pluralism, their early poetry shows something else for each man as a motive for revolt.

Pound's first good poem, "Cino," portrays his antagonist and target in the form of two fat burghers of the Italian middle ages, conversing about an itinerant poet.

> Once, twice, a year—
> Vaguely thus word they:
> "Cino?" "Oh, eh, Cino Polnesi
> The singer is't you mean?"
> "Ah yes, passed once our way,

A saucy fellow, but . . .
(Oh they are all one these vagabonds),
Peste! 'tis his own songs?
Or some other's that he sings?
But *you*, My Lord, how with your city?"

This bourgeois attitude might be found anywhere, yet it appears to be one Pound associated especially with America (he wrote "Cino" while teaching at Wabash College in Indiana), that "mass of dolts" to which he refers in "To Whistler, American." Being a poet, he believed, was in itself a serious occupation; based on its importance, he was to remonstrate with Eliot's father when his compatriot first came to England to make his fortune. Living as a poet and not, as Eliot came to do, as a banker and then as a publisher, was something Pound succeeded at, finally with the aid of his wife Dorothy Shakespear's fortune. Self-justification against a perceived animosity in society permeates Pound's early work. "I," he writes in "And Thus in Nineveh,"

Am here a Poet, that doth drink of life
As lesser men drink wine.

He sees that poetry itself can bait the bourgeois and "Ruffle the skirts of prudes," and he commission his poems to:

go to practical people—
   go! jangle their door-bells!
Say that you do no work
   and that you will live forever.

As he aims at the sensibilities of a society that would dismiss him as a poet and dismiss poetry as a marginal activity, he sounds a note echoing the attitude of the French symbolists. But as he finds that the language of poetry itself must change from the late Victorian diction he favors in his early work, he begins to sound like his nearest American relative. As if to cast a spell to hide this proximity, he writes "A Pact."

I make a pact with you, Walt Whitman—
I have detested you long enough.
I come to you as a grown child
Who has had a pig-headed father;

I am old enough now to make friends.
It was you that broke the new wood,
Now is the time for carving.
We have one sap and one root—
Let there be commerce between us.

Pound's own father, Omar, the employee of the U. S. Mint, approved of his son and in his old age was a disciple of his son's craziest theories. If Pound was to revolt successfully, he had to choose another father. When later he was to write, "to break the pentameter, that was the first heave," he acknowledge implicitly that it was Whitman who heaved and broke it. Whitman's apparently artless excesses repelled Pound, but it was especially Whitman's inclusiveness, his democratic vision, that Pound recoiled from, as did Eliot. Pound would not model himself on Whitman. His model would be another American expatriate, the aesthete of the previous generation of Americans in England—James MacNeil Whistler.

You had your searches, your uncertainties,
And this is good to know—for us, I mean,
Who bear the brunt of our America
And try to wrench her impulse into art.

You were not always sure, not always set
To hiding night and tuning "symphonies,"
Had not one style from birth, but tried and pried
And stretched and tampered with the media.

You and Abe Lincoln from that mass of dolts
Show us there's chance at least of winning through.

—"To Whistler, American"

Nowhere else in his early poetry does Pound himself sound quite so American as here, with his directness, his colloquial invective, and his casual use of the iambic pentameter line.

In "L'Homme Moyen Sensual," Pound writes of his character Radway that he learned of Poe, Whitman, Whistler, and Henry James. He also asserts that their recognition they "got abroad." But America's poor taste in literature he ascribes to one of its greatest literary documents:

The constitution of our land, O Socrates,
Was made to incubate such mediocrities...

Compounded in his iconoclasm is an elitism that would also repel the likes of Louis MacNeice. America as it was founded, so Pound believes, is incapable of recognizing genius—the sort of genius, anyway, that must regard itself as special.

Eliot's iconoclasm is more subversive and really more devastating than Pound's, for it appears in *Prufrock and Other Observations* that he wishes to break with the very society that might acknowledge his special artistic gift. In poem after poem of the first book he depicts and demolishes an American society that aspires to gentility despite hopeless provincialism. Yet it is not to assert his role as poet that he does this, but simply to overturn and with much less discretion even than Pound shows. Women are clearly the pillars of the society that Eliot would undermine—caryatids as icons, if you will. In "The Love Song of J. Alfred Prufrock" they utter inanities and dismiss his own attempts at communication. In "Portrait of a Lady," the woman is seen as pressing her advantage, even if she were to die. In the figures of Cousin Harriet, Aunt Helen, Cousin Nancy, and the laughing woman in "Hysteria," woman is variously boring, irrelevant, mannish, and dangerous. But she is always or almost always in the company of the poet, making him feel ineffectual. When she is exposed to other, stronger forces, like Mr. Apollinax and the man who leaves the weeping girl in "La Figlia Che Piange," she wilts. In every case, even the exotic one of "La Figlia Che Piange," she looks American. Against her society, the poet can only pose the resources of his private imagination and his ability to sympathize. Thus, the tenderness of "Preludes" and the brief moment of empathy in "Morning at the Window" for "the damp souls of housemaids" and the surreal floating image of a passing woman's "aimless smile" are all the more shocking. The woman in "Rhapsody on a Windy Night" and the figure in "Preludes" with her yellow-soled feet clasped in her hands appear on the margins of society, where Eliot himself, in these early poems, has chosen to loiter and frame the world he assaults.

Eliot's background in America was clearly different from Pound's, not on the other side of the tracks but certainly higher up the social scale. Yet Eric Sigg has pointed out that growing up in St. Louis the son of a successful industrialist in a prominent family, still Eliot had to endure life in an area of increasing dilapidation, because of the family's attachment to the ancestral home. The meliorist attitudes of his Unitarian background have also been pointed to as motives for his revolt. Sigg indicates that the sensibilities of Henry James and Henry Adams, disaffected Americans who returned to Europe and a traditional and coherent culture, appealed enormously to Eliot. Unfortunately, the antidote of William James did not affect him. The author of *Varieties of Religious Experience* expresses more of the American ideal of inclusiveness and the relative virtues of diversity than does his brother. But Eliot had had a bellyful of that thinking by the time he was grown. His first poems not only clear ground but appear to burn the very ground beneath his feet.

To revolt is to reject. To smash an icon is rarely to put a new image in its place. Both poets rejected what America offered them and at the same time acted as if to some degree it had offered them nothing. By blaming America's mediocre literature on the Constitution itself, Pound showed his incipient political concerns and his belief that the poet had a role to play in the government of nations. By satirizing genteel American society, Eliot sought to put another sort in his frame of urban degradation. But as Americans, as the products of an eighteenth century revolution and its intellectual legacy, and as a new generation living in the memory of a civil war fought for the principles of the founding fathers, Pound and Eliot would have acted uncharacteristically if they had resorted merely to nihilism. Along with *E Pluribus Unum*, another motto of the nation was and is *Novus Ordo Seclorum*, "a new cycle of the ages." Eliot and Pound set about to make new unities and to bring to life a new confederation of ideas. Their ends were quite different, but the impulse towards those ends was distinctly American.

Eliot's new world is depicted in *The Waste Land*, where the fragments of the old order offer, in new combinations, another way to regard the world. It is clear from recent scholarship that the poem could almost be considered a collaborative effort between Pound and Eliot, for it was Pound's editing that gave the poem its distinct character. Still, it was Eliot's intention from the start to set his lands in order, lands that he had himself laid waste. He comes to the old world as an explorer, in a reverse of the pilgrim migration. Every act of Eliot, in these early years, though a negation, is actually a mirror image of the making of America. Eliot makes up a new world out of the old, but the materials and images with which he does so have analogues in America.

In part I of *The Waste Land*, the unreal city is surrounded by or approached through desert, the land of red rock. The island city surrounded by hostile terrain is, indeed, a feature of the American landscape. The land of red rock is in the southwestern part of the U. S., however, not in Eliot's Missouri. As in previous poems, Eliot invests desert margins of the city with more reality than the city itself. In part II, he depicts a woman at the heart of the unreality, a figure who seems to a reader today to represent Eliot's own unhappy relationship with his first wife. Demotic and vulgar as they are, Lil's friends in the pub have much more reality about them in their frankness and their appetites. Once again, there on the margins, Eliot feels free. He cannot connect with the world from which he derives; he cannot connect with it intellectually or physically. Part III is about connection, sexual connections in particular. Most of them appear to be distasteful, whether they be the one suggested by Mr. Eugenides or the one effected by the young man carbuncular. Yet the son of the Thames maidens, though it resolves itself in the anguish of St. Augustine's flight from his own sensuality, suggests pleasure, swelling with the Thames tide. The enigmatic fourth part of *The Waste Land* depicts the drowning of Phlebas. It is his role to drown, just as Prufrock drowns. Here Eliot leaves behind the old body and, in fact, all that is represented by body and mind in the previous sections. In the fifth and final part, and in the footnotes attached (which must be seen as a sixth part to the poem, as the Bill of Rights must be seen as a part of the U. S. Constitution), he makes the new world.

St. Louis, on the Mississippi River, is the gateway to the American west and what was once called the Great American Desert. The vastness of empty space around the American city must be considered in the milieu of *The Waste Land*; it is part of the American imagination. So much space must mean so much potential. It takes that sort of mind to work as Eliot does, implying that ruins can be propped up, shored up by fragments. It is interesting, as well, that at the end of the poem Eliot offers a spiritual resolution derived from India. This would seem to be further repudiation of his intellectual heritage, his family's Unitarian faith in works. Yet the wisdom of the East enters American thinking with Transcendentalists like Emerson, who also were engaged in the ongoing American project of, in Pound's phrase, making it new.

The Waste Land, then, like the U. S. Constitution, is a thoroughly American project, an attempt at making something new. Though the language is Europeanized and literary, though the city itself is London and the best dialect bits are take-offs on British speech, still the poem profoundly affected American poets on the other side of the water. Young poets like Hart Crane and Eliot's own contemporaries like William Carlos Williams felt obliged to respond. Older American poets like Frost and Stevens seem to have been unaffected. And yet we can find in their work poems like Frost's "Directive" and Stevens' "The Man on the Dump," poems about ruins and fragmentation, that read differently because of the existence of *The Waste Land*. In a century of American innovations, *The Waste Land* is that thing on which Americans pride themselves. It is a first.

Or is it a second? Pound had already written "Hugh Selwyn Mauberly," his attempt to write a Jamesian novel in verse. Perhaps this claim has obscured his own significant syncretic achievement. I think so. Humphrey Carpenter argues that much of what Pound wrote and much of the way Pound lived displays a love of the mask, the persona. So, we see Pound moving from the role of Provençal troubadour to Chinese poet, in his Cathay series, to Roman wit, in "Homage to Sextus Propertius." In "Hugh Selwyn Mauberly" he dons the mask of the French neo-classicist, Théophile Gautier. All of these masks form the shifting personae of *The Cantos*, and, in truth, that work bears more of an analogous relationship to *The Waste Land*, in terms of its syncretic structure and its status as a new vision of world history. But much occurs in "Mauberly" that anticipates *The Waste Land*. It may be possible that having made his own attempt at a major work that would hold a series of pieces together, Pound as Eliot's editor was all the more ready to recognize the direction Eliot ought to go in "He Do the Police in Different Voices," the original draft of what became the most important poem of the modern era.

"Mauberly" is just as ambitious as *The Waste Land*, and in one regard, more formally original. After the twelve sections plus the "Envoi" of the poem, "Hugh Selwyn Mauberly, Life and Contacts," the poem begins again, with a section entitled simply, "Mauberly," which Pound considered both an extension of the poem and a commentary on it, like Eliot's notes to *The Waste Land*. "Mauberly," the second part, in five sections, contains no narrative material, and the writing is both more compressed in places and windier, too. The epigrammatic wit of the last stanza of part IV,

> "I was
> And I no more exist;
> Here drifted
> An hedonist."

exists nearby the mushy-mouthed attempt at onomatopoeia and self-criticism of the previous section:

> Nothing, in brief, but maudlin confession,

> Irresponse to human aggression,
> Amid the precipitation, down-float
> Of insubstantial manna,
> Lifting the faint susurrus
> Of his subjective hosannah.

Throughout the poem there are macaronic combinations of Latin and Greek, French, allusions to the ancient world and to World War I, portraits of friends, like Ford Madox Ford, and suspect characters like the venal Mr. Nixon, modeled on Arnold Bennett. In other words, it tries out much of the same staging as *The Waste Land*. But Pound's poem is also an album of English memories and as such a farewell to England. In a way the memories are those of an American tourist, the sort Louis MacNeice accused both Eliot and Pound of being; they are the keepsakes of an American gone abroad and bent on looking for the best art of the day, like Henry James' Newman in *The American*. Pound's saving grace might be that he hopes also to remember who made the art and who condemned it. He manipulates Gautier's trim quatrains to create his own Attic grace with a practical American sense of workability, stretching and contracting the form as he sees fit. The stanzas are meant to last, to be, as Donald Davie has observed, carved in time, as an antidote to what the times demanded.

> The "age demanded" chiefly a mould in plaster,
> Made with no loss of time,
> A prose kinema, not, not assuredly, alabaster
> Or the "sculpture" of rhyme.

The poem represents what is for Pound the one integral good, his proposed replacement for a world turned upside down. That good is beauty, chiefly the beauty of art. His aim is "to convey the relation / of eye-lid and cheekbone / by verbal manifestation." When he imagines himself drowning, like Phlebas and Prufrock, it is for him "to designate / His new found orchid." When he pictures himself and his beloved as nothing more than "siftings on siftings in oblivion," still he insists that change will break down "All things save Beauty alone."

Beauty alone continues to be Pound's obsession throughout his poetry. How beauty is made and preserved leads him, I believe, to his disastrous economic theories and these in turn provide the growth hormone for his anti-Semitism. Pound wished, as he says in the final Canto, "to write Paradise," to create the heavenly city on earth. "Mauberly" gives us our first look at his values. The tragedy of Ezra Pound was his belief that beauty could be an accomplishment of the correct economic policies; thus, he projected the aims of art along vectors like Social Credit. His suburban anti-Semitism, as he was later to call it, developed monstrously because he perceived an enemy to his project. His foolishness stems from his mistaken belief that he could have a larger role in the world than the role of poet.

Though *The Cantos*, as I have said, are by rights the work that should be placed beside *The Waste Land*, I do not believe they add much to Pound's vision that is not already apparent in "Mauberly." Pound's sense of how things ought to be and of what ought to be preserved in the world is determined almost completely by his aesthetic judgments. These were often first rate and his expression of beauty, by "verbal manifestation," few have ever contested. Both his ear for language and his eye for the image are unparalleled. But it is Eliot whose vision holds together and continues to cohere, because Eliot has more than the good of art on his mind. I am not, however, particularly interested in creating a contest between them as poets, assigning place to each for various reasons. It is an American quality that made each wish to make a new unity out of the pieces he perceived and in some ways created. I think the success and failure in each case is related to how they dealt with another American trait they brought with them to England—their anti-Semitism.

American anti-Semitism, of the sort bred in Pound and Eliot, and English anti-Semitism are rather different strains of the same disease. Their biographers correctly locate Pound's and Eliot's in the American xenophobia resulting from the great increase in the country's immigrant population around the turn of the century. Americans extended their prejudices to the Irish as well as the Jews, but the hatred of Jews was all the more pernicious because it could be fed by notorious and ancient conspiracy theories. Books like *The Protocols of the Elders of Zion*, a proven fraud, did their damage. The English brand of anti-Semitism is fed by the general English disdain for the non-English, but mingled with it is the English fascination with and distaste for Mediterranean culture, a repulsion/attraction syndrome for the South, which includes the Levant. There is also the anomaly of non-Christians living in a country where Anglo-Catholicism is the state religion. And there is the larger European issue of Jewish residence there since the Diaspora. English anti-Semitism is older than the American type on which Pound and Eliot were weaned. But the ingrained prejudice that could lead Henry James to refer to all bank loan officers as "the Jews," as he does in *Roderick Hudson*, could be found on both sides of the Atlantic.

Eliot's anti-Semitism mars a number of his poems in *Poems, 1920*. In "Gerontion," "the jew squats on the window sill, the owner"; in "Burbank with a Baedeker; Bleistein with a Cigar," Bleistein is described gratuitously as "Chicago Semite Viennese," and once again "The Jew" is caricatured. This time the rats below the Rialto of Venice are given a higher place, for "the jew is underneath the lot." Princess Volupine entertains "Sir Ferdinand / Klein" who, caught astride the enjambment, is deflated by the pun on his German name. In this case, Eliot indulges in a typically English bêtise about the aspirations of such people, for whom a knighthood is no disguise. In "Sweeney Among the Nightingales," "Rachel née Rabinovitch," who tears at the grapes with her "murderous paws," is the last of the anti-Semitic cartoons to appear in Eliot's poetry in his lifetime. It is sad stuff to catalogue these weaknesses, but sadder still I think to excuse them, as critics have done.

In his poems, Pound's anti-Semitism is worse; it is the tragic flaw running through and undermining his great work, *The Cantos*. Though his letters were often laden with references to "kikery" and all his life he entertained a belief that during his days as a railroad magnate his father had to endure the conspiracies of Jewish bankers, Pound's own first poetic expression of his prejudice appears in "Mauberly," in the section called *"Brennbaum."*

> The sky-like limpid eyes,
> The circular infant's face,
> The stiffness from spats to collar
> Never relaxing into grace;
>
> The heavy memories of Horeb, Sinai and the forty years,
> Showed only when the daylight fell
> Level across the face
> Of Brennbaum "The Impeccable."

Compared with Eliot's caricatures, this one is mild, a curious sketch speculating on what forms the mind and manner of someone perceived to be Jewish. For Pound is depicting here the author and artist Max Beerbohm, whom he mistakenly took to be a Jew. This mistake is related to the much larger disorder that Pound enjoyed. His theories about Jews ranged widely and outlandishly and ran the gamut from believing the dulling effect of circumcision led to a desire to make money as a compensation, to the issue of racial purity touching on his own background. He was anxious to make it clear that he had no Jewish ancestors. But Pound always had to have a theory or theories to knit together. His anti-Semitism enters forcefully into *The Cantos* in the 1930's, when he discovers Douglas' theory of Social Credit, and thus he begins to elaborate a petty prejudice into a social vision. Fascism helps him, too. Many who came into his sphere caught the anti-Semitic bug, like his American publisher James Laughlin, but were able later to shake it. Only the nasty bunch of sycophants surrounding him at St. Elizabeth's, described in a devastating memoir by his daughter, persisted in their prejudice. Humphrey Carpenter reports in his biography of Pound that Ernest Hemingway wrote to Allen Tate: "[Pound] ought to go to the loony bin, which he rates and you can pick out the parts in his cantos at which he starts to rate it." He starts to rate it, I would argue, in "Canto XXXV," which begins, "So this is (may we take it) Mittleuropa." He proceeds in that poem to describe the Jewish family in absurd terms (its warmth is "intravaginal," for example) and to depict European Jews as the pivot of artistic commerce, involving the production of art in the production of money. From there on, he is in the grip of his obsession, and it works a vein of rot through the poem which, from the 1930's until his death, was his primary literary endeavor.

Prejudice begins in childhood. Few would look back nostalgically to the roots of their prejudice, yet Pound's reported remark to Allen Ginsberg about his "suburban anti-Semitism" does look back. "Suburban" does actually describe Pound's American experience. Though born in the state of Idaho, where his father was constructing railroads, he was bred in Pennsylvania where his family lived on the edge of Philadelphia. As his biographer mentions, there was little "immigrant blood" in the neighborhood around him. He and his family were members of a Presbyterian church and he made his confession of faith there when he was about 12. His father's work in the U. S. Mint in Philadelphia seems to have excited Pound most when he reflected on his childhood. This association with the making of money had an ominous relationship with his later obsession. But his association with the West, the influence of his father's telegraphic style of writing letters, Pound's exposure to the Uncle Remus stories as a boy, and his grab bag Americanism, which he could reach into at will for the rest of his life, all color the character who wrote his own letters in phonetically Americanized English and gave himself the name Br'er Rabbit after dubbing his friend T. S. Eliot even more memorably, Br'er Possum. (For both men these nicknames were like calling cards from their American past.) One looks in vain, however, for a nostalgic or searching reminiscence of childhood in Pound's poetry. That sort of self-knowledge is absent in most of his writing and his life and may account for the moral lapse of his unrepentant prejudice.

There is one interesting story about Pound's relationship to his childhood. While Pound was incarcerated in St. Elizabeth's, the mental asylum where he lived after World War II after it was decided that his psychological state made a trial for treason impossible, Humphrey Carpenter mentions that Pound had gotten in touch with the family that occupied his old family house in Wyncote, Pennsylvania. In 1958, when he was released, they invited him to visit and Pound amazed them at how much he remembered of his childhood. He excitedly inspected the house and during the night he went down the road to the Presbyterian church where he had made his first confession as a boy, to see if a tree he and a friend had planted still stood. Hugh Kenner, at the end of *The Pound Era*, tells the story like this:

> At Wyncote, last, a summer night, in 1958, St. Elizabeth's freshly behind him, in bed in his old house for the last time (and aged 72), he had somehow wakened—always a brief sleeper; genius enjoys long days—and tiptoed downstairs in his pajamas, out into the dark street, and down to the Presbyterian Church, to sit on its steps looking over the moonlit lawns of great estates: sitting where a boy had sat 60 years before, his eye on trees before dawn, his mind on a poet's destiny, which should be that of dreaming old men's silences; the old man's memory now in turn accessible to the still older man in Venice, to be guessed at but never experienced by any comer. "Shall two know the same by their knowing?" Thought is a labyrinth.

Pound himself never wrote any such poetry about his childhood in America. But Kenner's assumption, lavishly as it is expressed, closes on a kernel of truth. The boy who made his confession of faith in that church, who grew up in that suburb of Philadelphia, became the poet Ezra Pound, a figure of such dimensions that his most unquestioning followers, like Kenner, are able to create myths out of his life without contradiction from the man himself.

Eliot as he grew older showed more of the actual roots of his imagination. Perhaps, because his childhood was the beginning of a lifelong unhappiness, not really assuaged until his marriage to his second wife, he could return to parts of it when he knew he was happy and he could recall its painful loneliness as well. Eric Sigg quotes these lines from "Animula" to give an oblique but sharp portrait of the boy, Tom Eliot:

> The pain of living and the drug of dreams
> Curl up the small soul in the window seat
> Behind the *Encyclopedia Britannica.*

Eliot also offers, in contrast, portraits from landscapes associated with his childhood and adolescence, not in St. Louis but in New England. Thus, "New Hampshire," in "Landscapes,"

> Children's voices in the orchard
> Between the blossom- and the fruit-time:
> Golden head, crimson head,
> Between the green tip and the root . . .

and the beginning of "Cape Ann,"

> O quick quick quick, quick hear the song-sparrow,
> Swamp-sparrow, fox-sparrow, vesper-sparrow
> At dawn an dusk. Follow the dance . . .

modulate into the children's voices woven through *Four Quartets*:

> Go, said the bird, for the leaves were full of children,
> Hidden excitedly, containing laughter.
> Go, go, go, said the bird: human kind
> Cannot bear very much reality.

And these voices from his childhood echo as well in the line of Verlaine quoted in part II of *The Waste Land*—"Et O ces voix d'enfants, chantant dans la coupole!" The human voices that wake and drown Prufrock become, as Eliot strains to hear them again, voices of the past and of another place. And behind these voices, like the river Wordsworth heard in his nursemaid's song, are, for the Eliot, both a river and a sea. Both these natural features figured in his growing up: the Mississippi River, the "strong brown god" of "The Dry Salvages," and the Atlantic off the northeast coast of Cape Ann where he enjoyed sailing as a teenager and young man. "The river is within us, the sea is all about us," he writes, convincingly, locating his understanding of this metaphysical condition in this original experience. Eliot's poetry seems to quest after something which he discovers; in practical American terms, he finishes what he starts. Pound's failure—his life ended in silence and his work in pieces—is just as American as Eliot's success. That I choose these terms at all to describe the work and life of the two poets betrays an American affliction, the desire to divide the world between winners and losers.

Eliot found his end, in his poetry at least, in his beginning. Pound in his touching last Canto acknowledges his original plan, too, way back at the beginning, which was to write Paradise. He asks to be forgiven, invoking the language of his Presbyterian background, by the gods and those he loves. Eliot, too, ends his final great poetic work with a vision of paradise.

> And all shall be well and
> All manner of thing shall be well
> When the tongues of flame are in-folded
> Into the crowned knot of fire
> And the fire and the rose are one.

Both endings come from a need to create a unitary vision. In Pound's case, it was of this world, where art would be made in the perfect society it needed, to be unblemished by financial practicalities. In Eliot's, it was of a transcendent reality. In the case of both poets, the pursuit began with an American belief that the attempt was possible and that its accomplishment could be measured in terms of success or failure.

Postscript

When I began drafting this essay in the first weeks of December 1990, I opened with the following paragraph:

> It feels unreal to be looking back across the century at two men who had so much to do with how we experience the daily fragmentation of our lives, if we are readers of poetry, and yet who believed, in their poetry, that they were trying to put the pieces back together in a new way. As the century's third global conflict begins, it feels strange to try to apprehend a quality—Americanness—in two Americans who left their country to escape characteristics they carried in their genes and social make-up. It is, in part, something in Americanness that has brought the world to war this time. So, it feels unreal, strange, and yet as the century looks back at us, through the eyes of Ezra Pound and T. S. Eliot, it seems all too familiar, all too real, all too in keeping with this era of catastrophes.

The actual outcome of the Gulf War, the end of the Cold War, and the state of the globe racked by the AIDS epidemic, all persuade me that the world described prophetically by Pound and Eliot has come and gone. Modernism is over and has been over for a long time. Even the term Post-Modernism is anachronistic. We read Pound and Eliot for their artistry—What music is like Pounds? What voice is like Eliot's?—and for their historical importance. Would either of them recognize the world as a global village that is also torn by conflicting cultural desires? As Americans they might suffer the same bewilderment Americans are now suffering, even as their system of government innately encourages diversity. But as poets, I think they would offer the same redemption as they did before—art and faith.

3

John & Randall, Randall & John

In the chambers of the end we'll meet again
I will say Randall, he'll say Pussycat
and all will be as before
whenas we sought, among the beloved faces,
eminence and were dissatisfied with that
and needed more.

—John Berryman, *Dream Song 90*

What more did they need? Talent they had in abundance. They received am-
ple recognition in their lifetimes. Yet both John Berryman and Randall Jarrell, as poets, labored in the shadow of Robert Lowell. Even as we cast our
gaze back to their careers and forward to assess their present status, Elizabeth
Bishop adds her shadow to Lowell's. But Berryman and Jarrell deserve special
attention. Two recent biographies, William Pritchard's of Jarrell[1] and Paul
Mariani's of Berryman[2], plus a collection of Berryman's poems, excluding *The
Dream Songs*, edited by Charles Thornbury[3], and a slim, rather idiosyncratic
selection of Jarrell's poems edited by Pritchard[4] make it time to look again at
these two writers. The value of Jarrell's poetry has been lessened by a regret-
table notion that his criticism is so far superior as to make the poetry almost
superfluous. And John Berryman's unique persona Henry and the poems that
recount his adventures have been losing currency, unfortunately, almost since
the day after his death.

Talent is god-given, or so we tend to believe, but the ease with which it man-
ifests itself depends entirely on the will of the individual to recognize the gift
and allow it to do its work. The Jarrell Pritchard gives us knew from a young
age, at least from his college years at Vanderbilt, that he was better read than
just about anybody; he would realize further that he was wittier than any-

---

[1] *Randall Jarrell, A Literary Life*, by William Pritchard Farrar Straus, and Giroux, 1990
[2] *Dream Song: The Life of John Berryman*, by Paul Mariani, William Morrow & Co., 1989
[3] *Collected Poems, 1937–1971*, by John Berryman, edited and introduced by Charles Thornbury, Farrar, Straus, and Giroux, 1989
[4] *Selected Poems*, by Randall Jarrell, edited by William Pritchard, Farrar, Straus, and Giroux, 1990

body, too. Allen Tate's acerbic caricature of Jarrell, made after Jarrell's death at the age of fifty-one in 1965, as a "gifted, self-adulating little twerp" is never really contradicted by Pritchard. However, the biographer does go a long way toward describing Jarrell's gift, which was, in part, the ability to make his own reading seem of paramount importance. Yet the wit he displayed in his early reviews, writing for *The New Republic* and *The Nation* in the early 1940's, does not appear in his verse until much later. When it does, Pritchard argues, the poetry becomes truly memorable and deserves to be considered alongside that of the best of his contemporaries. Still, toward the end of his life, Jarrell was to acknowledge ruefully a compliment paid to him that if Lowell was a Beethoven, he was a Robert Schumann. Jarrell did nothing to himself to obstruct the blossoming of his talent, except to be, perhaps, too smart, too much the ephebe of T. S. Eliot, but even wittier, even more fluent with allusions to his reading, abler to make many an unforgettable phrase stand on its head. Pritchard makes a point, in response to Berryman's elegiac Dream Song for Jarrell, that quite the contrary to Henry's claim that Jarrell "never loved his body, being full of dents," as an avid tennis player, Jarrell took great care of himself physically. It was, in fact, Berryman who exhibited a physical self-loathing—if, that is, his alcoholism and cigarette addiction were any sign.

It is amazing to regard what Berryman had achieved even as he commenced the decades of abuse that led eventually to the bridge in Minneapolis, where in 1972 in his fifty-eighth year he took his own life. Unlike Jarrell's, Berryman's gift was not obvious from the start, no matter what he and his mother might have thought. Despite certain successes and the recognition of the literary establishment that here was a talented, hardworking young man, a promising scholar and an excellent craftsman of poetry, nevertheless, it is "Homage to Mistress Bradstreet," published in *The Partisan Review* in 1953 and in book form in 1956, that announces his arrival. Looking back at his two most significant achievements in poetry before "Bradstreet"—the "Sonnets to Chris," a sequence of Petrarchan fireworks about his adulterous affair during his first marriage, and the superb "Nervous Songs," based on his reading of Rilke—it is hard to see more than a similar approach to disrupted syntax, hard to see where the extraordinary originality arises that makes "Bradstreet" a great poem. In Jarrell we can see that if he could only bring his wit to bear on his poetry in the lucid way it does in his prose, he will have made something unique. But for Berryman, "Bradstreet" has a profound dimension he had never before achieved. He brings *himself* alive in a multifaceted characterization, both as the colonial poetess and as her dream lover, while at the same time telling a story that resonates with the American psyche in every single line.

More than anything Jarrell ever wrote about poetry, Berryman's remarks in his criticism serve as revealing insights into his own ambitions and their eventual achievement. He is best when his subject turns him to his own concerns as a poet. Thus, on Ezra Pound, he asks, "Does any reader who is familiar with Pound's poetry really not see that its subject is the life of the modern poet?" As much could be asked of Berryman's poetry, especially of *The Dream Songs*. And doubly acute, as an angle on Pound and *The Dream Songs*, Berryman writes, "*The Cantos* have always been personal, only the persona increasingly adopted, as the Poet's fate clarifies, is Pound himself." I doubt that we can find anywhere such self-revealing observations as these in the criticism of Jarrell, although his preferences for Eliot and Frost can be linked to his own poetry. In his finest essay, "Shakespeare at Thirty," Berryman establishes his link with his most distant precursor. Writing of Shakespeare's sonnets, he claims:

> The sonnets do not tell a story, still less do they follow a fashion, though a habit of sonnet writing will produce occasional exercises; they reflect interests, pieces of living . . .

Part of Berryman's gift was to know, eventually, just who his forerunners were and what works preceded his great work as models—Shakespeare's sonnets, Whitman's "Song of Myself," Emily Dickinson's poetry of the 1860's, Ezra Pound's *Cantos*, and most importantly the middle and late poetry of Yeats. Jarrell never seems to perceive the connection between his critical passions and his art. Curiously, both poets begin with an obsession with W. H. Auden, the most talented poet of the preceding generation, only seven years their senior. Neither could be farther from that poet in sensibility and sheer genius. Their range was narrower. But for Berryman, Yeats was a wise choice for master. Jarrell may have known too much to be anybody's apprentice.

Strangely, Jarrell did not think it a good idea that a poet know too well what he was up to, although when Berryman knew, he was at his best. Criticizing the Beat Poets in "Fifty Years of American Poetry," Jarrell wrote that their "conscious social manifestoes . . . make it impossible for the artist's unconscious to operate as it normally does in the process of producing a work of art." And as part of the same dismissal he tosses of the profound observation: "their poems are direct as true works of art are indirect. . . ." Both of these statements may seem to come naturally from a reader of Freud, such as Jarrell. They suggest that not only the composing of a poem but the poem as a finished work of art has some connection to the unconscious—the writer's as he made it up and the reader's as it is read. Perhaps that is why, reading Jarrell's "A Girl in a Library," which Pritchard considers his signal work of poetry, I suspect that lurking below the surface is a hungry vehemence that at any minute or line is going to rise up and eat the subject in one gulp, then slither back into darkness. It is all the poet can do to protest his love for what his attendant sprite, Tatyana Larina, calls "a fat thing." The atmosphere of the poem so crackles with this electricity—the energy of displaced desire—that the librarian should be bawling for quiet.

When Berryman or his representative enters "Homage to Mistress Brad-street" no such tension exists, though there is plenty of drama. Seduction is his aim. Seduction is the aim of Berryman in many of his poems, of a woman or, in the end, of a distant God. Seduction is planned, deliberate, calculated, dramatic, and it either succeeds or it does not succeed. Coyness is a ploy but not an accident (as it can be sometimes in Jarrell). We can tell from Mariani's biography, as we could from Haffenden's, and from the collection of Berryman's letters to his mother, *We Dream of Honor*, that this drive to seduce is associated with her. For Berryman this urge, often leading to embarrassing moments in his life because of his drinking and poor timing, becomes the strongest motivating force of his poetry. It is part of his talent that he recognized and used.

The disappointment of many biographies of artists is that the biographer gives us everything, especially if he is a modern biographer, except insight into the talent. How did Jarrell and Berryman write their poems? Mariani reveals the mystery and excitement of composition, in chapter sixteen of his biography, when he describes the final drafting of "Homage to Mistress Brad-street." As both his biographers, Haffenden and Mariani describe it, Berryman invented a crude computer screen for himself, the "glassine covered wax pad" where he could place fragments he had written already beneath the glassine and then work to connect them, without touching them. It was a period, as well, when Berryman showed incredible insensitivity to his own wife, Eileen, who was recovering from a myomectomy, and interrogated at least one woman on the sensations of giving birth. He called back fragments of conversation from years before, like a story his wife told about her nephew's response to the death of a relative. He faced his own role as seducer and created a woman who could resist him but who would have to suffer and die as a result. He worked like a novelist, making a fictive whole of the world's fragments. As a poet he made a language as dense as anything in Hopkins and as revealing, possibly more revealing because of his worldliness, as anything the Jesuit father ever composed.

"Homage to Mistress Bradstreet" is a great poem, indeed, worth the pains of reading, and enough to have written Berryman's name into the pantheon he sought to be a part of. Chosen for praise by its critics, the section on childbirth is magnificent and accurate, Anne's cry "I did it with my body!" an unforgettable moment in literature. But consider too this simple stanza about her first winter in the new world.

> Winter than summer worse, that first, like a file
> on a quick, or the poison suck of a thrilled tooth;
> and still we may unpack.
> Wolves & storms among, uncouth
> board-pieces, boxes, barrels vanish, grow
> houses, rise. Motes that hop in sunlight slow
> indoors, and I am Ruth
> away: open my mouth, my eyes wet: I would smile . . .

The movement from the unfinished settlement, in its hostile surroundings, to the relative peace of domestic inner space is marvelously compressed. And the poet's way with inversion has found a voice that suits it. Saying "open my mouth" for "my mouth open" forms a heartrending chiasmus with "my eyes wet." The attempt at cheerfulness, "I would smile," is suitably bleak. Everywhere in this poem the language lets us look closely to admire its making and its aptness. This is not transparent diction by any means, but highly wrought, and if forced, forced into bloom.

> —It is Spring's New England. Pussy willows wedge
> up in the wet. Milky crestings, fringed
> yellow, in heaven, eyed
> by the melting hand-in-hand or mere
> desirers single, heavy-footed, rapt,
> make surge poor human hearts. Venus is trapt—
> the hefty pike shifts, sheer—
> in Orion blazing. Warblings, odours, nudge to an edge—

Besides doing Roethke fine here, Berryman writes one of the long periodic sentences that make the poem's ply on ply of meaning unfoldable. The "Milky crestings" of the clouds—as they break, outlined by sunshine—move the hearts of couples and single individuals, laden with winter's weight and enchanted to see spring again. The night sky reflects the movement in the human being as well, and earth responds with its sexuality. One stanza, and pages could be written. The poem contains fifty-six others, waiting like time capsules to be rediscovered.

In his introduction to Berryman's *Collected Poems*, Charles Thornbury makes much of poetry's power to transform a poet and of the poet's love for the process of composition. He even makes a cogent argument that change is central to Berryman's poetry (an argument Pritchard makes for Jarrell but develops more fully). Though poetry may have kept Berryman alive longer than his father, whose suicide at thirty-seven Berryman turns to again and again for a subject, it finally neither saved nor changed Berryman. And in the end we read and honor Berryman's poems for an excellence they have quite apart from his life. As old-fashioned as this sounds, the biography of a poet in reference to his best work matters very little. It might serve to work up some themes—transformation, reformation—but finally it is gossip. Yet having taken this outdated new critical stance, I have to admit that without Mariani's biography, and the previous one of Berryman by John Haffenden, we cannot read Berryman's great work, his autobiography in verse, *The Dream Songs*. That is to say, we cannot read and fully appreciate the entire work. It is still possible to choose from among the 385 Songs those that are best.

The best of *The Dream Songs* are elegies or they are elegiac. In *77 Dream Songs*, the first installment that won Berryman the Pulitzer Prize for poetry in 1965, they are "A Strut for Roethke," the poems after the deaths of Hemingway and Faulkner, 34 and 36 respectively, and the moving homage to Robert Frost, number 37. The final stanza of the last, like the writing in "Bradstreet," shows Berryman's aim as a poet achieved—all that style to say a memorable thing. Out of fragments, dissonance, and incoherence, comes language that can only be called, to quote him from an earlier poem, "heartmating."

> Quickly, off stage with all but kindness, now.
> I can't say what I have in mind. Bless Frost,
> any odd god around.
> Gentle his shift, I decussate & command,

> stoic deity. For a while here we possessed
> an unusual man.

The elegist must speak out of a fully composed personality with a strong sense of community, so that grief is expressed not only eloquently but authentically. He must do more and less than wail. Berryman introduces the extraordinary "decussate," making the sign of the cross over the dead poet's grave, in an act of religious authority. His personal regard for greatly talented figures, among his elders and his friends, took him out of himself in necessary ways. "I love great men I love!" he exclaims, and it is a relief to hear it sometimes in contrast to Henry's many "plights & gripes."

The strongest section of *His Toy, His Dream, His Rest*, the book that included the remaining Dream songs and garnered the National Book Award in 1969, is the group of elegies for Berryman's old friend Delmore Schwartz. I would venture to say that this group of twelve poems, Songs 146 through 157, this "solid block of agony," which Henry incorrectly refers to as "Ten Songs," is the best stretch in all of *The Dream Songs*. Schwartz was the first poet of his generation, the generation that would come to be dominated by Robert Lowell, to receive recognition and the blessing of such elder masters as T. S. Eliot and Allen Tate. Berryman remembers "his electrical insight as the young man, / his wit & passion, gift, the whole young man / alive with surplus love." In the final poem of the group, the voice of Berryman-as-Henry sets an ultimate tone which the best of *The Dream Songs* match. It is grave and tender and merciful:

> Ten Songs, one solid block of agony,
> I wrote for him, and then I wrote no more.
> His sad ghost must aspire
> free of my love to its own post, that ghost,
> among its fellows, Mozart's, Bach's, Delmore's
> free of its careful body
>
> high in the shades which line that avenue
> where I will gladly walk, beloved of one,
> and listen to the Buddha.
> His work downhill, I don't conceal from you,
> ran and ran out. The brain shook as if stunned,
> I hope he's over that,
>
> flame may his glory in that other place,
> for he was fond of fame, devoted to it,

and every first-rate soul
has sacrifices which it puts in play,
I hope he's sitting with his peers: sit, sit,
& recover & be whole.

Any elegy follows closure—and it is those poems in *The Dream Songs* which consider the afterwards of events that may also be admired by and in themselves. These include Song 22, "Of 1826," in which Henry's personality is contrasted with those of Adams and Jefferson; number 46, in which the Apocalypse is imagined; 48, in which the death and resurrection of Christ are shown; and 55, in which a tenuous heaven is depicted. Otherwise, *The Dream Songs* must be taken as open-ended, linked by the uncertainties of one man's fate. Berryman suggests this with his epigraph for *77 Dream Songs*, quoted from Olive Schreiner: "But there is another method." Charles Thornbury explains this method as being different from "the stage method" of dramatic inevitability with its closure; it is "the method of the life we all lead," whose end we cannot foresee. Berryman's life recorded in *The Dream Songs* follows this second method. Yet as uncertain as its end might be, certain patterns arise, one being the consequence of not drinking and thus losing poetry. In Song 76 Henry confesses to his interlocutor, "Nothin very bad happen to me lately. / How you explain that?" He explains it in "terms o' your bafflin odd sobriety." Downcast by this lack of event, Henry says:

in a modesty of death I join my father
who dared so long agone leave me.
A bullet on a concrete stoop
close by a smothering southern sea
spreadeagled on an island, by my knee.

His foil retorts, "You is from hunger, Mr. Bones." But the theme that undercuts his sobriety, his father's suicide, will return obsessively, even after he writes the elegy of Song 145, beginning, "Also I love him: me he's done no wrong / for going on forty years—forgiveness time." In the penultimate poem of *The Dream Songs* he will respond less tenderly, less forgivingly, with rancor and violence. In the final act of his life, he will echo his father's despair.

The Dream Songs is a glorious work and much more difficult to describe than "Homage to Mistress Bradstreet," its virtues more difficult to praise or enumerate. It must be taken as a whole, read straight through; later one can return to favorite parts. It lacks the clarity of purpose of Whitman's "Song of Myself" and the individual successes of Dickinson's most productive period, during the Civil War. For its strengths and weaknesses, it is closer to *The Cantos*, but even so it lacks the thread of an aesthetic vision that runs through Pound's poem; furthermore, its composition takes place over a shorter span of time. Unlike any of its predecessors, it is merely personal. A frantic, at times hilarious, often obscure, and occasionally sublime journal of a soul, an individual soul, whose yearnings and embarrassments and triumphs are its own, *The Dream Songs* seems to have been written to record a voice that would, otherwise, be lost. Writing about *Macbeth*, Berryman typically throws light on his own project:

> We know people, perhaps, chiefly by their voices—their individual, indescribable, unmistakable, voices . . . and the creation of an individual tone for each of his major characters is of course one of the clearest signs of a good playwright.

Praise for Shakespeare's multifarious talent can be narrowed to admiration for Berryman's achievement: his major character, Henry, speaks in an unmistakable voice.

The loss of Henry in the last two books, *Love & Fame* and the posthumous *Delusions, Etc.*, is a serious blow to Berryman's verse. It is not enough that the poet's sensibility unites the concerns of these poems. Diction and syntax relax in *Love & Fame*, so that what we get is mainly gossip, much of it self-regarding gossip, too. The "Eleven Addresses to the Lord" are often touching, but the final one, in its compression, with the poet peripheral until the last stanza, speaks adequately for all of them. Whenever Henry Pussycat makes a reappearance, the verse rises, as in the final, parenthetical qualifications of "'How Do You Do, Dr. Berryman, Sir'" and in the late Dream Songs "Henry by Night" and "Henry's Understanding." Otherwise, a short poem such as "King David Dances" is an eloquent achievement, where a new persona is taken on, with a new dramatic voice. The elegy for Dylan Thomas, "In Memoriam (1914–1953)," is as fine as any written around the time of the poet's death, and perhaps better than most, having taken so long to appear. One of the most interesting of Berryman's last poems is the atypical "Washington in Love," made up apparently of notes for a longer poem. It shows Berryman's intuitive feeling for the American psyche, also present in "Bradstreet." Berryman's sense of American history was every bit as keen as Lowell's, though he less often brought it to bear on his poetry. Among the last poems, the most moving speak of exhaustion. The ending of "The Facts & Issues" is a cry to be united with the God Berryman had come to believe in, whom he called "the God of rescue." And "He Resigns" is so barren of hope that Berryman's old and dear friend William Meredith was moved to observe in his review of *Delusions, Etc.* in *Poetry*, in 1973:

> This was the kind of resignation we had not expected, this final resigning *from*, by one who had so long managed just to resign himself *to*, the world. There had been so many wrestlings with the dark angel of suicide, and always at least to a respectful draw.

Berryman's suicide, in January of 1972, turned Olive Shreiner's other method back into the stage method. As a blunt, biographical fact, it seems to have been prepared for by the return to the father's suicide, and looks, with sickening irony, like an inevitable act of belatedness. It does not, however, change the stature of "Homage to Mistress Bradstreet" or *The Dream Songs* as Berryman's two essential works.

Because his mind was subtler, suppler, less self-absorbed, and because his ear was tuned to so many other sounds in his reading, besides those that fed his own poetic needs—in a word, because of his greater *openness* to the variety and excellence of literature, Randall Jarrell as a poet suffers by comparison with Berryman. Like Berryman, Jarrell was artfully aware of voice, though his influences come through the voices of Frost and Chekhov, and these lack the pitch of Shakespearean rhetoric, which Berryman assimilated. Thus Jarrell's rhythms and syntax—straightforward and prosy—are less dramatic in their effect. When, in his mid-thirties, he began to play more with rhythm and syntax, this master of voices began to speak more clearly to us through his own character and other characters, usually women. And yet (the phrase "And yet" became one of Jarrell's favorites) always Jarrell's characters seem to speak in quotations. Somebody's reading is clearly on their minds. Though Berryman invented the most memorable voice of his generation, Jarrell invented the most distinct train of thought.

John Crowe Ransom and Robert Penn Warren were immediately impressed with the knowledge that Jarrell brought with him to Vanderbilt as an entering student in the early 1930's. Warren noticed that Jarrell had "read everything," but also felt he had to take young Randall aside after class and request that he modify his responses to what other students said, especially when they had been obtuse. Jarrell tended to hide his face in his hands and groan. His fellow students saw Jarrell as perfectly happy with his own company; he would later characterize his own nature as generally "gay." His gaiety was based on a fully sufficient imagination and view of the world. As a critic, he was able to create from his own taste a complete literary canon, ranging from German fairy tales to Chekhov to Kipling to Rilke to Frost. He was F. R. Leavis without class bitterness, but with more than enough cruel wit.

As Pritchard tells it, there is not much of event to report in Jarrell's life, except for the saddening breakdown that occurred before its abrupt end. Almost as much can be learned about the life from reading the handsome collection of letters that appeared in 1985 as from reading Pritchard's biography. His divorce from his first wife remains a mystery; his affair with the Austrian woman Elisabeth Eisler can be explained in part as an expression of his love for Europe itself, during his first visit there. His second marriage, to a woman with two daughters, also retains its elements of privacy. And when Pritchard tells us that Jarrell tended to think of himself and his second wife, Mary, as brother and sister, one truly begins to wonder about the erotic side of Jarrell, especially when he is compared with Berryman. Yet the sensuality of the poem "A Man Meets a Woman in the Street" is obvious:

> Women were paid to knit from sweet champagne
> Her second skin: it winds and unwinds, winds
> Up her long legs, delectable haunches,
> As she sways, in sunlight, up the gazing aisle.
> The shade of the tree that is called maidenhair,
> That is not positively known
> To exist in a wild state, spots her fair or almost fair
> Hair twisted in a French twist; tall or almost tall,
> She walks through the air the rain has washed, a clear thing
> Moving easily on its high heels, seeming to men
> Miraculous...

This is all the more striking, given the chasteness of so much of Jarrell's life and poetry. Pritchard insists that Jarrell was often afflicted by prudery. Lowell observed that his friend seemed unsoiled by the dirt of human living. Only during his breakdown—when he appears basically to have suffered a full-blown midlife crisis exacerbated by an over prescription for the antidepressant Elavil—does Jarrell seem cast in the mold of his generation. Off the

Elavil, deeply depressed, he attempted suicide by cutting his left wrist. One night, coming home from a visit to a physical therapist, where he had been working to restore his wrist to health, he was struck and killed by a car in circumstances that are still ambiguous. Pritchard makes the best possible case for an accident, as does Mary Jarrell in the collected letters. We know his contemporaries, like Lowell and Berryman, thought otherwise. Yet unlike Berryman's death, Jarrell's, even if it were an act of self-annihilation, lacks the prepared-for dramatic closure that would shed light on his life or work.

Jarrell lived a life of the mind, of reading and writing. His biography is far less valuable to the reader than is Berryman's, though Pritchard does manage to describe the uniqueness of both Jarrell's mind and his talent. He does this by assessing the working of Jarrell's wit, which made its debut through his reviews of poetry and quickly became an instrument of cruelty feared and resented by American poets. Karl Shapiro was certainly putting on his best face when he reacted to a Jarrell review by saying he felt as if he had been run over but not hurt. For Jarrell could hurt painfully. What he wrote about Gertrude Johnson, the novelist in his comic masterpiece *Pictures from an Institution*, could have been said of him as a critic: "Gertrude's bark *was* her bite; and many a bite has lain awake at night longing to be Gertrude's bark." In one of his first reviews, his analysis of Conrad Aiken's work was so remarkably wounding that Malcolm Cowley felt obliged to write an extensive rebuttal. Jarrell responded, "I feel as if my decision had been overruled by the Supreme Court." Pritchard is right to point out that some of the things Jarrell said showed an original cast of mind. "It is one thing to abuse Kenneth Patchen's poetry," writes Pritchard. "it is a rather different thing to speak of it as 'Original Swinburne-with-a-dead-baby.'"

Pritchard follows the lead of Jarrell—who quoted extensively in his essays—by quoting Jarrell whenever possible. Ultimately, we reach *Pictures from an Institution*, published in 1952, which Pritchard argues is hardly a novel at all when compared with, say, Mary McCarthy's *The Groves of Academe*. Jarrell flings barb after barb, and the shower is like Agincourt, too much for a single sitting. What the novel shares with Jarrell's best poetry, however, is a profound and humane view of the world, about which the poet found it almost impossible to generalize. For him, as for Wittgenstein, whom he admired, the world was everything that was the case. The narrator of *Pictures* tries to explain this philosophy to Gertrude Johnson in a discussion about university life:

"It's like people. People aren't like anything, there are too many of them. Professors aren't like anything, they're like everything. I'm a professor; why, Gertrude, right now, you're a professor."

It was a queer thought: Gertrude looked at it, moved it with her paw, and let it stay there.

Despite the skill he brought to the arts of caricature and condemnation, Jarrell was also a master of the essay of praise; his re-evaluations (Frost and Whitman) and evaluations (Marianne Moore, Elizabeth Bishop, and Robert Lowell) of poets he consistently admired are among the best we have.

William Pritchard's aim in his biography and edition of selected poems is to bring new attention to Jarrell—whom he feels is too narrowly known for a single poem, "The Death of the Ball Turret Gunner." Though Pritchard is correct in believing that this poem is not representative of Jarrell's best work, Jarrell remains a key poet of World War II. Jarrell's fluency in poetry of all sorts was so great that he rarely brought anything much to bear upon the rhythm of his verse. This makes him very different from Berryman, who always struggled toward the highly charged, nervous phrasing that clings to memory like a lightning flash. Jarrell instead is master of the voices of his erudition, which play back and forth, charming the reader, reiterating important points. In "Woman," for example, Jarrell moves from Disraeli to Freud to Genesis:

> When, like Disraeli, I murmur
> That you are more like a mistress than a wife,
> More like an angel than a mistress; when, like Satan,
> I hiss in your ear some vile suggestion,
> Some delectable abomination,
> You smile at me indulgently: "Men, men!" . . .
>
> Let us form as Freud has said, "a group of two."
> You are the best thing that this world can offer—
> He said so. Or I remember that he said so;
> If I am mistaken it's a Freudian error . . .
>
> Did not the angel say to Abraham
> That he would spare the cities of the plain
> If there were found in them ten unjust women?
> —That is to say, merciful . . .

Jarrell's problem, if it is a problem, is that he can go on like this forever, and does in many poems. And yet not to have these chains of voices—the voices of one person's reading and his changes on it—is to miss the vision of a mind at play on the field of the page, a player who seeks not to dramatize but to expose in a monologue as many voices as possible, for the sake of association and then for the shape of the poem, or until the poem finds its shape.

Behind this method, as I have hinted earlier, is the allusiveness of a modernist such as T. S. Eliot. In Jarrell's longer poems one also might feel the influence of Frost's Horatian discourses, but with this distinction: the older master had a stronger dramatic sense. Not that Frost could not be discursive as well; in the early poem "The Black Cottage," he discourses about The Civil War, The Declaration of Independence, race relations, the power of the imagination, family life, and the cyclical and pragmatic nature of truth, all on the pretext of looking at an abandoned house. On similar pretexts, again in "A Man Meets a Woman on the Street," Jarrell writes:

> Following this new
> Body, somehow familiar, this young shape, somehow old,
> For a moment I'm younger, the century is younger.
> The living Strauss, his moustache just getting gray,
> Is shouting to the players: "Louder!
> Louder! I can still hear Madame Shumann-Heink—"
> Or else, white, bald, the old man's joyfully
> Telling conductors they must play *Elektra*
> Like *A Midsummer Night's Dream*—like fairy music;
> Proust, dying, is swallowing his iced beer
> And changing in proof the death of Bergotte
> According to his own experience; Garbo,
> A commissar in Paris, is listening attentively
> To the voice telling how McGillicuddy met McGillivray,
> And McGillivray said to McGillicuddy—no, McGillicuddy
> Said to McGillivray—that is, McGillivray . . . Garbo
> Says seriously, "I vish dey'd never met."

Such writing would be self-indulgent only if the quality of mind were less brilliant. Though Pritchard includes this poem in the *Selected*, others like it—for example, "Woman" and "A Conversation with the Devil"—he does not.

Pritchard wants us primarily to appreciate a Jarrell of lambent voices and tones, the Jarrell of "A Girl in a Library." But we also need the Jarrell who translates the psychology of the fairy tale and the Jarrell who knows the at-

mosphere in which one reads a fairy tale and remembers it as an adult—the
Jarrell of "A Hunt in the Black Forest":

> After the door shuts and the footsteps die,
> He calls out: "Mother?"
> The wind roars in the leaves: his cold hands, curled
> Within his curled, cold body, his blurred head
> Are warmed and tremble; and the red leaves flow
> Like cells across the spectral, veined,
> Whorled darkness of his vision.
> The red dwarf
> Whispers, "The leaves are turning"; and he reads
> The dull whorled notes, that tremble like a wish
> Over the branched staves of the wood.
>
> The stag is grazing in the wood.

We hear this voice as well in "The End of the Rainbow":

> And the voice of a departed friend, a female
> Friend, replies as crystal
> Replies to a teaspoon, to a fingernail:
> "A *strange* man . . . . But all men are, aren't they?
> A man is like a merman." "A merman?"
> "Mermen were seals, you know. They called them silkies."
> "You mean the Forsaken Merman was a seal?"
> "What did you think it was a merman?
> And mermaids were manatees." "The things you know!"
> "The things you don't know!"

Jarrell knows both sides, always, the things we know and the things we
don't know, and is willing to follow one or the other until it leads him to
light. Sometimes he ends nowhere, in pain, in darkness. I believe there are
times when he honestly does not hear the implications of his language. In "A
Girl in a Library," he writes, "The trap is closed about you, and you sleep," describing his subject with several delectable terms—the nose like strawberries,
the limbs "Dusted with cinnamon, an apple dumpling's"—before gradually
raising the evolutionary status of the sleeping student, dozing on her physical
education text and home economics homework, from coed to orangoutang
and finally to peasant. His disembodied cohort, his Tinkerbell, Tatyana

Larina, her "gray eyes nickel," looks at the girl with the combined spirit of Gertrude Johnson and Nero. Civilization and its discontents keep the poet's own desires in check: "I am a thought of yours: and yet, you do not think . . . ." The poem contains some of Jarrell's best writing and some of his most unconscious.

Pritchard's Jarrell is a poet whose central theme is change. The cry at the heart of his work is given voice in "The Woman at the Washington Zoo," the title poem of his most celebrated book, published in 1960:

> Vulture,
> When you come for the white rat that the foxes left,
> Take off the red helmet of your head, the black
> Wings that have shadowed me, and step to me as man:
> The wild brother at whose feet the white wolves fawn,
> To whose hand of power the great lioness
> Stalks, purring . . . .
>
>   You know what I was,
> You see what I am: change me, change me!

And indeed the women who speak many of his finest poems, such as "The Face" and "Next Day," stand before a mirror that tells them, "You are old." Age or aging breaks the spell. But what spell is it? In Jarrell's last book of poems, *The Lost World*—published in 1965, the year he died—we see a poet who desires changelessness, especially in the nostalgic title sequence about his childhood in Los Angeles, living with his grandparents among the vivid unrealities of Hollywood, in the only American climate that, on good days, foreshadows the weather of heaven. In "The Lost World" the poet is like the child in Dylan Thomas' story, who dreamed that he flew above his school, his town, his childhood, and there was no time. Whatever the spell was for Jarrell, poetry, a form of magical speech, kept it alive by staving off as long as possible age, growing up, death, the end.

Berryman's muse was a playwright—or better yet a director for the stage, ordering, "Dramatize!" He chose his subjects as if casting them and approached Mistress Bradstreet and himself with the same deliberate planning. Albeit willing to see what the future held, he was ready for the future armed with the Dream Song as a form, and while it worked he made the future fit it.

Jarrell's muse, on the other hand, was a psychoanalyst, or a poet's version of a psychoanalyst, that murmured, "Keep talking."

4

In Memory of Orpheus:

Three Elegies by Donald Justice

Anyone familiar with it knows that an elegiac mood pervades Donald Justice's poetry. Many of his best known poems have been written in memory of friends and relatives or to commemorate places, like Miami, Florida and South Georgia, where he grew up and which have changed so much that to remember them instills the pain of nostalgia. The elegiac and the nostalgic are, in fact, so closely related in his poems, at times they are impossible to tell apart. None of this is news for those who know and love Donald Justice's work. I am sure that each of us has a favorite Justice poem that represents this intimate wedding of two, powerful emotions. Mine is "On the Death of Friends in Childhood," from his first book, *The Summer Anniversaries*, published in 1960.

ON THE DEATH OF FRIENDS IN CHILDHOOD

We shall not ever meet them bearded in heaven,
Nor sunning themselves among the bald of hell;
If anywhere, in the deserted schoolyard at twilight,
Forming a ring, perhaps, or joining hands
In games whose very names we have forgotten.
Come, memory, let us seek them there in the shadows.

Memory is invited to re-encounter not only the lost friends but the lost childhood in a place made meaningful by that loss. We can find the same compelling feeling in Justice's poems about Miami and the South. This sense of loss is so perfected in Justice's work that I cannot think of another poet who has equalled his expression of it, though there are many, all in the Romantic tradition which he proudly embraces, which we might put beside him.

Having begun with the most salient and important aspect of his work—its emotional charge—I am now going to talk about something a little different. Or rather, in order to understand, perhaps, why his invitation to memory in the last line of "On the Death of Friends in Childhood" is so moving, I am going to talk about a special aspect of the elegiac that I have found in a few poems which I believe are central to Justice's work. Two of them, "In Memory of My Friend, the Bassoonist, John Lenox" and "In Memory of the Unknown Poet, Robert Boardman Vaughn," are from Justice's 1987 book, *The Sunset Maker*; the third, "Invitation to a Ghost," is included in the section of new poems in the 1995 *New and Selected Poems*. Each of these three poems alludes in some way to the life and death of the mythical musician and poet Orpheus, a figure of some importance to Justice whose newest book includes as an epigraph an epigram about Orpheus's attempt to retrieve his beloved Eurydice from death. On the dedication page of the *New and Selected Poems*, we find the following three lines:

> Orpheus, nothing to look forward to, looked back.
> They say he sang then, but the song is lost.
> At least he had seen once more the beloved back.

I hope to show that the emotive power of Orpheus's ancient story, the story of an artist's excellence and loss, as it is echoed in these three elegies by Donald Justice, provides them with some of their own emotional impact. I want to suggest as well that the role of the elegist, one Justice has taken on many times in his career, parallels the descent of Orpheus as he attempts to bring his love back to the world of the living, to retrieve what he has lost.

~ ~ ~

IN MEMORY OF MY FRIEND, THE BASSOONIST, JOHN LENOX

Coconut Grove

I

One winter he was the best
Contrabassoonist south
Of Washington, D. C.—
The only one. Lonely

In eminence he sat,
Like some lost island king,
High on a second-story porch
Overlooking the bay

(His blue front lawn, his kingdom)
And presided over the Shakespearean
Feuds and passions of the eave-pigeons.
Who, during the missile crisis,

Had stocked his boat with booze,
Charts, and the silver flute
He taught himself to play,
Casually, one evening.

And taught himself to see,
Sailing thick glasses out blindly
Over some lily-choked canal.
O autodidact supreme!

2

John, where you are now can you see?
Do the pigeons there bicker like ours?
Does the deep bassoon not moan
Or the flute sigh ever?

No one could think it was you,
Slumped there on the sofa, despairing,
The hideous green sofa.
No, you are off somewhere,

Off with Gaugin and Christian
Amid hibiscus'd isles,
Red-mustached, pink-bearded
Again, as in early manhood.

It is well. Shark waters
Never did faze you half so much
As the terrible radios
And booboiseries of the neighbors.

Here, if you care, the bay
Is printed with many boats now,
Thick as trash; that high porch is gone,
Gone up in the smoke of money, money;

The barbarians . . .
            But enough.
You are missed. Across the way,
Someone is practicing sonatas,
And the sea air smells again of good gin.

"In Memory of My Friend, the Bassoonist, John Lenox" is not Justice's only elegy for a musician, that is, if we count "Variation for Two Pianos," which recalls the pianist Higgins who has gone, taking both his pianos and leaving the entire state of Arkansas without music. There is also the fictional Eugene Bestor of "The Sunset Maker," whose entire *ouevre* has been reduced to a single, haunting phrase remembered by the narrator. All three musicians are linked to the natural world, the one enchanted by the music of Orpheus. The birds are Higgins' pupils and Bestor's music brings to mind the landscapes of Bonnard and the creation itself. When alive, John Lenox presided over Coconut Grove and the "Shakespearean / Feuds and passions of the eave-pigeons." He was possessed of a unique excellence as a "contrabassoonist," since at one time he was the only one "south / Of Washington, D. C.," but he was also an "autodidact supreme" who taught himself to play the flute. The loneliness such artistry creates is also a theme we find in these poems, and certainly it is one we can associate with Orpheus. As the critic Paul Breslin has observed in an essay in a recent issue of *The American Poetry Review*, Orpheus is unaware of just how his music moves other people until he meets Eurydice. His love for her changes that. But after he loses her the second and final time, he immerses himself once again in his art, disengaged from the world he moves through and affects. Breslin speculates that it is for this reason that Orpheus is torn to pieces by the Thracian women. For Justice, the death of Orpheus makes the pursuit of art all the more precious.

In Justice's poetry nothing is loved so much as what is lost. In the story of Orpheus, this loss includes both Eurydice and Orpheus. And it is the latter's death, the death of the artist, that Justice depicts in these elegies. Like the head of Orpheus, borne along on the Hebrus, John Lenox is imagined sailing out "blindly / Over some lily choked canal." He is replaced by "the terrible radios / And booboiseries" of his neighbors whose boats make a bad poetry, "printed . . . / Thick as trash," on the bay that was his kingdom. His "high porch," where he ruled creation, is gone, destroyed by greed. And the poet accuses in one elliptical phrase, "The barbarians . . . " Odd as it might seem, I think we can also hear an echo of Milton's flare of temper in "Lycidas" as he condemns the Church of England. And like Milton's Edward King, Justice's John Lenox is translated to a higher condition. He is imagined restored to youth, the genius of some South Pacific shore.

> Off with Gaugin and Christian
> Amid hibiscus'd isles,
> Red-mustached, pink-bearded
> Again, as in early manhood.

In his entry on the elegy in *The Princeton Encyclopedia of Poetry and Poetics*, Stephen Fogle observes that the form often includes "the consolation of some permanent principle." The idea of consolation may sound a religious note that, despite the echo of Milton, we do not associate with Justice. He could hardly be called a religious poet, except as he shares Wallace Stevens' affirmation in "Final Soliloquy of the Interior Paramour"—that "God and the imagination are one." Yet the absence of the Orphean Lenox is not filled in by crass substitutes alone. There is also a hint that his kind of artistry persists in the face of vulgarity. "Someone," the poet informs his lost friend, "across the way . . . is practicing sonatas." And as if to dispel the drunken after effects of those local barbarians and the smoke of their money, the smell of the sea air is reminiscent once again of "good" not bad gin. The endurance of the craft and charm of genuine artistry is indeed a consolation.

~ ~ ~

IN MEMORY OF THE UNKNOWN POET, ROBERT BOARDMAN VAUGHN

But the essential advantage for a poet is not, to have a beautiful world with which to deal: it is to be able to see beneath both beauty and ugliness; to see the boredom, and the horror, and the glory.
    —T. S. Eliot

It was his story. It would always be his story.
It followed him; it overtook him finally—
The boredom, and the horror, and the glory.

Probably at the end he was not yet sorry,
Even as the boots were brutalizing him in the alley.
It was his story. It would always be his story,

Blown on a blue horn, full of sound and fury,
But signifying, O signifying magnificently
The boredom, and the horror, and the glory.

I picture the snow as falling without hurry
To cover the cobbles and the toppled ashcans completely.
It was his story. It would always be his story.

Lately he had wandered between St. Mark's Place and the Bowery,
Already half a spirit, mumbling and muttering sadly.
O the boredom, and the horror, and the glory.

All done now. But I remember the fiery
Hypnotic eye and the raised voice blazing with poetry.
It was his story and would always be his story—
The boredom, and the horror, and the glory.

It may be a stretch to imagine the connection between a contrabassoonist and the lyre-strumming Orpheus, but the association between Robert Boardman Vaughn and Orpheus is one that Justice has made himself in another poem. In "Portrait with One Eye," from the 1973 book *Departures* and dedicated to Vaughn, Justice addresses him playfully as "Orpheus,"

Imperishable liar!
Your life's a poem still,
Broken iambs and all,
Jazz, jails—the complete works.

That poem recounts the outlandish, comical, even poetic behavior of a living individual, whose style of life seems to be a reproach to the speaker's. In contrast, "In Memory of the Unknown Poet, Robert Boardman Vaughn" is laden with a tragic sense of loss, not only of a life but of a talent. A villanelle, it has to be one of the handful—and by that I mean five or six—essential poems in the form in English. Start thinking of the others worth remembering and you'll see what I mean.

The Orpheus of "In Memory of the Unknown Poet" is a poet and not a musician, though music is still strongly associated with him. His story is "[b]lown on a blue horn, full of sound and fury." Yet the Orpheus we see here is not the witty, rakish figure of "Portrait with One Eye." This one is bereft, "[a] lready half a spirit, mumbling and muttering sadly" in the nether world of Manhattan. In this case the barbarous throng is represented by the "boots . . . brutalizing him in the alley." Though the poet has lost his gift, the elegist can remember its enchantment, "the fiery / Hypnotic eye and the raised voice blazing with poetry." Ironically, Vaughn's life is "a poem still," as Justice claims it is in "Portrait with One Eye," but this poem is the one T. S. Eliot describes in the epigraph and which the villanelle employs as one of its refrains. The Orphic Vaughn, degraded to a mere ghost of himself, still embodies a story that signifies "magnificently . . . [t]he boredom, and the horror, and the glory" beneath the beauty and ugliness of life.

Vaughn's fate as Orpheus is moving in part because he is obscure. Fame did not spare Orpheus, of course, but a certain obscurity is an aspect of those Justice celebrates in these elegies, as if it were part of their uniqueness, each of them, like John Lenox, being somehow "the only one." They are located in unlikely places, like Arkansas, or Coconut Grove, or in an alley in lower Manhattan, or in the case of Henri Coulette, though it is unstated, Los Angeles. Gray's "Elegy Written in a Country Churchyard" comes to mind, in which he mourns "[s]ome heart once pregnant with celestial fire" and otherwise unknown. In a sense, Justice is bringing each of his departed friends to light, to a kind of fame. He performs an Orphean task himself by descending into that bleak underworld, the alley, where he pictures "the snow as falling without hurry / To cover the cobbles and the toppled ashcans completely," and retrieving the brutally murdered, unknown poet. His villanelle for Robert Boardman Vaughn along with "Portrait with One Eye" and the poem "Hell," from New and Selected Poems in which Vaughn himself speaks, recall Berryman's sequence of Dream Songs for Delmore Schwartz, another Orpheus who signified magnificently and died in obscurity.

The achievement of an artist and the loss of that achievement, the loneliness of excellence, especially excellence in obscurity, are all reflected in the life and death of Orpheus. They are conditions that move Justice and, because of his own excellence as a poet, they move us, too. I would actually like to consider sometime what it means to be moved by a poem, since emotion seems so central to Justice's poems, but I am going to assume that you agree with me about what it means. So when I say that I think the third of these elegies, "Invitation to a Ghost," dedicated to the poet Henri Coulette, is the most moving of the three, I assume you will know what I am talking about, even if possibly you don't agree.

~ ~ ~

INVITATION TO A GHOST

for Henri Coulette (1927–1988)

I ask you to come back now as you were in youth,
Confident, eager, and the silver brushed from your temples.
Let it be as though a man could go backwards through death,
Erasing the years that did not much count,
Or that added up perhaps to no more than a single brilliant forenoon.

Sit with us. Let it be as it was in those days
When alcohol brought our tongues the first sweet foretaste of oblivion.
And what should we speak of but verse? For who would speak of such things
now but among friends?
(A bad line, an atrocious line, could make you wince: we have all seen it.)

I see you again turn toward the cold and battering sea.
Gull shadows darken the skylight; a wind keens among the chimney pots;
Your hand trembles a little.
                          What year was that?

Correct me if I remember it badly,
But was there not a dream, sweet but also terrible,
In which Eurydice, strangely, preceded *you*?
And you followed, knowing exactly what to expect, and of course she did turn.

Come back now and help me with these verses.
Whisper to me some beautiful secret that you remember from life.

"Invitation to a Ghost" is based in part on "The Coming Back of the Assassi-
nated Poet," Rafael Alberti's poem for Federico Garcia Lorca which begins,
in the translation by Mark Strand,

> You have come back to me older and sadder in the drowsy
> light of a quiet dream in March, your dusty temples
> disarmingly gray, and that olive
> bronze you had in your magical youth,
> furrowed by the passing of years, just as if
> you lived out slowly in death
> the life you never had while you were alive.

Adopting and reversing the strategies of poems he admires have been techniques Justice has employed in other poems, especially those in *Departures*. Whereas Lorca appears unbidden to Alberti and Alberti imagines him continuing to age, even in death, Justice on the other hand invites Coulette to return as a young man. Both poems are also moving because they are about ghosts, so, in a sense, their subjects are not utterly lost but still present in some form. Contrast this with Robert Boardman Vaughn who is depicted after the fact of his death or with John Lenox whose whereabouts are imagined vividly in some island paradise but who is inaccessible to the grieving poet. Coulette is invoked and summoned, and the poem implicitly returns both poets, himself and Justice, to their youth.

The story of Orpheus is alluded to directly in this poem, and in a wonderful passage Coulette takes on the roles of Orpheus and Eurydice both. In the penultimate stanza, Justice reminds his friend of a dream he may have had. The poignancy and tact of the following passage are characteristic of Justice.

> Correct me if I remember it badly,
> But was there not a dream, sweet but also terrible,
> In which Eurydice, strangely, preceded *you*?
> And you followed, knowing exactly what to expect, and of course she did turn.

Reversal, the very mechanism of irony, is a favorite strategy of Justice, as I have said. Orpheus changes places and, it appears, fates with Eurydice. This reversal and pairing may be related to the repetitions which function as a web of correspondences, like an improvised, erratic rhyme scheme, in this masterful free verse poem. Nearly a dozen of its words and phrases are repeated at least twice. As always Justice's virtuosity is subtle but unmistakable. The poem reads like a performance of one poet offered for the pleasure of another.

(Surely every Orpheus that the elegist seeks in the underworld is also a Eurydice. I have not forgotten the memoiristic poems in *The Sunset Maker* that recall Justice's music teachers, Mrs. Snow, Mrs. L, and Mrs. K.)

Orpheus must be defeated by barbarians, of course. We have seen that in the poem for John Lenox and in the villanelle for Robert Boardman Vaughn. Here they go without saying and exist outside the charmed circle of young poets Justice wishes Coulette to return to:

Sit with us. Let it be as it was in those days
When alcohol brought our tongues the first sweet foretaste of oblivion.
And what should we speak of but verse? For who would speak of such things now
  but among friends?
(A bad line, an atrocious line, could make you wince: we have all seen it.)

We may or may not envy the sensitivity that would make someone respond
physically to bad poetry. And there is another threat, too, less clear but much
more ominous. Just as Orpheus descends into hell and even, one might add,
goes among the mad, murderous Bacchantes, Coulette is depicted turning
"toward the cold and battering sea" as his hand "trembles a little." This image
of alienation and annihilation takes its place darkly at the center of the poem.

I find this poem moving also because it assumes there is some value present
but secret in life. Why else would Orpheus or anyone wish to bring a loved
one back from death? Whereas this secret is identified in the villanelle as
boredom, horror, and glory, and in "In Memory of My Friend" as good music,
gin, and company, in "Invitation to a Ghost" it is simply "beautiful." My guess
is that the secret has to do with poetry and the invitation to share the secret is
based on the assumption that the dead possess knowledge denied to the living
or that the living should know but have forgotten. Orpheus descends to rescue Eurydice in order to conquer his grief, but also for consolation, as Justice
implies in his epigraph to the *New and Selected Poems*. Though it may be essential, as T. S. Eliot says, for the poet to see past beauty and ugliness to what
lies beneath them, it is just as necessary to believe there is some value inherent
in experience which is good or beautiful. For Orpheus as he is embodied in
John Lenox, Robert Boardman Vaughn, Henri Coulette, and Donald Justice,
this good and beautiful secret is art, specifically music and poetry, and the
work that goes into making them, an endeavor of the living. When, in the
final line of "On the Death of Friends in Childhood," the poet says, "Come,
memory, let us seek," it is understood that the poet's means of seeking, even
in the realms of the dead, is through his poetry.

5

Robinson, Frost, and Jeffers
and the New Narrative Poetry

There is a twofold difference between those Americans writing narrative poetry today, especially among the younger generation who make up what is being called increasingly the new narrative movement, and their forerunners, Edwin Arlington Robinson, Robert Frost, and Robinson Jeffers. First, whereas Robinson might have looked to George Crabbe for his example, and Robert Frost might have looked to William Wordsworth and over his shoulder at Robinson, and Robinson Jeffers might well have had in mind the anonymous border ballads and the poems and novels of Thomas Hardy, today's young American narrative poet must look to Robinson, Frost, and Jeffers. If he or she looks beyond them, to their own English masters, these modern American figures intervene. The second difference is that modernism itself intervenes between Robinson, Frost, and Jeffers and the contemporary view of them. Unlike Eliot or Pound, neither Robinson, Frost, nor Jeffers was part of a transatlantic axis or took part in describing the modernist aesthetic. Only Frost proposed a poetics, his modest but sheerly original method of sentence-sounds. Robinson and Jeffers worked by example and neither would be included among what is now called the high modernists. Their narrative approaches, like Frost's, were linear and not spatial, coherent and not fragmented. Their intentions, too, in telling their stories might have been recognized by Crabbe, Wordsworth, or Hardy as moral, formally reflecting humanity's proper relationship to the world. It is doubtful that these older English poets would have recognized much in Eliot's and Pound's deliberately skewed and fragmented approaches to the narrative mode.

Although I am convinced that Crabbe, Wordsworth, and Hardy would have looked kindly on Robinson, Frost, and Jeffers, would Jeffers, Frost, and Robinson approve of what is going on in the narrative movement today? I am not sure. In fact, I have some serious doubts about whether they would. However, despite the doubts that I can imagine they would have, I think their skepticism might be applied to real virtues in the new narrative movement and only a few shortcomings.

The successes of these three masters of American narrative poetry are notable for their difference in length. Robinson is best short, Frost at a medium stretch, and Jeffers, who reserved his narrative skill for his longer poems, is best when extending himself.

Although Robinson could and did write long narrative poems, his greatest stories are told in poems that are often shorter than "The Ballad of Sir Patrick Spens." Sometimes they are sonnets, like the one about the butcher Reuben Bright or the mysteriously happy Cliff Klingenhagen. There are the brief poems in quatrains about Richard Cory and Minniver Cheevy; there are the lyrical tetrameters about the miller and his wife who kill themselves; there is the old anthology piece, "Mr. Flood's Party," which is still a great poem, despite our familiarity and the undergraduate contempt it may have bred. Robinson's forays into the longer poem, like his Tennysonian retellings of the Camelot stories, are about as interesting, now, as Tennyson's own. An argument for the resurgence of narrative verse cannot be based on *Lancelot* as it could not be on *Idylls of the King*. There is a friendly, ambling, yet profound movement to the medium-length "Isaac and Archibald," but for narrative compression that pivots on a fully created character, sometimes complete with tragic flaw, Robinson is the master. He is Dickens in fourteen lines.

One looks around today for anyone who chooses to work in his mode, to set out the entire story, naming the names resonantly, in a small space. When a contemporary narrative poet works that small, and that formally, the story is usually an autobiographical portion of the life or it is a series of events involving a persona. T. R. Hummer's marvelous "Carrier," a sonnet sequence from his first book *The Angelic Orders*, is an example of the latter. Hummer displays Robinson's compassion for his characters, for their tragic as well as their comic fates. Here is "Looking in His Rearview Mirror, the Rural Carrier Thinks He Catches a Glimpse of the Angel of Death Hanging over George Gillespie's Mailbox."

> A clear day, not even a crow in the air
> Over George Gillespie's as I put the mail
> In his box. The usual stuff, except for the one bill,
> The one he's been waiting for, from the funeral parlor.
> He's asked about it twice. The first time was the day
> After his wife was buried. He came to the road

When he saw my car. Asked if I had it. Said he owed
Somebody something. Said he was ready to pay.

The second time was some days later. He just stood there,
And when I shook my head he walked off, nodding.
I haven't seen him since, though every morning
When I come by, his curtains tremble. He knows I'm here.
He knows my moves, how I hang out my window to slip
Something in his box. He knows how to add things up.

When a contemporary poet interested in telling a story invents a character as rich as Hummer's mail carrier, he is more likely to give him an entire series of poems than to compress everything into one sonnet. Certain characters of Robinson's make more than one appearance in his poems (one thinks of Flammonde), but he would have made the one story work—as Hummer makes the story of George Gillespie work, albeit as an episode in the mail carrier's life. Robinson's legacy to the new narrative is the episodic power of the short form, which has now been extended to the sequence through the contemporary interest in personae. Our current extension of character through sequence may have been seen by Robinson as an attenuation, either in search of a moral center or in flight from one. The intervention of modernism may be seen in not wanting to round off the life—to send Richard Cory home to the pistol or Minniver Cheevy and Eben Flood to the bottle. The dilemma for the new narrative poet, then, is whether or not to commit himself to a character's fate. Unless he does commit himself, he may find he has created characters more like Edgar Lee Masters' small town stereotypes than like Robinson's sharp-edged yet three dimensional human beings.

In fact, it may be Masters who appeals to us, though I say so with great reluctance. What intervenes between us and Robinson is modern relativism, the reticence to judge, unless the character is part of a historical sequence (consider the numerous historical poems of late, for example, about Nazis) and history has already judged. Perhaps the most successful Robinsonian character created in a narrative poem in recent years is Robert McDowell's bootlegger in "Quiet Money," the title poem of his first book. Named "Joe," as in "average Joe," this character flies the Atlantic before Lindbergh; his job is to bring liquor in from Sweden. Joe is forced to endure his obscurity while Lindbergh enjoys celebrity then suffers the tragedy of his child's kidnap and murder. Joe must come to terms with his own absence from history, which he decides is preferable to Lindbergh's place in history, and thus enjoys the rounded fate of a Robinsonian character. "Quiet Money," however, is a poem of over 200 lines and hard to imagine as a sonnet.

Robert Frost's approach to narrative, in his poems of medium length in his early books, *North of Boston*, *Mountain Interval*, and *New Hampshire*, may be better suited to contemporary workers in the form. Many of Frost's narratives are based on the classical eclogue, a conversation between rustics, as in "Home Burial" and "Death of a Hired Man"; in others, a single voice dominates, although a narrator usually introduces the speechmaker and lets him or her go on, as in "The Black Cottage." Another example is the conversation between the mother and son for the benefit of their overnight guest in "The Witch of Coös." The dramatic monologue takes an interesting form in Frost that can be seen in today's monologue poems. Unlike Browning's dramatic monologues, in which we can imagine the stage and the other characters, Frost's dramatic monologues tend more to be voiced ruminations about the speaker's life or inner life with no audience in mind, except the reader, as in "Wild Grapes" and "The Pauper Witch of Grafton." Only "A Servant to Servants" has Browning's sense of the full stage being acknowledged and the play being stopped for the speech, but there the poor woman uses her audience as an excuse to talk to herself. Frost rarely makes a point with names the way Robinson does, unless the name is the point, as in the Starks who gather in "Generations of Men" and chat about the streak of madness in the family or the little girl in "Maple" who must contend with people who do not believe that "Maple" is a proper name for a child. One exception, though still different from Robinson's mode of characterization, is the name Toffile Lajway in "The Witch of Coös." It is the name of the witch's dead husband, which the narrator verifies the next morning on the mailbox. As a corruption of "Théophile Lajouer," its implication that God loves a joke shows us a kind of word play and reflexivity that I, for one, have never found in Robinson. Frost is usually more interested in what his people *say* than in what happens to them or what their fates are or are to be. What they say and how they say it in blank verse are the pleasures of Frost's narrative poetry, more than the stories he is telling. As the critic Vereen Bell has pointed out, one does not go to Frost for his plots. This is not to say that plot does not exist in Frost's narrative poems, but it is more as a portion of a life, an episode with the rest of the life left to speculation, sometimes certain, more often not.

Frost's narrator is rarely central, but usually is along for the walk or the ride, as in "A Fountain, a Bottle, a Donkey's Ears, and Some Books," or he is the scene-setter, as in "The Witch of Coös" or, again, the person who goes along with the minister in "The Black Cottage" or who serves as an ear for the cranky mother-in-law in "The Housekeeper." This is an appealing role for the contemporary narrative poet who cannot, as Frost rarely could, completely dispense with himself or herself in a narrative poem. To serve as witness, bringing his own character or situation to bear while letting the subject shine forth, shine brighter than the poet in word or deed, was Frost's goal in his narratives, one he abandoned, as he abandoned narrative, as his fame increased and he realized that it was his pithy lyrics people wanted.

Two poets who are working particularly well in that narrative tradition that Frost adapted from Wordsworth and made his own are Andrew Hudgins and Garrett Hongo.

Since Hudgins works primarily in the blank verse line, I will look first at him. "Sotto Voce," from his first book *Saints and Strangers*, adapts its title from music and gives the phrase dramatic meaning. Hudgins presents himself as our narrator, but in more of a comic light than Frost ever would have shown *himself*. Like Frost, Hudgins wants to turn a phrase into a dramatic moment, to make the emotion of the poem come from the way he tells the story. Here are the poem's opening lines:

> I'm standing in the university
> library, staring at the German books
> and I don't parle eine word of Allemand.
> Actually I'm listening to a girl named Beth
> call her boyfriend in El Paso.
> He's leaving her for work in Mexico
> and other reasons. She doesn't understand,
> repeats out loud the things he says, as if
> the sound of her own voice will help make sense
> of what is happening. And even now
> her voice is airy, cool, and beautiful;
> only her humor perks into uncertainty
> as she tries to turn around his serious
> long distance voice.

Although I am not arguing that Hudgins *sounds* like Frost, it is hard not to see the Frostian touch in how the girl repeats what her boyfriend says out loud, "as if / the sound of her own voice will help make sense / of what is happening." The simple language and the sense of that phrase fall out along the blank verse arrangement as Frost would have had it. Also, we are given a multiplicity of view points: the speaker's, the girl's, the imagined party on the other end of the line, and the poet's. We're not supposed to be overhearing the girl's conversation, but how can we help it? One thinks of Frost's late and brilliant short poem, "Loud Talk," in which the speaker and his companion overhear an argument coming from a house at night as they pass by. Frost reports the substance of the fight between a married couple and some of its actual phrasing, because the phrasing contains the truth of the matter.

Hudgins watches Beth "pull pink tissues from her purse":

> With practiced hands she shreds them into strips
> then floats them to the phone booth's tiny floor,
> the phone held lovingly between her ear and shoulder.
> As if it were already painless, she's
> reminding him of the evening they made love
> (her alto—half in music—lingers on
> the simple words) in her parents' queen-size bed.

Clearly, it is the way she is talking, the "alto" of her "sotto voce," as much as what she is talking about that moves the poet. She tells her boyfriend that she had to change the sheets and make up an excuse for her mother, saying she'd fallen asleep there herself and, for the first time since she was a child, wet the bed.

> She talks until he starts, I think, to laugh,
> and she laughs back in harmony with him,
> the laughs oddly resonant though his
> is still in Texas and I can't really hear it.

Almost everything is imagined here. When the girl glances up and catches the poet watching, he quickly sticks his head in a copy of *The Tin Drum*, "Which by fifty-fifty chance is right / side up." The poem ends with a parting word and a final dramatic scene.

> *Regret*
> is the only word I can make out clearly,
> and even then I can't decide if it's hers
> or if she's repeating what he said.
> But with a smile she hangs the phone up and

> clicks down the hall to the elevator, leaving
> the bottom of the booth fluffed with pink tissue.
> Over the whole of German literature
> I see her smiling, framed in the closing doors;
> her afterimage holds the same sure pose,
> floating on air, in the empty shaft, and fading.

Earlier in the poem Hudgins admits, having regarded her with a stranger's intimacy, that he can understand why the boyfriend "had to run to El Paso / to leave her." The poet has fallen in love with her a little himself, as I think we do as readers, and the final depiction of her smiling and in a sure pose, floating on air, is an imagined triumph. But the poem ends, as it began, in a kind of *medias res* for the speaker, though the episode is over, the portion of the subject's life has taken shape in the speaker's own. This provisional quality, which characterizes much of Frost's narrative poetry, is attractive in a way that Robinson's fuller, tragic version may not be.

Yet Hudgins' comic self-portrait is in conflict, somewhat, with the character of the girl. It asks for our sympathy, too. Usually Frost's narrator has little or no character, and may seem much less vivid, much less alive than the character he allows us to meet. Garrett Hongo puts himself in a perfect situation to observe in this way in "Metered Onramp," from his second book, *The River of Heaven*. All that he observes in the poem, which he claims "pursues [him] through sleep / and waking daydream," originates from his car window as he waits to get on the freeway in L. A. on the "Alondra onramp." There, he would see, in "a swale of new field grass . . . / sloping under the powerlines":

> the bums and ragpickers,
> the shopping bag people
> with their makeshift rakes
> and scavenged handtrowels,
> sifting through the loose dirt and refuse piles
> for whatever treasure they could find . . .

If this seems to be a typical urban desolation, consider again its roots in Frost, who could give us equally defeated places and people in New England, or Wordsworth who could show the moors dotted with dismal little ponds where leeches bred. From such unpromising material, these poets work with a faith that meaning is inherent. Hongo discovers his leech-gatherer, his mud-time tramp, his pauper witch.

> Her name was Sally, I think,
> and she reeked of wine and excrement
> but always had money, wadded up
> like pads of Kleenex mixed with carrot tops
> and cabbage leaves stuffed in the deep pockets
> of her long Joseph's coat.

Hongo's prosody is not the traditional one of counted feet, the one Frost could have recognized, but rather of repetition, parallelism, increment, and the laying down of compelling sentences over lines. The poem ends with a long cadenza of such free verse techniques as he remembers one day seeing Sally launch herself from the crest of the hill, as if for the delight of those waiting their turn to enter the freeway:

> She seemed to stop more than a couple of times,
> blocked by a tie or a trough in the dirt,
> splashing in the puddles,
> but kept going, shoving herself downhill
> flinging her body shoulders first
> and scuffling over the crusts of mud
> and small piles of broken fencing.
> All the while she flailed her arms,
> billowing her open coat that,
> now drenched in fresh doses of mud,
> slapped and whispered sexually
> against her spindly things.
> *Hallelujah*, she was saying,
> *A-le-leu*, over and over
> as we marvelled, crouching in our cars.

Certainly Frost might have cited more than one opportunity to make Hongo's poem metrical. In Hudgins, he would have taken exception to the count in some lines. But the example present in both poems is of the Frost who trusted the narrative and the mystery of the story to which he might not be able to draw a conclusion. The marvelous life that goes on as we shrink from it was a theme Frost expressed himself. Think of the professor sliding down his pillow at the end of "One Hundred Collars." It is also the life that draws us out of ourselves, out of our hiding places, like Hudgins behind his ridiculous book or Hongo in his car.

It is much more difficult to discuss Jeffers' relationship to the new narrative movement in American poetry because his example is at once the most daunting and least appealing. His characters act out dramas unmitigated by Robinson's compassion or Frost's moral relativism, but determined by Jeffers' merciless vision of humanity as an aberration of nature. Jeffers' determinism derives from Thomas Hardy's "Immanent Will," from his own Calvinist background (his father was an ordained Presbyterian minister), his belief in contemporary science, and his Spenglerian vision of western civilization's decline. He preferred to see man as a biological phenomenon rather than as little less than the angels. His philosophy is the moral foundation of his poetry, especially his narrative poetry. He set about in his long narratives to make humanity enact social and biological forces that he saw working to bring about the end of civilization. It is a much simpler matter to find the influence of Robinson or Frost at work today than of this austere soulmate of Thomas Hardy. Would Jeffers be more appealing if, like Hardy, he had written novels instead? For if one considers Jeffers' narrative poems beside Hardy's bleakest books, *Jude the Obscure*, *The Mayor of Casterbridge*, *Tess of the D'Urbervilles*, *The Return of the Native*, one finds the same fools damned by much the same fate. In Jeffers' case, the isolation on a coast too grand for their aspirations twists his characters to madness: man does not measure up to nature, to the creation. Whether we like it or not, this profound moral vision is the motivating force of Jeffers' narrative poems.

Though it is impossible to find anyone working on Jeffers' terms, some do see the long poem as a way of exploring a unified deterministic vision. Chase Twichell's "My Ruby of Lasting Sadness," from her second book, *The Odds*, is held together by a scientific understanding of fate. Part narrative, part meditation, the poem relates a love affair the poet had when very young and her reunion, later in life, with the man who broke her heart. He has "laid claim / to the demimonde" and deals drugs in Southeast Asia. She has "retired / to the regions of the north," a poet living in New England. Though the two have "divided the world" between them, a deep connection remains, one that seems to have determined who they are, and which is symbolized by a ruby in a golden lotus that he gives her as a gift. To explain their connection, Twichell appropriates one of the most speculative theories of recent physics, Bell's Theorem:

> that at a fundamental level,
> disparate parts of the universe

may make an intimate connection,
and furthermore
that things once joined remain
even over vast distances
and through the shifts of time
attached by an unknown force
its speed exceeding that of light,
a force which Bell called
"that-which-is."

Like Jeffers, Twichell has found her own definition of God. Instead of "I am that I am," which is close to Jeffers' belief that the creation itself is God, it is "that-which-is." Thus, Twichell echoes Jeffers, but in a reductive way that resonates with a pathos I believe he would have recognized:

The physics of connection
is all that matters.
The heart matters, and the mind.
Sensation matters, as long as it lasts.
The world does not think of us at all.
It is animated dust, and that is all,
a flower of atoms pulsing in space,
a flower of ash, a flower of soot.

And there are some poets working on Jeffers' scale, that of the book-length poem. Recent attempts include Frederick Turner's *The New World* and Frederick Pollack's *The Adventure*. But these poems are more properly considered epics and make use of the hero as a central figure. Both require us to imagine a science-fiction world where man is remade. Their visions are political, especially in Pollack's long poem, and veer away from Jeffers' moral absolutism for very good reasons. Jeffers' book-length and other long narrative poems hew closer to the drama and, I believe, the dramatic form of novels like Hardy's. If we think of them as naturalistic, then we can see why they must occur in their local confines. Jeffers' northern California coast is his Wessex. Thus his locality (I hesitate to say regionalism) is also essential to his vision. For Jeffers' work to be of more use to the new narrative movement, the terms of his great story-telling verse may have to be changed. But since those terms—the enormous beauty of creation, particularly around Carmel, California, and the insignificant ugliness of humanity—inhere in his stories, it is hard to say what a new narrative poem in Jeffers' style would look like without them.

My aim here has been to sketch briefly the relation of each of the American masters of narrative poetry to the current scene. It should be clear that I believe Frost is the one we find most engaging to younger poets, whether or not they recognize the influence, because of the fluidity of his medium-length narratives, especially their moral relativism when compared to Robinson's narratives or Jeffers'. Frost's own moral vision is perfectly clear in his body of work, and we might infer from it that the characters he has created express his belief in self-reliance. Still, I would argue that because of the nature of narrative as Frost uses it, there is an essential mystery of character and motivation and, in the end, meaning, that appeals to many working in the narrative verse form today. E. A. Robinson requires a fuller, more rounded story, with a manifest plot and a strong sense of closure. He feels love for his characters as human beings and pity for their fates, emotions we do not see as clearly in Frost. Finally, as I have tried to suggest, the challenge of Jeffers remains to be met. Only now that we have passed his centennial year is he being reconsidered, critically reevaluated, in a way neither Frost nor Robinson has had to be. This is all to the good. But if Jeffers is going to have the powerful effect hat I, for one, believe he can have, he will have to be recognized for what he is—the most troublesome and imposing of the three figures.

6

Aspects of Robinson

Edwin Arlington Robinson, Robert Frost, and Robinson Jeffers represent the three r's of American narrative poetry in this century. Anyone writing or reading narrative poetry needs to come to terms with all of them. Robinson shows us how narrative works in the small, elegant space of the lyric. By contrast, Robert Frost's narratives, usually written in blank verse, and often more like dramatic monologues than narratives, are open-ended. Robinson Jeffers' narratives while varying in length tend toward the loose, baggy monster of the novel. While these three are together the masters of narrative in modern American poetry, it is Robinson who manages best to wed the lyric with the story, especially as he takes one lyric form—the sonnet—and turns it into a narrative vehicle. We remember the stories of Reuben Bright the butcher who, after his wife died, "tore down the slaughterhouse," of Cliff Klingenhagen who baffled his friend by drinking a glass of wormwood at dinner, and of Amaryllis, the beauty buried in a shallow grave in the woods. All of these characters are embodied in Italian sonnets. These sonnets share with Robinson's famous short narratives in quatrains, like "Richard Cory" and "The Mill," a sense that an entire life has been elegantly, faithfully, and sympathetically rendered.

Those characteristics are related not only to Robinson's artistry, but to his humanity. The American poets who have worked in the short narrative like Robinson, sometimes in the sonnet, sometimes in quatrains, sometimes in forms reminiscent of these Robinson favorites, have succeeded most when they have shown an elegance, faithfulness, and sympathy, like his. There is also a typically American metaphysics at the heart of Robinson's poetry, derived from pragmatism, the philosophy that influenced so many of Robinson's contemporaries among modern American poets. It is a recognition that meaning is practically based on whether it is worth something or not. Thus failure and success, those measures of American life, measure many of Robinson's characters, too. In Robinson this pragmatic metaphysics, always a source of pathos, is often expressed in negative terms. In fact, since narrative itself is a mode of meaning, like a trope or figure of speech, it is not unusual to find a poet who uses it deferring, through negation, to the inherent meaning of his or her story. Certainly, poets who show Robinson's influence tend also to employ negation as he did, not only in metaphysical but in moral terms.

The Robinson poem that might serve best as a model for his short narratives is the sonnet "Reuben Bright."

> Because he was a butcher and thereby
> Did earn an honest living (and did right),
> I would not have you think that Reuben Bright
> Was any more a brute than you or I;
> For when they told him that his wife must die,
> He stared at them, and shook with grief and fright,
> And cried like a great baby half that night,
> And made the women cry to see him cry.
>
> And after she was dead, and he had paid
> The singers and the sexton and the rest,
> He packed a lot of things that she had made
> Most mournfully away in an old chest
> Of hers, and put some chopped-up cedar boughs
> In with them, and tore down the slaughter-house.

Reuben Bright is summed up in the first four lines as an honest man with a profession associated with brutality (cutting up carcasses), yet the poet assures us that his profession has not coarsened him anymore than yours or mine. That admonition in line three *not* to think is like being told not to picture a white bear. By means of negation Robinson places before us the most tragic way to think about this character. The signal event that shows us Reuben Bright's humanity (which is always the point in a poem by Robinson) is his wife's death and his response to it. Big Reuben the butcher is weaker than the women, perhaps members of an extended family. They may be the ones who have given him the news that his wife is dying, and now they are overcome by his response. Like a Greek chorus they reflect the communal sense of tragedy. The Robinsonian touch is first to depict this devastation in a man who deals with dead bodies every day, then to dramatize the extremity of his response. Though he has assured us that Reuben Bright was not a brute (no more than anyone who earns an honest living), still Reuben feels compelled to prove it himself by destroying the brutalizing way he made his living. It should not be necessary to emphasize the poignancy of the "chopped-up cedar boughs" he puts in the "old chest" with the things his wife had made. Still, his final act of grief is touched with violence, if not brutality.

All of this occurs in fourteen lines, an octave and a sestet. The long *e*- and *i*-rhymes of the octave are the most intense, the highest pitched, in English poetry. (They were Emily Dickinson's favorites, too.) In the sestet only one rhyming pair ("rest" / "chest") eases up on the length of the vowel. The *b*-alliteration of the octave reinforces the claim that Reuben Bright is no more brutal than the poet or the reader and at the same time undermines it. The iambic pentameter is straightforward in the octave, and all of the octave's lines are endstopped except lines one and three. In the sestet the meter is not as straightforward. There are enjambments in every line but the second, and two of them, in lines twelve and thirteen, are wrenching. Line twelve pushes the stresses to either side with a Tennysonian emphasis on assonance and alliteration.

And yet Robinson manipulates all of these effects so that they seem secondary. We discover them when we go back to understand the poem's technique. First it is Reuben Bright's humanity and the exactitude of his story that strike the reader—not like an ax-blow, but like watching a man wield an ax or, better yet, work with a carving knife.

Among Robinson's descendants who show his humane and artistic way with narrative within the confines of the lyric, the first to come to mind is James Wright. His sonnet "Saint Judas" is indeed a Robinsonian narrative and transforms the Robinsonian narrator in an utterly original way. Usually Robinson's narrators speak for a community (true of "Reuben Bright" but also of "Richard Cory"). Occasionally the narrator is a single witness to an event and a character's fate (as in "Cliff Klingenhagen" or "Amaryllis"). Always there is a sense, and this is Robinson's form of sympathy, that the narrator is implicated in his subject's tragedy.

SAINT JUDAS

When I went out to kill myself, I caught
A pack of hoodlums beating up a man.
Running to spare his suffering, I forgot
My name, my number, how my day began,
How soldiers milled around the garden stone
And sang amusing songs; how all that day
Their javelins measured crowds; how I alone
Bargained the proper coins, and slipped away.

> Banished from heaven, I found this victim beaten,
> Stripped, kneed, and left to cry. Dropping my rope
> Aside, I ran, ignored the uniforms:
> Then I remembered bread my flesh had eaten,
> The kiss that ate my flesh. Flayed without hope,
> I held the man for nothing in my arms.

James Wright makes his narrator the ultimate criminal in Christian mythology, doomed despite an ultimate act of humanity, which is all the more saintly because it will not benefit him in eternity. Like Robinson's, Wright's language in this poem is straightforward, and like Robinson at the moment of most intense mystery Wright puns on a large abstraction. "Flayed without hope," says Saint Judas who has rescued the victim of a beating, "I held the man for nothing in my arms." The relative values of "nothing" and "something" are central in Robinson's work. They are the poles of his pragmatic metaphysics, in which his characters have either made something or nothing of their lives. So it is in James Wright's poem.

When Wright turned from the kind of traditional verse that Robinson wrote, he did not abandon the way he employed narrative. The late poem "Hook" in which the speaker begins, "I was only a young man / In those days," includes the kind of encounter we often find in Robinson between a witnessing, sympathetic "I" and a lost or baffled soul. The stanzas of various lengths in free verse lines of various lengths should not deflect our understanding that the story is told in the same small space, the same confines, that Robinson employed, and with the same fullness. In "Hook" the young Sioux with the prosthetic hand, standing with the speaker on a bitterly cold street corner one night in Minneapolis, decides that the speaker needs sixty-five cents for bus money. The mysterious act of kindness, in which he places the coins in the speaker's cold hand with his hook, is narrated with Robinson's economy and his sense of completion.

HOOK

> I was only a young man
> In those days. On that evening
> The cold was so God damned
> Bitter there was nothing.
> Nothing. I was in trouble
> With a woman, and there was nothing

There but me and dead snow.

I stood on the street corner
In Minneapolis, lashed
This way and that.
Wind rose from some pit,
Hunting me.
Another bus to Saint Paul
Would arrive in three hours,
If I was lucky.

Then the young Sioux
Loomed beside me, his scars
Were just my age.

Ain't got no bus here
A long time, he said.

You got enough money
To get home on?

What did they do
To your hand? I answered.
He raised up his hook into the terrible starlight
And slashed the wind.

Oh, that? he said.
I had a bad time with a woman. Here,
You take this.

Did you ever feel a man hold
Sixty-five cents
In a hook,
And place it
Gently
In your freezing hand?

I took it.
It wasn't the money I needed.
But I took it.

Compare Wright's insistence on "nothing" in the first stanza of his poem with the word as we might find it employed in Wallace Stevens, say in his poem "The Snow Man." Both poets draw the word from the same belief that meaning comes not from transcendent values but from nothing or next to nothing. Meaning is another product of the human imagination, like the sixty-five cents offered by the young Sioux. But when Wright says, "there was nothing," he gives the word a human dimension of frustration and abandonment, along with the physical sensation of cold, that contrasts vividly with the way Stevens says it. Wright's expression of failure, the palpable feeling of being godforsaken, is another legacy of Robinson.

It is always a pleasure to find a poet writing today who combines not only the Robinsonian technique of telling a story in a short lyric, but also Robinson's temperament. Two recent poems, neither of them a sonnet nor a formal lyric, that seem to show both how the witnessing *I* is implicated as the story is told, how brevity gives the story shape, and how feeling is located in negation—all aspects of Robinson—are Chase Twichell's "Silver Slur" from her book *The Ghost of Eden* and Kate Daniels' "Sorrow Figure" from *The Niobe Poems*.

In Twichell's poem compression has much to do with the duration of the event, a desolate, urban scene she has glimpsed from the train. But this is not merely an impressionistic anecdote. The poem is fraught with the desire to understand, to comprehend, even as the speaker insists that she cannot understand or comprehend.

SILVER SLUR

Nothing stays attached to what I saw,

what I glimpsed from a train.
It has no magnet for meaning.

Four men sat on a wall shooting up,

companionable. One waved at me.
Waved the needle. Ten feet away,

a man was fucking a woman from behind,
controlling her with her heavy necklace,

a bicycle chain. The budding sapling
shook as she clung to it,

her orange dress hitched up in back.

People there throw garbage out of windows.

Who cares? Four arms, four rolled-up sleeves.

The silver slur of light along the tracks.
Four arms, four rolled-up sleeves.

The orange dress hitched up in back.

Something does stay attached to what the speaker saw, and that is the sardonic, "companionable" wave one of the men gives her. It invites her to be more than a spectator, but a witness, a sympathizing witness, too, for the drug addicts and for the pair copulating out in the open. "Who cares?" the speaker asks, and as if to show her answer, the poem ends with an echo of the formal closure we would have in a Robinson lyric, accomplished by the repeated line, "Four arms, four rolled-up sleeves" and the rhyme of "tracks" and "back." The story itself is the magnet of meaning, and this poem clings to it with the symmetry of iron filings. Where Robinson at the grave of Amaryllis states, "It made me lonely and it made me sad / To think that Amaryllis had grown old," Twichell repeats the bleak detail of "the orange dress hitched up in back." To deny comprehension, as she does, is not to deny empathy. And the poem's very first word, "Nothing," carries the moral weight Robinson himself attached to it.

Kate Daniels' "Sorrow Figure," a poem in prose, is shaped by an encounter between the speaker and a child who owns a set of toys she has studied. When the child addresses her, it is like the moment in a Robinson poem when a character, by thrusting himself into the speaker's consciousness, insists on being recognized and given his due.

SORROW FIGURE

The toys are lying on the floor. They're some kind of doll, plastic and bendable, blue and green, about six inches tall. The little boy calls them his "figures" and plays with them every day, imagining family romances with complicated plots. One blue figure is always placed off to the side, standing on its feet but bent over with its hands pressed to its face. From a distance, no one can tell what separates this one from the rest of the group—whether he's an expatriate, an exile, a pariah, a leper. "Let me introduce you to the sorrow figure," the little boy said one day. "He's so sad no one can help him." It was

then I noticed the sorrow figure in the sunshine, glowing, a haze of blueness
rising from its bent-down body. I leaned closer. I heard its little toy
wail trapped inside the plastic body. I heard the shudders, the sobs,
the oaths. And I heard, too, all the other toys chattering and enjoying
being played with as if nothing like this could ever happen to them.

It is the purpose of the Robinsonian narrator to understand or to admit his inability to understand, both of which are forms of sympathy. Here the speaker has only a cursory interest in the child's toys until he makes her look closer, makes her see that for him they have a meaning more profound than she expected. She sees that the difference between innocence and experience is grief, and that a child may himself understand that difference. Reminiscent also of Robinson is Daniels' own final figure about the toys "chattering and enjoying being played with as if nothing like this could ever happen to them." Our own humanity responds to this, since we know what causes sorrow. Yet, there is that word "nothing" again. Robinson's "An Evangelist's Wife," begins "'Why am I not myself these many days, / You ask? And have you nothing more to ask?'" The woman speaking in Robinson's poem is aware that her husband is unfaithful. The word "nothing" is laden with her knowledge. Daniels also employs the word to convey knowledge—the knowledge that loss ("nothing like this") can occur to anyone.

Though not a sonnet or a lyric in any traditional sense of the word, still Daniels' poem is replete with a humanity and has an elegant sense of closure that recall Robinson. His short narrative poems, with their sympathetic focus on human behavior, especially in dramatic situations, combine the power of the story and the emotion of the lyric in a way that is highly compressed and formally beautiful. Twichell's "Silver Slur" and Daniels' "Sorrow Figure" share these qualities and suggest that today when narrative and the short lyric combine to be a study in character—both the poet's character and his or her subject's—Edwin Arlington Robinson may be the presiding spirit.

7

Sheathed in Reality: The Fact of Clare Walker
in Robinson Jeffers' "The Loving Shepherdess"

Recently I heard an exchange between a young critic and a young novelist concerning characters in the novelist's latest book, which she said dealt with gender. The critic asked the novelist how she "gendered" her characters. The novelist responded that she would never think of working that way. She said she began with characters who happened to be male or female; presumably gender followed from there. Though the novelist left herself open for such a question—"How do you gender your characters in a novel that deals with gender?"—I liked her answer. Of course, she wouldn't think of gendering a character anymore than she might think of portraying a character as a symbol or an archetype. I should add that this novelist works primarily in the realm of realism. If she does anything it is to make us believe her characters conform to a world of everyday reality based on conventions of fictional representation that go back—how far? Nearly 200 years? Or all the way back to the beginning of storytelling?

My point is that Robinson Jeffers, who can hardly be called a realist, has in his poem "The Loving Shepherdess" created in his main character, Clare Walker, someone who first conforms to a world of everyday reality, even though it is the heightened reality of Jeffers' central California coast. Clare Walker may indeed be the embodiment of a female archetype or "archetypally Christian," as R. W. (Herbie) Butterfield argues, but without the reality in which Jeffers sheathes her, she would embody nothing.

"The Loving Shepherdess," published in 1929 in the volume *Dear Judas*, is unlike most of Jeffers' other narrative poems, since the most dramatic action has taken place before the poem begins. Clare Walker's lover and father have had a violent confrontation, resulting in her father's death; privateers have sacked the family ranch; Clare is alone, as the poem begins, leading about ten sheep, the remnants of her family's flock. And she is pregnant with a child she knows she is physically incapable of bearing. The Oedipal conflict which Robert Zaller has pointed out is the heart of many of Jeffers' narrative poems is in the background of "The Loving Shepherdess," but it has resulted in Clare's dilemma. Clare may be a Christ figure, a mother figure, an ironic figure of the waning moon, the final phase of Robert Graves' White Goddess, she may even be the muse herself. First, she has to be someone we can see and believe, and there are passages in this poem where I think we do.

We see and believe Clare Walker for many reasons but I will concentrate on four of them. First is the way other characters respond to her. Second is the way she responds to them. Third and most important is the physical fact of her body; Jeffers has spent more precise details on her than on any other character except Hoult Gore, the walking corpse in "The Love and the Hate." Fourth is her place in the landscape, that "intense realization of character rooted in place" that Zaller has said marks Jeffers' work at its best. Here she is rootless or uprooted, like Hardy's Tess or the traveling shepherdess referred to in Walter Scott's *Heart of Midlothian*, which Butterfield has noted as a possible model for Clare Walker. As she moves through the landscape it gives her life while taking it away and finally assimilating her.

The first characters Clare Walker encounters are a group of school children who taunt her. One of them shouts, "'You killed your daddy, why don't you kill your sheep?'" Not only is this the untruth of gossip, but it has the logic or illogic of a jeer. At the end of the poem, divested of her flock and "heavily swollen / Toward child-birth," Clare camps with some outcast men. Hearing her call her absent sheep, one smiles "without mockery." That he is a "sickly, sullen boy" recalls the boys of the schoolyard, even the boy Will Brighton, a young ranch hand that she sleeps with. It is both a symmetrical moment and one that, because it has no explanation, stabs with poignancy. When the rancher Fogler aids her by giving her a pair of his wife's old shoes, then furtively kisses her knee; when Will Brighton first encounters her and says, "'Where did you drop from?'"; when Onorio Vasquez warns her that with the onset of the spring rains she ought to think of herself; when an old man who has given her shelter in his barn catches her foot in the straw and scratches her sole with his thumbnail, then declines her offer of sexual comfort; finally, whenever her sheep turn to her, follow her, even though they have an air of the fabulous about them; in all of the ways other characters respond to her, Clare Walker is given further depth, reality, believability.

Her responses to others are easier to interpret, to see as emblematic of a meaning beyond simple fact. I suppose what interests me about Clare Walker (even her name is a combination of lucidity and physicality, saintliness on the road) is the fact of her rather than her meaning. We know she loves and pities her flock, though in her current state, homeless, wandering, and due to hunger and illness not entirely sane, she leaves her flock vulnerable to disaster and one by one its members are destroyed. Still, when bathing in a pond she feels a ewe's chin on her shoulder and draws "the bony head against the soft breasts." The scene I find most affecting and that relates most clearly to my argument occurs after Clare has spent the night with her sheep in a barn.

> . . . two coughing sheep
> Brought her to a stand; then she opened their mouths and found
> Their throats full of barbed seeds from the bad hay
> Greedily eaten; and the gums about their teeth
> Were quilled with the wicked spikes; which drawn, thin blood
> Dripped from the jaw. The folds of the throat her fingers
> Could not reach nor relieve; thereafter, when they coughed,
> Clare shook with pain. Her pity poisoned her strength.

I think this passage is equal to any in Jeffers. It has an exact homely sadness, especially about the unreachable folds of the sheep's throats, worthy of a stylist like Flaubert. Fact speaks for itself. Jeffers adds his note about human weakness ("Her pity poisoned her strength."), for if Clare is a Christ figure, it behooves Jeffers' inhumanism to underline the detrimental effects of human sympathy. Yet the passage shows that Clare Walker is aware of her desires— to help her sheep—and her limits—her inability to pluck out all the barbed seeds. At the very end of the poem, when she goes into labor, knowing she will die, "she called / The sheep about her and perceived that none came." This passage, too, gives her the dignity of factualness. She may have behaved in a deluded way and have deliriously thought her dead flock had accompanied her, as the outcast men have observed, but her final response to her absent flock is awareness. Simply, they do not exist to answer her call any longer and she knows. She knows she is alone.

Clare's body as a physical fact is central to the poem and to her fate. Jeffers' very first description of her marvels how "Her thin young face / Seemed joyful, and lighted from inside, and formed / Too finely to be so wind-burnt." Variations on this description continue through the poem, including comments on her chapped lips and the brownness of her skin. A few details stand out as remarkably real. At evening sitting among her flock Clare combs her hair with a "gap-toothed comb" and "the thick blond strands" hiss. When she attempts to bathe in a shallow stream she is described as "Flattening herself

to find the finger's depth water." Like the bodies of other Jeffers heroines, hers
is lean, boyish, with "flattened flanks / Hardly a woman's." Her leanness has
to do with hunger, in part, though I detect in these women of Jeffers a certain narcissistic projection of his own physicality. In any event, when taking
shelter in the barn where her sheep eat the bad hay, Clare smells the fried
grease clinging to the old man who has given her shelter when he comes after
his meal to visit her; she hungrily believes he is bringing her food. Elsewhere,
describing her love affair with the man who has killed her father, she speaks
of her first experience of orgasm as a "sweet fire." Jeffers gives her a body that
includes appetites, even vanity—human realities. Most important is her understanding of herself as a pregnant mother. The passage which occurs in the
tenth section of the twelve-part poem is, to my mind, the climax; it also contains an element that seems purely Jeffers and, therefore, disturbing. Upon
learning that Clare is pregnant and doomed because of the shape of her pelvis
(she has had one miscarriage already), Onorio Vasquez who has tried to help
her urges her to abort the baby. She refuses to do this. She has had a mystical
insight into "The golden country that our souls came from." Onorio Vasquez,
a visionary who appears in other Jeffers poems, knows this place well; it is the
country of his visions. But Clare, physical creature that she is, believes it is the
womb. In her womb her child is experiencing that golden country. She tells
Vasquez:

> When I was in my worst trouble
> I knew that the child was feeding on peace and happiness. I had happiness here in
>   my body. It is not mine,
> But I am its world and the sky around it, its loving God. It is having the prime and
>   perfect of life,
> The nine months that are better than the ninety years. I'd not steal one of its days
>   to save my life.
> I am like its God, how could I betray it?

Here she speaks of herself in terms that other Jeffers characters might use,
characters like Barclay in "The Women at Point Sur" who denies God by taking on the responsibilities of God, Hoult Gore in "The Love and the Hate"
who imagines his body is as large as the world, California in "Roan Stallion"
who thinks that by killing a murderous horse she has killed God. The element
these characters share is what the Greeks called *hubris*. Clare Walker's lines
disturb me because they reveal the magical reasoning of someone who has

included the fate of another with her fate. When Vasquez remembers or almost remembers that the Caesarean section operation would be a resolution of Clare's dilemma, it is futile. Besides, Clare, sick, starving, insane, is determined to die; many of her references include a foreknowledge of death. When she dies, all of creation, as she sees herself to be, will expire with her. The death of the fully formed infant is still a moral dilemma, even if the child has enjoyed a few more months of the womb's golden country. Like all of the admissions of Jeffers' great obsessed characters, Clare's fascinates and repels me.

If there is anything Jeffers truly loved that went into his art it was the natural landscape where he set most of his poems: the California coast stretching from the north end of Monterey Bay as far south as Morro Rock, the coast range of mountains, and the meadows, rivers, deltas, and canyons among these features. Along with them there were the sky, sun, moon, stars, and the Pacific Ocean itself. These are the most fully realized of any of the parts of his poems, be they his short lyrics or longer narratives. This seems to be so obvious that any reader of Jeffers, even one who knew the poet only from passages quoted on a Sierra Club Wilderness Calendar, would know it to be true. But as with references to Clare Walker, I want to dwell on small touches that represent her connection to this landscape and the loving transformation of it as fact. The first is the reference to Clare's walking stick, "the bent staff of rosy-barked madrone-wood / That lay in her hand." Anyone who knows the region knows the madrone and its peculiar beauty. For Jeffers the phrase "rosy-barked" with respect to madrone or manzanita is almost as much a mnemonic motif as Homer's rosy fingered dawn. The staff connects Clare to the landscape, even as she drifts through it aimlessly. The Pacific is a constant presence as well and is described at one point when the sun streams through a cloud as "the lank striped ocean," terms that almost could be applied to Clare. She makes her way through Jeffers country and the poet refers to landmarks by the names of characters he has associated with them in earlier poems, "Cawdor's Canyon" and "Point Lobos, by a gate / Where Tamar Cauldwell used to lean from her white pony / To swing the bars." One of the last signs of Clare caught by Vasquez is "in the yellow mud / Prints of bare feet, dibbled about with many / Little crowding hoof-marks." In this regard, Clare is a visitation to the entire Jeffers landscape, like the poet's love itself walking with clarity and unusual sweetness over the places he has transformed and set down in his poems.

If Clare Walker is an embodiment of the female archetype, then I might draw strength from Robert Graves and say that not only is she Jeffers' own interpretation of Christian charity, as well as a version of human tragedy as he represented it time and again in his great landscape, but I think she represents the muse. Sadly, she is doomed, like other Jeffers heroines. He has derived this convention not from Greek tragedy but from 19th century narratives where female characters who step outside of social norms are also lost. That deserves a much longer treatment. My aims here are modest: to me Clare Walker is one of the most vividly imagined of Jeffers' characters, even as in some ways she is the most imaginary. He brings her to life by the ways in which he makes her a fact.

8

Letter from Leeds

Dear *Hudson Review*:

During the past school year, 1989 to 1990, I have been director of Vanderbilt University's junior year abroad program at the University of Leeds in north central England and have taught in that university's School of English. My main teaching duties have involved tutoring sections of a course called Practical Criticism, based originally on I. A. Richards' classic study of poetry. The course has another title as well, Introduction to the Study of English Literature, since the genres covered have included fiction and drama as well as poetry. During the past two years the course has undergone a radical change. Instead of introducing first year college students to the study of poetry, fiction, and drama, it has been redesigned to introduce them to the study of the 20th century's most sophisticated critical theories of literature, excluding Anglo-American New Criticism.

None of my students this year was an English major, though I don't think that teaching what are called honors students here would have made my task any different. I was asked to teach first year English minors or subsidiary I students, subsid I's for short. Along with them, there were the students of North Riding College. This is a teacher's college in Scarborough, a resort town on the North Sea in North Yorkshire, famed as the residence of the playwright Alan Ayckbourn and his acting company. It is less well known for the fact that North Riding College's English department had, as I was told, "run away together." The North Riding students were farmed out to various northern universities to pursue their specializations for a year before returning to their education courses. English specialists come to the University of Leeds. Among their courses is Practical Criticism. It is generally believed that they should have less expected of them than honors students or subsid I's. Still, the new Prac Crit/Intro to Eng Lit could not be altered just to suit them. What to do, i.e. how to divide them among those teaching tutorial sections? There were some two dozen North Riding students. I agreed to take them all.

Classes began in October. By then, the heat of England's unusual summer and the continued balminess of its early fall were replaced by days of cold rain and frequent grim overcast. I had five sections of Prac Crit to tutor, each of about ten students. They would attend lectures and discuss them and their reading in their tutorials. Typical English university procedure. For the first term, our reading would include the works of the Russian Formalists, the semiology of Ferdinand de Saussure, and essays by structuralists, like Roland Barthes. After a month long break over Christmas, we would return to the many theories grouped under reader response criticism, the many applications of Marxist thought in Marxist literary criticism, and the quickly evolving theories of feminist literary criticism. We would also look ahead to post-structuralism and the slippery hindquarters of Jacques Derrida. In the third term, we would wrap things up, finish papers, and the students would study for and take their final exams.

We would not be reading anything by the New Critics from either side of the Atlantic or applying their methods, because their approach to literature was already well known by the students. So went the reasoning of the planners for this course.

The School of English offices and classrooms are contained in older red brick buildings on the southern side of campus, facing downtown Leeds. Most tutors have offices large enough to contain a class of a dozen or so students. Mine was not large enough, so I met my tutorial sections in a regular classroom. Throughout the year, the room would be cold when we entered it. There was a gas heater, with a pilot light that did not work. To light it, I would thrust a lit match through the grill and carefully turn on the gas. The first time I did this, the igniting *whoosh* sizzled the hair on the back of my right hand into smoking black punctuation marks. I fell back with a yelp. It broke the ice with my students.

I began by expressing my reservations about the course. We had only one literary work to read and discuss, Tolstoy's short story, "Strider, the Story of a Horse." Victor Shklovsky had examined this story in the early years of the century and discovered in it elements of "defamiliarization," that *sine qua non* of Russian Formalist criticism, the combustion in the matchhead. Otherwise our texts included collections of essays and a glossary of literary terms. Often the essays made no allusion to literature or they discussed works with which the students were unfamiliar. Presumably the students would apply these theories in their other literature classes, like their class in Shakespeare. But in our class, we had only "Strider, the Story of a Horse."

We also had Roland Barthes's *Mythologies*, his essays about popular culture in France in the early 'fifties, including his long discourse on how he applied Saussure in order to demythologize contemporary bourgeois myths. But contemporary French culture of the early 'fifties tended to elude my students. They had long lived with things made of plastic, of much more advanced kinds than the sort Barthes deplored. And popular culture itself, which Barthes sniffed at like an oenologist, they knew as *vin ordinaire*. No reason for excitement or censure, particularly. Or for analysis.

The challenge was to find a way to discuss literature as well as literary theory. There was only so far Tolstoy's story could be stretched. And though we ran it long and hard, we read other things, too. Because they are compact, easily portable, and, in their range, more various than any other genre of literature, poems became the main source of class discussion.

Yet language itself was often our subject, if not always a manifest one. As an American with an accent created by numerous influences, including the regional one of growing up in Southern California but also a period during my childhood when I lived in Scotland, I admitted that I must sound pretty strange to my students and that perhaps my speech defamiliarized the English language for them. But they were more familiar with American accents from T.V. and movies, than I was with theirs. I heard broad northern accents from either side of the Pennines, the flat inflections of the Midlands, West Country sounds that reminded me of Tennessee, and an assortment of toffee-nosed speech from the Home Counties.

A woman with the flaming red hair and pale blue eyes left here by the Vikings spoke up in class early in the year and I asked her to repeat what she had said. I was sure it was my fault, but her blush made her freckles run together, and she insisted that she was to blame. It was embarrassing to ask her again to repeat herself. After a number of conversations with her, now I can hear the English I am listening for in the Geordie dialect that she speaks as a native of Newcastle-upon-Tyne. We agreed it was odd knowing that as soon as we opened our mouths in Leeds we would be identified as strangers.

Moments like these brought Russian Formalism and Saussure to life, in a way, while at the same time making semiology problematic. Wasn't there some essential thing—communication—we hoped to achieve that language was failing? Certainly, with deference to Saussure, we would hear the arbitrary differences in our habits of speech, but we also wished to impart information, and we both thought we were speaking the same language.

For the Russian Formalists, I showed the class Craig Raine's poem "A Mar-

tian Sends a Postcard Home" and we discussed the *ostranenie* of its riddles.
For Saussure and his formulas of the signifier and the signified, of paradigm
and syntagm, of word values based solely on difference, we read "Jabber-
wocky." It was fun detecting the shiftiness that existed between the sounds
of words and their potential meanings, especially since Carroll's nonsense
invited us to play with it. On late afternoons, after the time changed, night
began falling as quickly as, later this spring, it would tend to hold off. We
read David Wagoner's "Song to Accompany the Bearer of Bad News" and
talked about how sentences put together in one order could seem just as inevitable cut up and appearing in another order, if they made sense. On evenings
when we stood with collars turned up in the bus queue below the limestone
neo-classical façade of the university library, I reflected on how successful or
wise it had been to apply Barthes's structuralism to Rupert Brooke's "The Soldier" or Robert Frost's "The Gift Outright." I felt much better talking about
the narrative theory of Genette and Raleigh's sonnet "Three Things There
Be That Prosper Up Apace." I even said excitedly to my drowsy late Thursday
tutorial, dozing in the swollen heat of the gas fire as sleet pattered like rice
on the windows, that Raleigh's understanding of his son's behavior and its
consequence—hanging—was its own critique. We didn't need structuralism
when the poem itself was its own key! I read them Stevens' "The Man on the
Dump" to demonstrate further, but felt a barrier between us after the silence
of "Where was it one first heard of the truth? The the." It was time for Christmas break.

We all attended lectures during the first term, as well. An introductory lecture, a lecture on Russian Formalism, and one on Saussure. There was to have
been a lecture on structuralism, too, but rumor had it that the lecturer, a part
time cross country coach, was with his team abroad. He called in sick. These
lectures were held in part of the modernistic complex that occupies about
one third of the campus. Gazing upon this area I tended to think, because
of his recent criticism of modern architecture, "Prince Charles is right." Inside the complex are long corridors with rubber floors. Down these corridors
the human figure diminishes to a speck, with shoes squeaking. The building
that housed the lecture rooms has enlarged fluted bulges and looks like a pipe
organ knocked askew on one side. On the other side, near the roof, a statue
made of bronze or some other metal hangs. A figure in academic robes, it
appears to be in rapid descent toward the fountain below. We met in a lecture
theater and sat in long rows of fold-down, padded pews. Each row with its
own door. Our lecturer on Saussure was well informed and endowed with a

strong, clear voice, but he puzzled us all with the visual aids on the overhead projector. Our lecturer on Russian Formalism mumbled to the first row.

Throughout the course I wondered what I was doing. But during the first term I looked ahead to the second term, particularly to Marxist literary theory. I thought my English students must have grown up with a more objective view of Marxism than I had. After all, outside the Safeway in our neighborhood in Leeds, hawkers sold *Marxism Today* and *Living Marxism*. But my students had little or no familiarity with Marx and his theories. We all watched the collapse of the Soviet empire in Eastern Europe with a good deal of excitement, though some among my colleagues and in the media rued the passing of the opportunity for real socialism. But when it came to their actual associations with Marxism, the best my students could come up with was the color red and Marx's grave in London.

My students at the University of Leeds were, in fact, very much like my students in America. They were part of a culture, indeed, but it was not the one they were learning about in the university. The university culture was full of facts and assumptions, ideas and beliefs, that were either unfamiliar or had never been named within my students' hearing. University was the last chance to pass on a set of values for which, it was very possible, they had no use, not to say need. Their culture was signified in the black, skin-tight clothes some men wore, the deliberate pallor some women affected, and a general post-modern raggedness, as if they all had roles in a play by Samuel Beckett. My North Riding students, as future primary school teachers, tended to make less of a statement with their dress. But except for the gorgeous saris and pantsuits of the Asians, my English students dressed drably or in sooty attire that made them resemble old tattoos. Many assumed a kind of languor as well. Yet the flash of an earring in a male ear or a jewel drilled into the side of a female nostril or the change overnight of hair from blonde to magenta suggested an undercurrent, something important that was probably none of my business.

But why was I teaching critical approaches to literature instead of literature? Was it to teach my students how to read one another instead of books? Russian Formalism, semiology, structuralism, and Marxist literary theory all pretended to be scientific. Marxist theory went so far as to claim for itself alone a detached view that no other humanist criticism ever achieved. Some feminist critics abjured humanism altogether, with its corrupt sense of the universal. All seemed to say that literature was devious and untrustworthy, but literary theory was a science. It would explain the world.

We began the second term with reader response theory. The sublime baloney of Stanley Fish was a big hit. Reader response theory suggested that all readings were valid, all equally authentic. It penetrated to the heart of something about literature that had been planted in my students. Literature had to be studied because it made no sense. A theory made sense, especially one that said, "Don't worry. Whatever comes to mind is *your* reading of the poem and no one should intimidate you into thinking you are wrong." We read James Fenton's scathing, surreal, narrative poem "The Skip." I explained that if I had not learned that a British skip was different from an American dumpster, I might have had some fairly erroneous notions about the poem. We read Donald Justice's "Poem" and John Ashbery's "Paradoxes and Oxymorons." I believe this was the only time during the course when I felt obliged to tell a student, after he interpreted a poem, that he was wrong.

Our weeks back after Christmas, during January and February, took us on a wild carousel of weather that made it into the international news. The hurricane hit on January 25. As I descended from my bus that night a tree snapped off by the gale fell on a car in front of the bus, pinning a young nurse inside it and severing her arm. Throughout February we had days in which all the known weather of this island would revolve—sun, rain, sleet, snow, sun again, all sped by bitter wind. I could hear Stanley Fish saying it was all valid, neither bad nor good. One kind of weather was the same as another. But the British said, "Global warming."

Marxist literary theory stimulated some of the most curious responses. The lecturer himself, when he discussed Lukács's reflection theory and Althusser's schemes of the repressive state apparatus and the ideological state apparatus, confessed that given recent events, it might seem irrelevant to consider Marxist literary theory at all. But he insisted that its use of dialectic made it a potent oppositional tool. While he spoke he made sweeping motions with his arm as if brushing crumbs from the long countertop in front of him. He described *Hamlet* as a play that dealt with English worries about Elizabeth's succession and *Lear* as a pessimistic view of Jacobean optimism. One of my smartest students, an otherworldly and usually silent young woman, said she thought the lecture was "brilliant." This word is the current superlative and is often abbreviated. My children use it to describe an especially good birthday party:

"It was brill!" But Marxism also baffled my students. One asked if "dialectic" referred to the role of one's dialect in determining social and economic class.

We ended our course with readings in feminist literary theory. Contemporary feminists are involved in the gender issues embedded in language and look to Derrida for guidance, or they are Marxists. But my students, especially the women, included few if any feminist sympathizers. For many *feminist* meant a woman with an extreme political position. The grossest comment was a caricature of "crewcut lesbians on motorcycles." I had hoped to discuss poems by Elizabeth Barrett Browning and Christina Rossetti, together with contemporary poems by the young Scot Carol Ann Duffy and the Irish poet Joan McBreen. But I couldn't imagine a sensitive response to issues of gender in their poems, when feminism had been personified that way. My landlady had left us a house full of books; among them (she is the mother of two grown children) a copy of the English edition of Dr. Spock's *Baby and Child Care*. It dated from 1973. Its passages about the working mother and the role of the father appeared to have been little revised from the first edition in the late 1940's. I copied them and showed them to my students. The women, especially those who had the cartoonish view of feminists, hooted at the good doctor's advice. "This is what your parents were reading when you were toddlers," I said. After that we were able to talk about the poems without too much prejudice.

The lecture dealt with genre in *Richard III*. It was a look at the cross over of the masculine and feminine in Shakespeare's day. But the power went out in the lecture theater as the lecturer was concluding her remarks and though the doors at the end of each row were opened to admit light, still she spoke to us from a dark well, and we were a sparse audience.

Toward the end of the second term the English department chairman asked me how I thought the course was going. It had been a bad day. She had noticed me in the general office and I think had asked me the question only in passing, not expecting much of an answer. I told her the course was a boondoggle from start to finish. No one should be expected to teach or take an introduction to English literature based only on critical texts, especially *these* critical texts. I said it was bass-ackwards, goofy-footed, out-in-left-field. I expressed myself in additional foreign clichés. She asked me if I would be so kind as to put my thoughts in writing.

Now in the third term we have entered the period of final examinations. It is mid-spring and the hazy warm days remind me of the Los Angeles basin at this time of year. The air is full of gnats. The rhododendrons, especially vivid in overcast weather, are blooming. A mildness has come in which most things can be forgiven, but with it, sadly, a fear that ahead lies another dry summer and the threat not only of drought but of drastic climatic changes. The North Riding students and subsid I's that I taught were equally qualified, although the former had more motivation to pass, since their careers as teachers depended on it. The year has had a full measure of events totally unrelated to modern critical theory. Yet I think I can see how some of the most important ones do relate. The events in Eastern Europe. The sequestration of Salman Rushdie. And the popular response to Britain's new community charge, the poll tax.

To my surprise, my students' final evaluations of this course have been overwhelmingly positive. They felt it gave them a freedom to look at literature in new ways. They had no idea that so many ways of reading literature existed. Freedom was the word that turned up in more than one conversation I had in our last conferences. I told them I was amazed, but I supposed I had to be pleased. "Didn't you find it confusing," I asked, "when I told you I didn't understand our reading?" No, that had been refreshing, they said. Human. They weren't used to it. And they weren't used to such freedom.

I don't think I am referring here to Derrida's idea of play. That idea proposes that a word has no essential meaning or value. The freedom my students were responding to *is* something essential and its meaning cannot be deferred for long. It is something the people of Poland, Hungary, Czechoslovakia, East Germany, and Romania clearly wanted. It is something Salman Rushdie has clearly lost. And it is something the British consider they might be lacking, since the poll tax has been imposed upon them without their consent. It is an essence and the desire for it is universal. Taking their lead from Saussure and Derrida, the hippest of the critics we read this year scorned "essence" and "universality." Though they may have shown my students new ways to read, I think they're still missing something.

Part II

Reviews

9

Contemporary Mannerism:
American Poetry Slips into Something Comfortable

The mannerist is confused with the mannered. At a reading a poet introduces a poem by mentioning that before the poem appeared in *The New Yorker*, the editor suggested its title be changed because it seemed mannered. The poet laughs ironically, "What could be more mannered than *The New Yorker*?" By mannered, he may mean overrefined, unless for him what is mannered is also mannerist. But there are poems at any time which are overrefined or *vers precieux*. Usually, they are the work of imitators; often these taggers-along ape the styles of writers Pound dismissed as "the starters of crazes." Having no style of their own, they adopt a manner; of course, a manner in fashion. Furthermore, the mannered poem can be encouraged by editors. An established magazine with a history of editorial taste is often accused of fostering mannered writing—*The New Yorker* poem, the *kayak* poem. A magazine's strongest contributors influence this work, too; sometimes it is they themselves who write it.

But mannerism, as I mean it, is something else. The term comes from art criticism and applies especially to certain Italian painters of the 16th century. John Rowland in his book *Mannerism—Style and Mood*[5] offers a correlative definition which I would like to use here. Mannerism is a reaction against tradition; it creates forms which are ends in themselves and which lack a focus. A mannerist poetry is being written in American right now and even seems to be the predominant style, if not the latest craze. The poems are reactions against the contemporary emphasis on the self, with its traditional roots in Whitman and Dickinson; as poems they point only to their form, and the focus they lack or evade is any emotion original to the poet.

What is important to understand first is that the self has been so emphasized in recent American poetry that some sort of reaction against that emphasis is inevitable. The self has become so emphatic that its poetry has reached a *reductio ad absurdum* of content and form: to be desirable, the self

---

[5] *Mannerism—Style and Mood*, by John Rowland, Yale University Press, 1964

must be shown as vulnerable (this leads to sentimentality) and its poem minimal (*this* will not do).

Three poets who exemplify this reaction and whose recent work is correspondingly mannerist are Norman Dubie, Ai, and James Tate. Naturally, they are not alone, yet of poets in their thirties these three have the most distinctive styles. By distinctive, I mean that peculiar phenomenon where if a poem by Dubie, Ai, or Tate were published anonymously, we would know the author at once (granted we were not slipped a piece of mimicry by an imitator).

In *The City of the Olesha Fruit*[6], Norman Dubie in one poem comes as close as he ever comes to telling us what he is up to.

> The new for us is the last thing our worlds
> Have forgotten, brought back by someone, not
> Out of necessity, but
> Out of the *otherness* of invention which has an unforgiving
> Mother, and no father.
>
> —"Winter Woods"

Dubie's own manners, as it were, are evident: the italics, the enjambment, and the relative clause, "which has an unforgiving / Mother, and no father," which personifies and imbues with secret meaning the already secretive phrase "the *otherness* of invention." What does that phrase mean? It means mannerism. It means the mannerist creates not out of necessity or the urgency of the self, but out of "the *otherness* of invention," a bastard with such parents.

Dubie hopes to reveal as little of himself as possible. And in the lines above, he offers only an aesthetic position. What this position generates are poems which must then have no relation to himself, or none that we can find, and will stand as ends in themselves. Therefore, Dubie often writes poems about other art forms. "Winter Woods" is *after* the murals and bottles of Dina Yellen. Another poem is titled "After Three Photos of Brassaï." Another, "Elegy to the Pulley of the Superior Oblique" (a note at the beginning of the book states that the pulley "is just part of the musculature of the eye") has as its acknowledgment simply "Weston photograph of a border bridge." In each of these poems Dubie displays his genius for fictionalizing. He is at his best when using a persona: Chekhov dying of tuberculosis at Yalta, in the poem

---

[6] *The City of the Olesha Fruit*, by Norman Dubie, Doubleday, 1979

"The Seagull," or a concentration camp prisoner in "Aubade of the Singer and Saboteur, Marie Triste: 1941." No one employs the cachet better than Dubie. In "The Seagull" Chekhov ruminates,

> The drunken visitors laughing
>
> In my kitchen, eating my duck and venison, while I hide
> From them here in the dark garden.
> The daughter of one of these gentlemen is pretty.
> I saw her through the window drinking
>
> Champagne from a clay mug—just under her thin blouse
> I saw the blue points of her breasts . . .

What can we do but wink at the magic of verisimilitude? And, too, be fascinated by Dubie's fascination for other times and places, the subjects of many of his meditative pieces. Like reading a historical novel, reading a poem by Norman Dubie allows us to enter a world where neither we nor the writer need worry about emotional risk. The content is glamourous. The form, fulfilling itself, is an escape.

Like Eliot's, this escape is from emotion and personality, but Dubie's would have left Eliot gasping. Certainly Dubie is detached. Yet, the failure of most of the poems in this book to focus on an emotion original to him is his success as a mannerist. Two poems where an emotional focus is vaguely present suggest the reason. "Sacrifice of a Virgin in the Mayan Ball Court" attempts to relate the subject of the title to a series of brutal murders in the Southwest. The discovery of "the body / Of yet another nude girl" outside Phoenix seems to have led to the poem. According to Dubie, the reincarnation of the sacrificial priest is out there, "He is hated, he is *wanted*—and / Soon, perhaps, he'll be hunted . . ." And, Dubie goes on, this murderer is returning "To kill. *Again!*" This poem is followed by a short love poem, "You," also atypical of Dubie. It is about a fountain, and how the poet and his love are like the water of the fountain, etc. With sentiments such as we find in these two poems it is clear that Dubie's detachment in other poems serves him well.

Like Dubie, Ai favors the persona poem, and like him, too, she is fascinated by the exotic flavor of other times and places. Most every poem in *Killing Floor*[7] is uttered by a persona,—Yukio Mishima, Marilyn Monroe, the son of

---

[7] *Killing Floor*, by Ai, Houghton Mifflin, 1979

a mortician. The question is, what relation do these personae have to Ai herself? As presented, do they make their poems ends in themselves? At first, one is inclined to say no. Compared to Ai, Dubie seems to be an aesthete, meditating on history just as he would on a painting, for its form, for the picturesque in it. Ai appears to be in a constant state of bloody rage: no time for aesthetics or manners! However, the similarity between the two poets does exist. Ai uses other voices, like Dubie, and like his, her personae are often so remote it is hard not to see the poems as reactions against the self.

In "The Singers," a man who rode with Zapata is haunted by the dead revolutionary and when he kills a lover, by pushing her head in a cooking fire, he shoots the smoke rising from her body.

> Zapata. I raise my pistol.
> I'm not afraid of any sonofabitch on two feet.
> I fire, then jam the barrel in my mouth.
> Not even you, motherfucker, not even you.

Ai sounds hysterical, but she is not. She is thoroughly engrossed in the *otherness* of what is happening, so that its very form encloses the world described. Except as imagined history, the poem relates to nothing outside itself—not to you, not to me, and not, in any perceptible way, to her.

In the lines above, Ai displays her stylistic manners, too: the present tense, the straight narrative, the violent verb ("jam"). What gives her work an intensity missing in Dubie's is its tone. Like her constant use of personae, her tone is constantly violent. Even in one of the tenderer poems in the book, "She Didn't Even Wave," Marilyn Monroe, still Norma Jean, recalls her mother's death in a way that brings a shudder.

> It was a real nice funeral. Mama's.
> I touch the rhinestone heart pinned to my blouse.
> Honey, let's look at it again.
> See. It's bright like the lightning that struck her.

The form of violence, though coated with the poignancy of Norma Jean's mourning, is the end Ai seeks, the mannerist end in itself.

But violence, poured on heavily, as Ai pours it on, covers something else. Central to the sort of violence that obsesses Ai is sentimentality. In "The Kid" a boy tells how he murders his family, then:

In the house, I put on the old man's best suit
and his patent leather shoes.
I pack my mother's satin nightgown
and my sister's doll in the suitcase.
Then I go outside and cross the fields to the highway.
I'm fourteen. I'm a wind from nowhere.
I can break your heart.

A self grown sentimental, as it has in the poetry Ai will *not* write, is a pitiful thing. To avoid sentimentality, to obscure its focus, Ai goes to the extreme, violence, and meets it coming back in disguise.

James Tate knows that sentimentality is a thing to fear, and if that is all the self has to offer, then you must blur it, hide it, swirl around it, as he does, with brilliant evasions. Finally, the mannerist invests himself in form alone. Rowland in his book explains that some Italian Mannerist paintings seem to whirl vertiginously around a negative space central to the composition. This, to me, describes much of the poetry in Tate's newest collection, *Doggeries*[8]:

We wanted something: a nude instance
of gaga, a tern in a sunken hammock,
anecdotes that end with angry pigeons,
pinochle won. Should think profound—

profound was the wrong word. We won't
get anything so don't expect anything,
a babe in the mouth and knees sacked
dandling the natal muse, the hysterical

victim's bouquet in Springtime.

—"Nature Poem: Demanding Stiff Sentences"

Of these three poets, it seems to be Tate alone who is concerned merely with language. Shouldn't he alone be called the mannerist? Yet, because things fit together in something like a logical progression in Dubie's and Ai's poems, the narrative line fools us. Its absence in Tate's work makes him more difficult. His language spins in constant deflection—deflection from a central focus, an emotion at the core.

---

[8] *Doggeries*, by James Tate, The Ecco Press, 1979

Tate knows himself better than Dubie or Ai know themselves. Or, at least, he knows that the mannerist has nothing at heart, which is what Wallace Stevens, that grand master of mannerism, said misery is. And if you have nothing at heart, how can you trust your own feelings? Aren't they all received from elsewhere? Aren't they all clichés?

> The little Prince was trapped
> in his miniature life
> and chanted *fuk fuk*
> under his breath:
> in his heart he is a bandleader
>
> —"The Prince at Amherst"

In nearly every line he writes Tate is either approaching or ricocheting from sentimentality. To strike the romantic pose is what he *would* do, and what he winces to think he would do at all.

> I stood there on the bridge and watched
> the moonbeams . . .
>
>
> There is the sensitive gesture.
>
>
> . . . varnish the smirking crocodiles.
>
> —"The Responsible Romance"

And the snickering recoil.

Aim for and deflect, approach and ricochet, gesture and recoil, this is how James Tate generates one of the most dazzling private languages since Stevens. And at the center of each poem, each tour de force, is that negative space where the undesirable self hangs faintly focused with its secondhand sentiments. The cloud around it is the form created by a master mannerist.

> Already rasping machines are turning my
> life into a twenty-five word account.
> *It's none of your beeswax*, I want to say.
> Instead, slipping into something com-

fortable, I made haste, stumbled and bluntly
accepted the call, signal from the pit,
to return to my nook in the deaf opulence
of fossils mending their clocks.

—"The Responsible Romance"

Mannerism is both a reaction and an evasion. As I said at the beginning, the reaction has been inevitable. Through overemphasis, the self in American poetry has been reduced. It is something like a black hole. It no longer produces poetry; it eats it up. These three poets, and others, have responded with a style of poetry that will not be sucked in the "hungry self," as Norman Dubie has called it. Perhaps, Tate's poetry seems the most exciting of the three, the best really, because that conflict is acknowledged in it, a hint of personal risk. However, there is only a hint. And maybe for poets like these, the evasion suggests a dilemma. Without feeling, form is all we have. Will the form last? Isn't form a comfort, really? Yes, but it can be a grand thing, too. The discomfort I feel in reading the poems by these poets is the emptiness of mannerism. *And their apparent refusal to face it.* If Wallace Stevens is the great mannerist of this century, he is also one poet who faced the emptiness.

The empty spirit
In vacant space.
What wine does one drink?
What bread does one eat?

—"The American Sublime"

There is bread and wine somewhere, I think, but not in mannerism.

10

Singers and Storytellers

I am not going to assume that you trust or distrust my good taste as a reviewer of the following eleven books of poetry. I chose them because I have a special interest in them; the poetry written by these poets represents, more or less, a contemporary opposition that fascinates me—that between the lyric and the narrative. It is my suspicion that the lyric is either exhausted as a genre of poetry or is undergoing a necessary revitalization but in some very different directions. One direction seeks to destroy even the syntactic coherence that narrative cannot exist without, so that the consequential underpinnings of the lyric poem itself are kicked out. The other direction is toward more, not less, narrativity.

My title suggests a recognition of temperaments and, since I believe in the primacy, not the death, of the author, I wish to recognize individuality. I do not want to condemn or to praise because of distaste or preference, although I clearly am more excited by the possibilities of narrative in poetry than the destruction of continuity and genre and self. The act of writing poetry is still, to paraphrase Elizabeth Bishop, one of the most backward industries in the world; the poem is still a handmade thing, signed by its maker. That this tradition, coming to us at the very latest from the Renaissance, is under attack is something to take seriously.

It is difficult to say how Leslie Scalapino wants to apply the word *aeolotropic* which she uses to describe the title poem of her latest book[9]. Are we to take it as an expression of its Greek root, meaning "variegated"? That meaning offers a great deal of latitude. Yet the technological slant of much of the Language School of poets, of which Scalapino seems to be a member, suggests that this series may also be taken as *anisotropic,* like "crystals that exhibit properties with different values when measured along axes in different directions," according to *Webster's,* or "anything that assumes different positions in response to external stimuli." Finally, although only one of the four poems included in this book is called an aeolotropic series, since its title is the book's title, are we then to take all four of the poems as variegated series of one sort or another?

In fact, the poetry of Leslie Scalapino, though much of it is in prose blocks,

---

[9] *that they were at the beach—aeolotropic series,* by Leslie Scalapino, North Point Press, 1985

is like the poetry of the Language School generally; that is, it is a form of the lyric. Despite the critical opinion of Marjorie Perloff that the Language School buys into the death of the author and, furthermore, despite the apparent Derridean blurring of genres in assuming that Scalapino's paragraphs are poetry (not a new idea, anyway), there is still a central consciousness in her poetry which speaks with a lyric voice. Associations in her poems are with childhood and adolescence, sexuality, often faceless but lyrically repetitive, and though the emotion may be so subdued as to seem stoned or disoriented by protective apathy, emotion is the key. The fragmentation of the writing itself, often imageless and flat and redundant, provides the very chinks that allow us a partial view. What is most fascinating is how often Scalapino seems to choose not to show us anything interesting. Lest this sound like a circumspect way of saying this poetry is boring, I would hasten to add that her previous book from North Point, *Considering how exaggerated music is*, which stylistically has much in common with this new one, also is more interesting. Even its use of titles from the first line of prose paragraphs has an original wit that teases both the reader's expectations and typography itself; the narrative situations that do appear are more clearly delineated, too: "Driving down to Los Angeles a man who was in the lane on the freeway beside me began talking to me out of his window." And they are often funny, off the wall, and real. It takes an effort of good will to read and enjoy most of the writing in *that they were at the beach*. Personally, I believe it is an effort Scalapino's work deserves, but I must expose my traditional prejudices by saying that I prefer the section called "A Sequence" which seems to be a parable of sexuality built around an irreducible symbol, in this case of the leopard, a motif familiar from Eliot's "Ash Wednesday."

The gorgeous repetitions of his blank verse lines and the expensive Proustian landscapes, even of his persona poems, are characteristic of Herbert Morris's poetry. Two of the twelve poems in his new book[10] are in the voices of personae. In one Freud recalls his friendship with the notorious Fliess; in the other the fiancée of a frequently absent ship's captain reveals to her father that she has taken a young hired man for her lover. The rest of the poems, though they seem narrative at first, become lyrically repetitive, fixed in time, and are meant to be heartbreaking as song rather than story.

Despite its clarity and coherence, Morris's project is much like Scalapino's, except that his repetition is of conventional syntactical units, clauses that

---

[10] *Dream Palace*, by Herbert Morris, Harper & Row, 1985

we understand modify a clear but sometimes distant referent. The referent in Scalapino's writing is part of its enigma—to what is she referring? Where Scalapino can give a kind of dizzying pleasure through disorientation, Morris does so through baroque elaboration. When both poets fail, it is because they satiate the reader; as one gets lost in Scalapino one gets bored; as one sees a single image enhanced and elaborated yet remain static—a photograph or photographic memory—one wonders why Morris must go on.

The lyric, it seems to me, builds emotion through repetition. The narrative builds it through plot. The passions present in Morris are in part nostalgic. The first poems in his book depict his parents, then the poems go back even further in history, then they come forward to the childhood and youth of the poet, and end in the present. There is something of this in Scalapino, too, expressed in the title of her book and in its subject matter, if we can call it that. Repetition in Scalapino works at different angles or axes of measurement; in other words, as just what she says or means by "aeolotropic." In Morris, it is a hypertrophy of the lyric, going to extraordinary lengths to be inclusive, to grow out into all the possibilities of a single emotion. Length, which is associated with narrative in poetry, is then a kind of illusion in Morris, much as prose, which is associated with clarity, is in Scalapino. But the passion each shares is nostalgia, too. The possible subjunctive tense of Scalapino's title implies a wished-for condition; the symbolically resonant title of Morris's book hints at the wish fulfillment of the cinema. The location of emotion in the case of both poets, as it is with all lyric poets, is in the presence of a thinking and feeling human being represented on paper by words. And when there are only words, in the lyric mode, then the absence makes the poetry barren, jejune.

That the lyric poet has only himself or herself for company has been the cause for much discomfort for awhile now, and can be seen, naturally, in some of the formations of the language, even in a young poet like Matthew Graham and his accomplished first book[11]. *Someone*'s, *you*'s, *somewhere*'s, *something*'s, *sometimes*, all these unspecified pronouns abound in Graham's poems. This lack of specificity has been pointed out before as endemic to our poetry, and it is certainly not so much a flaw of Graham's poetry as a symptom of a larger disease. Leslie Scalapino's puzzling referents, I believe, are similar. It is, in other words, not so much that the lyric poet has suddenly discovered that he or she is all alone with these strong feelings but that the

---

[11] *New World Architecture*, by Matthew Graham, The Galileo Press, 1985

primacy of the self seems in doubt, too. What Mary Kinzie has called a shadow self must be constructed, which really is nothing more than a persona, a Yeatsian mask.

Matthew Graham's mask is as something (note my own vagueness) of an itinerant; this person has come from farm stock and has worked in many places and ways, always laboring, on barges or on the roofs of houses, and takes his leisure in bars. Wistful and witty, he is nobody's fool, and saves some of his most moving language for his father, and for his lovers, too, though often indirectly. The single most successful lyric in the volume, a sestina called "California," speaks of a woman who "used to practice patience by making me wait."

The two most compelling poems in the book, though perhaps not the most successful, are "To a Friend Killed in the Fighting: Dominican Republic, 1965" and "Translation." Both take foreign places at war as settings; the latter takes Saigon after the evacuation in 1975. In the former, as if talking to him in his head, a guerrilla explains his situation to his dead friend as he waits to ambush a convoy of U. S. Marines. The otherness of his experience, the warmth of the friendship he recalls and its legacy—the rifle in his hands—even the slightly florid language ("The black night is so long it could be the wind."), all are moving and make the poem almost too intimate, almost embarrassing in its exposure of emotion. "Translation" is written in the voice of a translator who assists a journalist—nationality unspecified in both cases—in greeting the North Vietnamese as they roll into Saigon. The queerness of a tank commander stopping to ask a journalist for directions to Doc Lap Palace and the memory of a woman the translator knew at the palace are compared to make a statement on the inevitability of change. Again, it is the strangeness of place and action in the poem that sets it apart from the lyrics of the rest of the volume. What I am saying is that with the exhaustion of emotion in the lyric self and its expression, a poet like Graham, coming through the door of the persona poem (like Morris), finds a new power in narrative structure. Yet it should be possible to find this power without recourse to the persona poem.

Elizabeth Spires's lyric poetry in her second book[12] is, at times, profoundly touching in the way it echoes the more traditional yet still modern music of a poet like Edna St. Vincent Millay. Here is the opening of the beautiful love poem, "Two Shadows."

---

[12] *Swan's Island*, by Elizabth Spires, Holt, Rinehart, and Winston, 1985

> When we are shadows watching over shadows,
> when years have passed, enough to live
> two lives, when we have passed
> through love and come out speechless
> on the other side, I will remember
> how we spent a night, walking the streets
>   in August, side by side . . .

This is not at all to say she sounds old-fashioned, only to praise the risk in composing such unequivocal music. This lyricism is present in a number of short poems, including "Angel," "The Falling," "My Daughter," "Bread & Water," and "Song of Renunciation"; none of these has quite the lilt of "Two Shadows," however. All do show the necessary compression required by the lyric and the emotional exposure of the self that makes the lyric work.

What is curious about Spires's poetry is that much of it in this volume displays the greater discursiveness sometimes associated with narrativity. Certainly this, and a sense of others, helps Matthew Graham break the lyric habit. I am not altogether sure that Spires improves at length, even though she is always competent and intelligent. The long "Storyville Portraits," based on E. J. Belloq's photographs, neither fish nor fowl, neither lyric nor narrative, exists in that shadow genre we might call meditative poetry, like much contemporary poetry that treats aesthetic subject matter. "Ever-Changing Landscape" about the Ladew topiary gardens in Monkton, Maryland is similar. At this many removes from experience, lyric poetry tends to be overlong and sententious.

The contradiction to these claims is that the very best poem in the book is the four-page title poem, "Letter from Swan's Island." Whoever the speaker of this piece of magic is, I, for one, would not have minded if she had taken up the entire volume. I have had this feeling reading a poet like Elizabeth Bishop, too, who possibly is the presiding spirit of the poem.

> Some mornings I wake too suddenly,
> the light on the wall
> brilliant and unfamiliar, and wonder
> for a moment, where am I?
> I answer myself, my disembodied voice
> high and far off
> like what I imagine saints and martyrs

heard in moments of ecstasy: *Swan's Island*.

On this island, the isolated narrator considers how "love struggles to perfect /
itself, and finally perfect, / finds it has no object." The solemn whimsicality of
the poem, with its serious understanding of this very dilemma, is addressed
to the problem of the lyric poet in our time. With a perfected form in hand,
on what object shall the poet apply it, besides language itself? Elizabeth Spires
is a valuable poet because she understands this problem. Like Matthew Graham, she attempts to solve the problem through greater narrativity.

Louise Glück is arguably the foremost lyric poet of her generation, and the
title of her fourth book[13] does make a certain claim, with its neo-classical
ring, imaginable as a title for a painting by David. But Achilles' triumph, and
Glück's triumph too it must be added, is to be, despite demi-godhead, "a victim / of the part that loved, / the part that was mortal." The book begins and
ends with two rather petulant responses to mortality. "Mock Orange" tells
us about flowers in a moonlit yard, "I hate them. / I hate them as I hate sex, /
the man's mouth / sealing my mouth, / the man's paralyzing body—." And
"Horse," which concludes the volume, is a reproach for the lover's animal nature and ends, "What is the animal / if not passage out of this life?"

At her best Glück is what might be called an academic poet in that many
of her poems are literary. "Mythic Fragment," "Hyacinth," "The Triumph of
Achilles" and "The Mountain" all allude to classical myths. "Winter Morning"
and "Day Without Night" are meditations on Christ and Moses, respectively.
The landscape of many of her poems is classical in another sense, too; it is the
psychoanalytical landscape of dreams and its painterly neo-classicism is de
Chirico's rather than David's

> I had come to a strange city,
> without belongings:
> in the dream it was your city,
> I was looking for you.
> Then I was lost, on a dark street lined with fruit stands . . .
>
> Then I was on a boulevard, in brilliant sunlight.

In the poem the preceding passage is taken from, part 6 of "Marathon"
called "The Beginning," Glück offers us this piece of dreamwork: "Then what

---

[13] *The Triumph of Achilles*, by Louise Glück, Ecco Press, 1985

began as love for you / became a hunger for structure." Is dream, as it so often is in Glück's poetry, structure enough with its odd narrative twists? She has made it so in the past, most notably in *House on Marshland*, still her finest book. A characteristic of that book, but only a minor one, was that along with the imagistic language and the compressed free verse was a hint of discursiveness, a willingness to let mere talk carry weight. In "Pomegranate," Hades seduced shy Persephone memorably, saying, "examine / this grief your mother / parades over our heads / remembering / that she is one to whom / these depths were not offered." Now that discursiveness not only predominates in a form not made for it, but often becomes persiflage, as in "Metamorphosis" about the death of her father: "Once, for the smallest / fraction of an instant, I thought / he was alive in the present again."

On the other hand, as contemporary poetry grows more discursive, in the narrative and meditative modes, Glück's condensed lyrics are beginning to seem less and less fashionable and, perhaps, more to be prized for their individuality. It is odd, but their address to matters of love and birth and mortality is being better handled at this time by the poet Sharon Olds, whose charged up, often headlong and even redundant imagery makes Glück's seem cautious, though more artful.

Where Louise Glück's world is the dream, James Schuyler's, in his latest book[14] is the waking life. Schuyler is so wide awake that he even tells us of a sleepless night and the roil of associations that pass through his head, crazily but consciously. Schuyler tells the reader everything he can think of, believing that in "the mess" is "all this beauty." He does not hunger for structure in the least; there seems to be no inner censor or editor; everything goes into the poetry, distinguished, it appears, only by the poet's taste for the names of flowers, friends, and musical compositions. Of all members of the New York School, Schuyler is still given to what his friend and contemporary Frank O'Hara called "the I-do-this, I-do-that poem." His poetry is a diary of daily life, and the name-dropping he does, off putting to some, is a part of that life and no longer seems to be making any inordinate claims, but simply to be documenting and rounding out a personality.

The poetry doesn't make much of a claim on the reader, either. One does not read it with a wrinkled brow, as one reads Glück, patient or impatient to receive wisdom through the slow exposure of the images. Schuyler throws the

[14] *A Few Days*, James Schuyler, Random House, 1985

shade up and the door open and lets light and air flood in on everything and anything.

> Because of the coolness in the air,
> because of the henna in your hair
> (it turned it orange, boy)
> because of Helena's perky boobs,
> because of Tom's insouciant buns
> (M. is really gone on them),
> I would like to celebrate today.

—"The Day"

By the end of *A Few Days* one seems to know quite a bit about Schuyler's everyday life and thus his life generally: the French doors of his apartment in New York City, his frustrated attraction to his assistant Tom, his insomnia, his fight with alcoholism and mental illness, his preference for Romantic music over Baroque, his cologne, his opinions about friends like Frank O'Hara and John Ashbery ("John is devoted to the impossible"), how many pills he takes before he goes to sleep at night, his brother's family, his mother's death. The title poem is set off by itself, loosely structured around his mother's final illness and death, but filled as is the rest of the book with Schuyler's commonplace, diaristic lyricism. Schuyler is so forthright he makes Allen Ginsberg sound literary. I think of the opening of John Ashbery's prose poem "The New Spirit": "I thought that if I could put it all down, that would be one way. And next the thought came to me that to leave all out would be another, and truer, way."

Schuyler chooses the first way. Nevertheless, peeking through all the newsprint and flowers and chit-chat is a genuine human being in a good deal of pain, somebody wide awake and feeling an inner pressure that makes him pettishly quibble with himself about how much cologne he will wear or whether rum cake will activate his Antabuse. Schuyler's poetry is the opposite of Glück's temperamentally, but both her constriction and his explosion may mark an end, a need for something new, in the lyric.

John Ashbery has, at last, published a volume of his selected[15]. Formally, Ashbery has been very well understood; no one has improved on David Shapiro's *Urgent Masks*, but I do not believe even Harold Bloom knows what the poet is saying, if indeed he is saying anything. Ashbery's approach is much like

---

[15] *Selected Poems*, by John Ashbery, Viking, 1985

James Schuyler's; he does put everything in, but most of it is abstract, symbolic, and the terms keep changing as an apparent lyric or narrative or meditative line of reasoning develops, so that he seems to be leaving everything out. For Bloom, Ashbery is the poet who claims, "We are happy in our way of life." For the rest of us, Ashbery adds, "It doesn't make much sense to others." I will not pretend to let anyone know what Ashbery is talking about throughout this handsome book, only that my experience of reading it straight through, having already read the books from which it was selected, was totally unlike James Fenton's, reported in *The New York Times Book Review*. I was not reduced to tears of boredom. Lying on a couch, reading steadily but without undue concentration, I let the poetry come in waves and concluded that one could describe it *only* in formal terms.

First of all, Ashbery is a magician of metaphor, especially when the object is humor: "I only slipped on the cake of soap of the air / and drowned in the bathtub of the world." The poem "37 Haiku," selected from *A Wave*, might just be what we search for in the larger bodies of the others. Its lines seem to have been flensed from the warm blubber of the big poems: "A child must go down it must stand and last," "The dreams descend like cranes on gilded, forgetful wings," "What is the past, what is it all for? A mental sandwich?," and so on.

In larger terms, I would call Ashbery a narrative poet *manqué*. The two best poems from his first book, "The Instruction Manual" and "Illustration," create a setting and characters, and though the former is without event and the latter is basically a lyric, the point is that a narrative structure is essential to both of them. Ashbery knows this; there is no more cunning poet writing; his voice has the dreamy persuasiveness of hypnagogic imagery.

> And meanwhile my story goes well
> The first chapter
> endeth
> But the real story, the one
> They tell us we shall probably never know
> Drifts back in bits and pieces
> All of them, it turns out
>
> —"Oleum Misericordiam"

It is not surprising that Ashbery is the preeminent poet of our time. He is the poet modernism has been headed for. Nor is it surprising that he is to the

Language School what W. C. Williams was to the Black Mountain School. The pleasure of his poetry is the deep, dazzling murk of it. We should buy this book and rediscover it years hence and understand what we had come to. Till then, like children listening to a conversation that doesn't concern them, we *are* likely to be bored, albeit pleasantly.

It is significant that Evan Connell's companion volume[16] to his classic *Notes Found in a Bottle on the Beach at Carmel* has also been reissued, for like its predecessor, it appears to be a book-length narrative poem, but its fragmentation may be the only sort of narrative acceptable to readers of poetry in the age of Ashbery. Actually, the book is a box of mind candy. One can alight anywhere among its 240 pages and find mostly fascinating comments on the vanity of human wishes, Connell's theme.

Page 11:

We suspect giantesses live beneath the sea,
just as we know dragons wait in grave mounds
and Valkyries eat corpses on battlefields.

Page 88:

Bohemond's warriors ate the flesh of Turks,
declaring it tastier than spiced peacock.
This, too, has contemporary reverberations.

Page 44:

Arabs compare women to camels, and say they are graceful
hideous creatures with magic in their way of walking.

Page 132:

Andromeda's stars aren't important, but opposite Mirach
is the Great Nebula, probably larger than the Milky Way,
visible as a hazy speck so faint that in order to see it
we must look a little aside.

Page 190:

I would say I resemble the King of Tsin at whose order

---

[16] *Points for a Compass Rose*, by Evan Connell, North Point Press, 1985,

the Great Wall was begun, who decreed that every book
composed before his time be destroyed.

I chose these passages at random, in full faith that I would be able to find
exemplary ones. This is a syndetic work and to explain the meaning of *syndetic* let me quote David Robertson quoting R. P. Armstrong in "The Book of
Proverbs" from the Winter 1986 issue of *The Hudson Review*:

> "Syndesis . . . proceeds by 'accretion' and 'repetition,' 'accumulation' and
> 'proliferation.' Whereas synthetic works of art are 'consequential,' syndetic
> ones are 'sequential.'

Even sequence might be misunderstood with respect to this work. Yet there
is a trope supported at intervals through the book that we are aboard a ship;
readings of latitude and longitude turn up; perhaps, we are reading a ship's
log. Thus, the poem may be seen as Archibald MacLeish's "Letter to Be Left
in the Earth" writ enormously large. It is also like a novel made up entirely of
the narrator's digressions, rhapsodies instead of episodes, poetry instead of
plot. Connell himself calls it "a song for a single voice. A monody." On page
224 the poet finally comments:

> Look. I appreciate your impatience
> with what must seem intolerably circuitous;
> it's just that affairs of supreme urgency
> like root-bound plants send out tentacles
> in a dozen directions.

One of the directions is an intrigue with conspiracy theory.

> Perhaps you know this, but an unspecified quantity
> of a gas designated "G-B" has been manufactured.
> Theoretically, 300 gallons would be enough
> to blot out one billion people.

But a dozen directions? That is either too few or too many.
How then is a book-length narrative poem to be written nowadays? Examples do exist, but their appearance is separated by years rather than months.
Most recently there is Alfred Corn's *Notes from a Child of Paradise* and some
would include James Merrill's *The Changing Light at Sandover*. The last major

book-length narrative poem to raise the problem of what form such a poem is to take was George Keithley's *The Donner Party* in 1972. Nobody has seemed to have trouble with Corn's or Merrill's poems on that score; they are traditional formalists. One of *The Donner Party*'s harshest critics, James Dickey, argued that the poem lacked rhythm and original imagery and figures of speech; for him, these are essential elements of poetry in any form. Daryl Hine and Frederick Turner have given us two book-length narrative poems that say a lot about how narrative poetry is currently conceived. Besides the fact that both are, in the end, quite readable, they also have historical importance.

For all its science-fiction prose and phony behavior of characters (an over solicitousness for feminine propriety, for example, especially with regards to obscene language); for all its space opera and pseudo-Medieval mores, which we are to assume we will return to after the apocalypse and the oil wells run dry; for all its pretentious mixing of traditional myths and legends, including Siegfried and Brunnhilde, Sohrab and Rustum, Arjuna and Krishna, Odysseus and Nausicaa, Arthur and Mordred, Adam and Eve, and finally, even the Jonestown mass suicides; for all this machinery to present us a single warrior-savior, an Oedipus as Christ, Frederick Turner's epic poem[17] is quite a read, absorbing and atrocious, tasteless and tactless, bloodcurdling and inconsistent (the invented language and coinages of the recent post-apocalypse novel *Riddley Walker* are more successful). There are moments that make a reader cringe, but times, too, when one is in the presence of real epic poetry and feels what the first auditors of Homer may have felt.

Yet the adrenalin that gets pumping through the vascular reader at the climactic end of *The New World* is no different from that secreted by reading a fast-paced pot boiler. The so called prosody Turner claims to be following really isn't demonstrable. The characterizations are often ludicrous, especially the retro-Nigger Jim speech of the Kingfish, the Krishna-like deity who presides over the poem's final internecine battle. Still, if we are to have a resurgence of narrative poetry, then a work like this should have a place in it, just as science fiction has a place more and more in serious fiction. I don't really believe Turner's intention is to capitalize on the Star Wars hokum that James Merrill refers to in a cover blurb, nor is it to write a kitsch epic, taking the risk others like Turner Cassity and Peter Klappert have of turning kitsch into culture rather than reducing culture to kitsch. Too much in Turner's poem

[17] *The New World*, by Frederick Turner, Princeton University Press, 1985

is in earnest, too little is humorous, the entire enterprise is solemn. As one who watches recent developments in narrative poetry, I read Turner's poem with chagrin, asking myself if this is, in fact, what one thinks of when one considers a contemporary epic? Must the dim past return as science fiction? Must the narrative poem of epic length be resurrected as pulp? It could very well be that a poem like Turner's, in which action and character are of heroic dimensions, is where it all has to start, again.

Daryl Hine solves the problem of form in his book-length narrative poem[18] mostly in traditional ways. First, his poem is divided into 12 sections, each named for a month and beginning, with the school year, in September. Then, since for Hine poetry is metrical composition, he has chosen to write what he calls an Alexandrine line of 12 syllables; this choice is a smart one allowing for a wider variety of beats per line, less predictability than page after page of blank verse, yet it risks doggerel. And the poem rhymes the even-numbered lines of each verse paragraph in a pattern of xaxaxbxb and so on. Since Hine is a poet of insistent wit, few opportunities to pun are passed up, at least when he is more or less marking time or developing a character or setting. A lesson at his junior high in British Columbia called "Taking care of our tools" is described as raising "a tumescent titter / in pubescent circles," for example.

But a narrative poem is supposed to deliver something more than the satisfaction of certain lyrical criteria. It has to tell a story. Hine tells a good one, one that grows more harrowing and solemn and sad as the book comes to an end. It is the story of a precocious junior high school boy, Hine himself, adopted son of a dour Scot, who as part of his sexual awakening falls in love with one of the class stars, a handsome young athlete. The path of their consummation as friends is a winding one. Much of the poem deals with narrator's anguish and precocity and provisional friendships between the ages of 13 and 14, during a single school year and into the summer. His father, his mother, and two librarians, a woman and a man, all figure importantly, all are touching, even in their perversity. It is Hine himself, represented straightforwardly with more than confessional fullness, who tends to grow annoying. This is a kid who is already reading Northrop Frye in junior high school; who, in fact, reads everything and begins his career as a poet. As I read, I kept wishing he would lighten up. But he never does, and by the end of the poem it seems clear why he doesn't. He has learned that "There is no hierarchy to unhappiness" once the boy he loves becomes seriously hurt. He learns, too, that his own

---

[18] *Academic Festival Overtures, A Poem*, by Daryl Hine, Atheneum, 1985

profound loneliness can only be shared by another who is, in a sense, handicapped by solitude. When Hine tries to console the crippled Donald Wisdom, the boy responds like any pre-teen.

> What, compared to the loss of function and sensation,
>   Was the fact that he was alive and not in pain?
> I spoke airily of intellectual pleasures,
>   But he muttered, "That's O. K. For you, you're a brain."

Hine's poetry suffices to give this story its haunting sadness, bad puns, and good, and all.

Currently, narrative exists best or most successfully in the lyric mode. Andrew Hudgins's first book[19] shows that he may be the foremost practitioner of the narrative lyric at this time. The book's epigraph from St. Augustine, "To blame the fault of a creature is to praise its essential nature," is right on target. In many of these poems, people who find themselves in extremity, including the author, are shown with all their flaws and still given their due. A warmth of this sort, a real vulgarity in the sense of the vernacular and the people who use it, has not been present in our poetry since James Wright's death, although Philip Levine has also shown it. And it is the story element of the poem, its narrative component, that shows it best.

Much of Hudgins's milieu is Southern, so when he brings anecdotes together in a lyric whole, as in "Prayer," he often begins with experiences of childhood in the South, where a woman in church might holler, "Hep me, Jesus!" Usually from that beginning point he travels, often ending himself among strangers, even when they are loved ones. There are 33 poems divided into four sections in the book; the fourth section is comprised of the eight-part title poem. In it, a daughter of a retired itinerant preacher recalls her life with him now that he has been debilitated by a stroke and is unable to care for himself. This poem is the most completely narrative in structure. Unlike many contemporary persona poems, its first person narration has more the thrust of a fictional convention. In poetry, this can bring up the problem of genre, of the precedent of dramatic monologue, but not here. Hudgins can create moments so pathetic all you can do in response is laugh. Marie, the narrator of "Saints and Strangers" (her daddy's name for Christians "in the world"), explains her father's failing mind and health.

---

[19] *Saints and Strangers*, by Andrew Hudgins, Houghton Mifflin Co., 1985

> He's scared to leave the house. Incontinence.
> When he's wet himself, he lets us know
> by standing grimly at our bedroom door
> and reading from his Bible.

On one occasion Daddy has run through the local Kroger's "pointing out demons." These late-life humiliations are complicated for Marie by her love for her father, of course, and his tenderness for her the years he was bringing her up, despite the obsession of his calling.

Two other poems stand out for comment, in part because they leave the South and yet bring that storytelling loquacity we tend to associate with it (Hudgins keeps his in check with an idiosyncratic iambic meter that gives his poems an original rhythm). One is "Sotto Voce," the only poem I know in which an overheard conversation is not presented to us condescendingly but with lyric sweetness and humor. The other, the book's masterpiece, is "Returning Home to Babylon" in which the poet writes of "The Eunuch who loves Daniel—Ashpenaz" and is able to get completely inside the Biblical story and bring along extraordinary details of his own life, understanding greatness and weakness of character in a way few poets have of late. Andrew Hudgins's narrative lyrics are the state of the art.

11

A Scale of Engagement, from Self to Form Itself

In her latest collection,[20] Marilyn Hacker uses the sonnet, much as Lowell did in *Notebook*, more as a section in a sequence than as a poem in itself. She tells the story of a failed love affair, but her real subject is herself. The strictness of the sonnet and the demands of the sonnet sequence and the other complex forms Hacker employs do not constrain her from self-exposure.

> First, I want to make you come in my hand
> while I watch you and kiss you, and if you cry,
> I'll drink your tears while, with my whole hand, I
> hold your drenched loveliness contracting . . . .

The story is of an older woman's love for a younger one, and the above passage is like many in the poems. Curiously, one of the few poems with a title, "Lesbian Ethics, or: Live Girl-Girl Sex Acts," invites us to consider the difference between the erotic and the pornographic. Lesbian ethics, as they are described, sound like any ethical sexual behavior; the lovers are waiting to be free before they can be together. And yet, the subject of some pornography aimed at the heterosexual market *is* "girl-girl sex acts." The healthy animal spirits of Hacker's love poems are, I presume, supposed to circumvent this dilemma.

The success of the sequence is not, however, its erotic motif but its representation of the dailiness of being in love. Hacker chronicles eating, drinking, living in New York City, sharing poems, teaching, raising her teenage daughter, traveling to France, mourning the death of a friend, all with her lover Rachel beside her or on her mind, until the final days of the affair. This journalistic approach is also found in Lowell's first version of *Notebook*. In a similar fashion, we see less a form taking shape than a form of person, the person of the poet, in Hacker's case, the poet in love. It is Hacker's gift to give us this in a kind of sensual fullness, that includes sex, but also includes banality and produces questions. Why do the lovers spend so much time apart? Just what brings about the end of the affair, which is terminated cruelly ("Who would divorce her lover with a phone / call? You did.")? What this sort of poetry requires is that the character of the poet engage us, for that is clearly

[20] *Love, Death, and the Changing of the Seasons*, by Marilyn Hacker, Arbor House, 1986

what engages the poet herself. All of the woman at this time in her life is illuminated by her passion, which means depths and heights, the sublime and the ridiculous are all present in this unique book.

> We do get headaches, but we don't get cramps.
> We take less than a half an hour to dress;
> need: pockets, details, stuffs that please the touch.
> We do it once like ladies, once like tramps.
> We love each other very very much.
>
> —"Symbiose II"

Like Marilyn Hacker, Richard Katrovas in his second book[21] has himself for his own best subject—or, rather, favorite subject. Actually, he is best when, writing about the marginal people of New Orleans (streetwalkers, transvestites, tourist hustlers), he marginalizes himself and brings to bear the art of pathos he has learned from James Wright. One of the most powerful poems in the first New Orleans section of the book is "I Feel" about overhearing a woman trying to explain herself to an outraged male companion, perhaps her pimp.

> Whatever she has done,
> it doesn't warrant his
> restrained passion,
> his noble posturing
> which is utterly absurd.
>
> Besides, whether they can
> acknowledge it or not, I
> am part of this,
> and I don't want to hear
> her tell him what she feels.

The role in which Katrovas announces his active emotional participation is extended sometimes to heroic or mock-heroic lengths. In one poem he describes beating up a stalker ("to them the earth is packed with angels who hate them"), then shaking hands with the woman who has enlisted his help; in another he helps a woman vomit in a gutter by putting his fingers down her throat; in "The Waiter" he serves a newlywed couple in a restaurant and "divine[s] their marriage will not last." In all these situations, he presents himself

[21] *Snug Harbor*, by Richard Katrovas, Wesleyan University Press, 1986

as a locus of moral authority and genuine feeling. This can grow a bit thick, as when in "Meeting Yevtushenko, July, 4, 1985," he measures himself against the Russian media-star: "I address him / as I would any other mortal / who has not had time to piss me off / or earn my reverence." He claims that he has developed this attitude because he has lived "so long / in Southern California / where everyone I knew / had star potential." But the tough guy shtick is pure Charles Bukowski, who lived in Southern California a long time, too.

Nevertheless, *Snug Harbor* is a compelling book and it is precisely because of the persona in these poems—although I am beginning to think that persona in the modern sense hardly applies to the typical autobiographical lyric today. The claim the speaker of Katrovas's poems makes is that they are records of the authentic experience of Richard Katrovas. There are attempts to find mythic allusions in the life of New Orleans, as in "Kings' Day, 1984" where three transvestites are seen as the Magi ("I imagine they are / bearing gifts to celebrate the birth / of something conceived in a glass beaker . . . / I burn with hope like a star.") . But the best of the poems are the most realistic.

Ruth Fainlight has a less theatrical sense of herself than Hacker and Katrovas, but like them she makes herself the center of her poems in this, her seventh volume[22]. The difference in Fainlight is that we are in the presence of someone engaged in understanding herself as an artist more than anything else.

> What I am working at and want to perfect—
> my project—is the story of myself: to have it
> clear in my head, events consecutive,
> to understand what happened and why it happened.
>
> —"Author! Author!"

The author of these poems engages herself on any number of levels, in any number of ways, from the aging of her own body, to her interest in the classical world, to her Jewish background, to being an average citizen of London who encounters a madwoman on the street. She is especially moving in her role as a daughter and as a mother, and as a sister, the elegist for her departed brother. The range of situations played out in her poems gives us a much fuller sense of a human being, in fact, than the range in Hacker or Katrovas. Recalling an event during her childhood, when her father was away at war, she tells how her mother used her as a shield in public so that she could mend a torn stocking.

---

[22] *Fifteen to Infinity*, by Ruth Fainlight, Carnegie-Mellon University Press, 1986

Her flushed face. My harsh stern eye. My impulse
to hurt and to love, towards and away. That rainy
winter day, my mother and I determined
a future no peace-time knowledge can assuage.

—"War-Time"

Addressing her brother on the day of his burial, she writes:

Harry, I know how much you would have enjoyed it.
I can see your mouth's ironic curve as the heavens
opened. The umbrella over my head was almost
useless—rain and hail at the same slant
as your amused imagined gaze darkened
the side of my coat and trousers.

—"The Storm"

And in the book's title poem, she describes her son's growing up in terms of his mastery of the camera and its f-stop.

...time
expands around you like the dizzying
crown of the tree and sky above:
fifteen to infinity.

To my mind, a poet with this warm sense of others, who at the same time hopes to recognize herself, is the lyric poet at her most mature. Fainlight's career has taken place in England, although she is an American. The English claim her, but it is a valuable service of CMU Press to publish her latest English book in this country, and American poets might do well to read it. Straightforwardness is a trait I have always valued in our poetry and missed in poetry from across the Atlantic. Lately, I miss it in ours, but find it in the work of this expatriate.

Robert Wrigley's poems in his third book[23] attempt to move closer to the experience itself, than to the self who had the experience, hence his narratives tend to be emblematic and at times obscure. The speaker is sometimes a persona (an arsonist in "Lover of Fire," a firefighter in "Volunteers") and sometimes a fictional narrator as in the baffling "The Secret Life in Every Living Thing."

---

[23] *Moon in a Mason Jar*, Robert Wrigley, University of Illinois Press, 1986

Access to the other and stricter formal considerations characterize the movement along the scale I have devised, from the poet's concern with himself to a
greater concern for his poem's form. Consider how many of Wrigley's poems
are about animals. The titles alone tell a good deal, "The Bees," "Nightcrawl-
ers," "Termites," "The Beliefs of a Horse," "Fireflies," "Pheasant Hunting,"
"The Skull of a Snowshoe Hare," "The Owl." The animal has a moral purpose
in poetry, as in all literature, but in the lyric, too, it has the romantic purpose
of accepting the self's projections, and, in my view, it offers a form.

> I found it in the woods, moss-mottled,
> hung at the jaws by a filament
> of leathery flesh. We have painted it
> with Chlorox, bleached it
> in that chemical sun, boiled loose
> the last tatters of tissue
> and made of it an heirloom,
> a trophy, a thing that lasts, death's
> little emissary to an eight-year-old boy.
>
> —"The Skull of a Snowshoe Hare"

I hope it is fair to say that Wrigley belongs at the heart of the American tradition that takes country things and understanding of them for the heart of
experience itself. His is neither an urban nor an urbane poetry; I do not mean
to assign a plus sign to this side of the issue (country +, city -), but merely to
characterize. Admittedly, the possibilities inherent when the isolation of the
country and the human intersect are rich ones, and Wrigley makes the most
of them. One of the best poems is the very first (it was reading this that made
me want to read the entire book). On a deserted road at night in the Ozarks
a family car collides with a chicken truck. Apparently only a small boy, the
speaker, survives.

> I walked, in the almost black of Ozark night,
> the moon just now burning into Missouri.
> Behind me, the chickens followed my lead,
> some fully upright, pecking
> the dim pavement for suet or seed,
> some half-hobbled by their wounds . . .
>
> —"Moonlight: Chickens on the Road"

Being drawn to the emblematic in imagery or narrative is, to me, not unlike being drawn to form itself or putting the formal properties of a thing first. This can lead to detachment in the writer, and for those who enjoy their poetry with the poet's full presence announced in every line, it may leave them cold. But Wrigley can follow his inclination with great feeling, as in the book's most beautiful poem, "Appalonea." Discovering the name of a forgotten relative leads him to a moving passage of association.

> Apotheosis
> of appellations, a plum of pure sound.
> Apollo, Apollonius, Apollinaire . . .
> that strong grayish horse
> across the field: Appaloosa,
> a portrait but not a picture,
> a prize, a poem, Appalonea.

Michael Collier is even more concerned with the form of his poems than Wrigley, and many of them in this, his first book[24] are organized around a central image. This keeps his poems shorter, under greater control, and clarifies the emblematic nature of narrative when it appears. Not only do his poems rely on a central image, often they are constructed around a conceit, and this frame of mind flickers with Collier's wit, which is impressive. The first poem, "Ancestors," plays both on the meaning of the poet's surname and on his forebears' profession—they were dentists.

> These most intimate colliers,
> with drill and bit and whir,
> black slag of old amalgam,
> the sear and singe of pulp.
> They wanted to come as close
> as they could to the fleshy rose
> pulsing in the root like the heart's
> faintest hint.

The challenge to such an imagination is to transform unpromising material. If Donne could turn a flea into a priest, then Collier can transform himself into a fishing lure to angle for his father, as he does in "White Bass." If Herbert can make his collar into a protest against his vocation, then Collier in

---

[24] *The Clasp and Other Poems*, by Michael Collier, Wesleyan University Press, 1986

his title poem can see an example of his own art in a serpentine necklace of pearls. He is clearly more interested in the dimensions of his subject, that is, its *form*, than in his own personality. This is not to say that personal concerns do not exist in the book. Collier is such a clean and scrupulous writer that we can find them—one being the memory of his father, already mentioned in "White Bass" and also dealt with in "The Point of No Return," "The Bird Feeders," and "Flyer."

What has a poet like this to give his reader, if it is not going to be the whole man, alive and in person and the star of these poems? His wit, of course, his ability to make connections, and—even though the alliteration sounds corny—his wisdom, too. The single most powerful poem in *The Clasp* is "Bruges." Its imagery is transfixing, and the news it brings is that "there is no way past death." News like this is hard to bear. Collier's poetry makes it bearable.

Alice Fulton's second book[25] is divided into six sections, each headed with a different definition of "palladium," running from the element to the music hall to the Trojan statue of Pallas Athena. The definition is the form her poems most often take; as if in acknowledgment that a single thing or word can have many meanings, she attempts to give as many as she can think up. For her all the fun's in how you name a thing. In this, her guiding genius is Marianne Moore. Although Fulton's exuberance is not as strictly controlled as Moore's, it could be argued that the great modernist's elaborate syllabic forms were disguises for a chaos of associations. Like Moore's poems, which she called her "things," Fulton's poems are also things, rather amazing ones, too.

They can include fanciful guidebooks to the lifestyles of hell ("Orientation Day in Hades") and phantasmagoric trips through contemporary underworlds as in "The Body Opulent." She is savvy about female and male forms of identity, in "Fictions of the Feminine" and "Men's Studies: *Roman de la Rose*." I like her poems best for the way they say a thing, as in these lines from "Everyone Knows the World Is Ending."

> Everyone knows the world is ending.
> Everyone always thought so, yet
> Here's the world.

Or the pun that closes "Days Through Starch and Bluing" ("Tomorrow's pressing."). I would like to show how Fulton puts a poem together, because a reader can get lost and one poem can seem very much like another, as if the

[25] *Palladium*, by Alice Fulton, University of Illinois Press, 1986

associations lined up in poem A could just as well have worked in poem B, but her poems are long and complicated. Two brief passages will have to do.

> born gorgeous with nerves, with brains
> the pink of silver polish or
> jellyfish wafting ornately
> through the body below.
> An invertebrate cooing
> on the mother
> tongue shushes and lulls them into thinking
> all is well.
>
> —"Babies"

> We feel
> heavily unconscious, submerged in colors dense
> as chloroform, distant
> effervescent riffles, the roar of boulders in a whirlpool,
> slight sandy agitations.
>
> —"Obsessions"

The subject of the first passage is clear in the title, but the second is not.

Reviewing her first book I complained that the poems were often overwritten. They still are, but to say so is also to object puritanically to their abundance. This long book covers quite a bit of ground, some of the best of it focused on Fulton's own family, mother and aunts, her father, and Troy, New York, her hometown, which she mythifies with a gossamer touch ("We loved a ruin"). As good company as these poems are, they are best when we can, to paraphrase Marianne Moore, admire what we understand.

> Oh, you will never know me. I wave and you go
> on playing in the clouds
> boys clap from erasers. I am the pebble
> you tossed on the chalked space and war-
> danced toward, one-leg two-leg, arms treading air.
>
> —"Fierce Girl Playing Hopscotch"

David Lehman's poetry[26] reminds me of the story about two vaudeville comics who were working on their act. Mike tells Maish a joke, to which Maish responds, "It sounds contrived." Surprised, Mike says, "I just contrived it!" There's a just-contrived feeling to Lehman's very carefully wrought poetry, a spontaneity within form that is reminiscent of Stevens and early Frank O'Hara.

> X distrusts actions; he has his *is*,
> His *was*, which shall be again, when
> The jangle of change is spent, the jingle
> Of jargon clicks off, and peace in the jungle
> Reigns in the tiger's snore, as before.
>
> —"Dominant X"

Lehman makes a good deal out of the "jingle of jargon," using, as he states in a note, a collage technique of "incorporating echoes and quotations."

> "Work shall set you free": a sensible sentiment:
> Marx would agree: Freud would give his assent:
>
> Yet take those words and put them on a sign
> And hang that sign upon the gate at Auschwitz,
>
> What happens then: it means "abandon hope all ye who enter here"
>
> —"Arbeit Macht Frei"

His feeling for the phrase, especially the debased one, leads him to construct an effective villanelle, like "First Offense" ("I'm sorry officer, I didn't see the sign. . . . The light was green. How much is the fine?") and a pantoum, "Amnesia," with these repeating lines: "The car pulled up and the driver said, 'Get in.'" and "'Wolves don't criticize sheep,' Cage grinned. 'They eat them.'"

The temper of Lehman's poetry is about as far away from Marilyn Hacker's as one can get within the mode that we might simply call the mainstream lyric. Ironically of all seven poets discussed here, it is Hacker and Lehman who most rigorously engage meter and rhyme, but their aims are totally different. On Lehman's end of the scale, forms of language are much more compelling

---

[26] *Alternative to Speech*, by David Lehman, Princeton University Press, 1986

than roles of the self. With his cerebral interest in clichés, literary modes, stock characters, and the styles of others, Lehman might be called a mannerist. There is nothing visceral in his poetry, nor is there meant to be; it is a superior amusement. It should not be surprising then that one outstanding poem in his volume is titled "The Difference Between Pepsi and Coke." It lists qualities and talents of one called "Pop" (Fulton might be just as likely to pun on the name and still mean an actual relative).

> Needs no prompting to give money to his kids; speaks French fluently, and
> tourist German;
> Sings Schubert in the shower; plays pinball in Paris; knows the new maid
> steals, and forgives her.

Pop can tell the difference between the two soft drinks, and could surely tell the difference among these seven poets. Even when their aims are similar, they remain distinct from one another.

12

The Pragmatic Imagination
and the Secret of Poetry

I

The great American contribution to the history of thought is pragmatism, attributed mainly to C. S. Peirce and William James and described wittily by José Ortega y Gasset in *What Is Philosophy?*:

> With that amiable cynicism which is characteristic of the Yankees, characteristic of every new people . . . pragmatism in North America dared to proclaim this thesis— "There is no other truth than success in dealing with things."

Two major American poets, Wallace Stevens and Robert Frost, can be linked directly to James's thought; the former was his student and the latter called James "(the) teacher who influenced me most (whom) I never had." And since Ortega's words seem almost to paraphrase William Carlos Williams' most famous credo—"No ideas but in things"—we really must add him to the list as well. Pragmatism's insistence that philosophy must deal with the empirical world is fundamental to the work of these three modernists and creates there a tension between things as they are—as they appear to the senses—and as they might be. That is to say, against the restraints of pragmatism the poet must pose his own imagination; to make statements about being, he must risk creating a metaphysics. Robert Frost would have called this trying to say a few things the world can't deny. He meant taking the risk of deducing—from things and their relationships—truths about being, or beliefs that might, as the preacher says in "The Black Cottage," cease "to be true" but "will turn true again, for so it goes." Pragmatism, bred in the bone of modern American poetry, makes us suspect metaphysics while trusting the imagination. We look to the imagination to express a unified ontological view of the world, while at the same time we see the world as fragmented, incapable of embodying a metaphysical reality. Thus the poet, encouraged by pragmatism to trust the imagination, takes a risk in trying to say something the world can't deny.

I call it a risk because, in simple American terms, we may not buy it; readers faced with the metaphysical statement, may not believe it.

And so I bring together books by three poets—Charles Wright[27], C. K. Williams[28], and Philip Levine[29]—who attempt to resolve the conflict between pragmatism and metaphysics. Their means of expression are very different, ranging from Wright's mystical, koanlike statements, to Williams' baffled and angry questions about mortality, to Levine's classically simple but elegant affirmation through negation. All three seem to want to come to terms —who attempt to resolve the conflict between pragmatism and metaphysics. Their means of expression are very different, ranging from Wright's mystical, koanlike statements, to Williams' baffled and angry questions about mortality, to Levine's classically simple but elegant affirmation through negation. All three seem to want to come to terms with another assertion by Ortega, also found in *What Is Philosophy?*:

> Life is not a mystery, but quite the opposite; it is the clearest and most present thing there is, and being so, being purely transparent, we find difficulty in studying it closely. The eye goes beyond it, toward wisdoms that are still problematical, and it is an effort for us to stop it at these immediate evidences.

From these words one can understand Ortega's admiration for pragmatism and the discomfort a poet might have at being told that "Life is not a mystery." And yet, I think this view is fundamentally shared by these three poets; it is the pragmatic ground of their imaginations.

II

As if nothingness contained a métier . . .

—Wallace Stevens

Kant believed that though a metaphysics of the immanent or empirical world was possible a transcendent metaphysics was not. Charles Wright subscribes to this belief but writes about the empirical world as if a transcendent metaphysics *were* possible. It is because of the tension between possibility and

---

[27] *Zone Journals*, by Charles Wright, Farrar, Straus, and Giroux, 1988
[28] *Flesh and Blood*, by C.K. Williams, Farrar, Straus, and Giroux, 1987
[29] *A Walk with Tom Jefferson*, by Philip Levine, Knopf, 1986

impossibility that he is able to make the statements he makes. The title of his book, *Zone Journals*, plays on this tension. The "zone" is unidentified, although image after image, poem after poem, locates it in this world. The "journal" is the form that these poems take, a form implicit as well in his two preceding collections, *The Other Side of the River* and *The Southern Cross*; it is the way in which this poet, with his distrust of narrative, still follows an ancient chronological pattern. Although time is fixed and place shifts, only in this zone can time be marked, in a journal, as passing.

Zone Journals includes ten poems divided unequally into three parts. The sixth poem, "Journal of the Year of the Ox," which comprises all of part two, is forty-eight pages long and its movement, like the movement of the entire book, is toward a greater understanding and the challenges this will require. The challenge to Wright is that his is a metaphysics of absence—what is most important to him is what is *not* in the picture. His journal entries appear preceded by a dash and many of his lines move in a staggered two-step across the page: a portion of a line, then a descent to the rest of the line, allowing a fullness to enter without running up against the margin (as C. K. Williams' lines do, spilling over time and again, a mark of his style as much as Wright's is of his):

> —Exclusion's the secret: what's missing is what appears
>   Most visible to the eye:
>   the more luminous anything is,
>   The more it subtracts what's around it,
>   Peeling away the burned skin of the world
>   making the unseen seen . . .

Thus in the first poem, "Yard Journal," he shows us his method for the entire book: to make the metaphysical statement, "what's missing is what appears / Most visible to the eye," and by elaboration of imagery, coming before and after, offer the world as proof:

> That rhododendron and dogwood tree, that spruce,
>   An architecture of absence,
>   a landscape whose words
>   Are imprints, dissolving images after the eyelids close:
>   I take them away to keep them there—
>   that hedgehorn, for instance, that stalk . . .

Wright acknowledges the idealism of most metaphysics that have come before, and against this he opposes his own vision, with a wistfulness at times that is part of the paradoxical nature of so many of his statements. "A Journal of English Days," set in London, fall 1983, shows Wright confronting the spiritual tradition from which his poetry derives:

> How sweet to think that Nature is solvency,
>   that something empirically true
> Lies just under the dead leaves
> That will make us anchorites in the dark
> Chambers of some celestial perpetuity—
>   nice to think of that,
> Given the bleak alternative,
> Though it hasn't proved so before,
>   and won't now
> No matter what things we scrape aside—
>   God is an abstract noun.

The final metaphor, "God is an abstract noun," expresses Charles Wright's metaphysical view, par excellence. It also expresses the pragmatic view, wherein "God" works only as a word—a powerful word, but existing apart from any concrete manifestation. Dante would not have agreed, we know that; nor would have Milton. It is important to understand that a metaphysics is possible without a transcendent or religious view of reality. The paradox of Charles Wright is that his is a religious poetry without a religion, but not without a metaphysics.

As Wright's metaphysics is based on absence, so it must acknowledge the limitation of presence or immanence. As he says at the end of "March Journal," "—Form is finite, an undestroyable hush over all things." The conclusion of the following poem, "A Journal of True Confessions," arrives at much the same point by describing "The last warm wind of summer" shining "in the dogwood trees" and "flamingoing berries and cupped leaves" as a "Veneer, like a hard wax, of nothing on everything." Even words are included in his austere metaphysics, for they are part of the things of the world in which that metaphysics does its work. In "Night Journal" (like the seventeenth-century metaphysical poets, Wright is fond of oxymoron, contradiction, paradox) he says, "—Words, like all things, are caught in their finitude."

In the central poem, "Journal of the Year of the Ox," Wright covers the year of his fiftieth birthday, 1985, from January to December. The use of the Asian name for this year is one indication of Wright's empathy with Eastern theories and systems. Another might be the combination of Christian and Zen views of the fundamental nature of reality that makes him speak of the immanent in terms of the transcendent. The poem begins with a trope Wright has used before, the persona of the pilgrim, a poor one this time, setting forth to remember. Wright begins, "Each year I remember less." Taking stock of memory has been Wright's theme in a number of his recent major poems—for example in "The Southern Cross," from the book of that name, and in "Lost Bodies" and "Lost Souls" from *The Other Side of the River*. It is a form of confession, of seeking absolution, but it may also be a mode of purgation, of setting oneself free or clearing the decks for action. Although "Journal of the Year of the Ox" includes memories of Wright's years in Italy (touchstone of his greatest creative and spiritual force), running through it is an account of and meditation on Long Island of the Holston River in eastern Tennessee where he grew up, "sacred refuge ground / Of the Cherokee Nation."

"Journal of the Year of the Ox" is about sacred places—those like the Island that are barely memorialized while being desecrated constantly, and others, like the homes of Emily Dickinson, Edgar Allan Poe, and Petrarch, that are kept in relatively decent repair for visitors. He also recalls the beginning of his metaphysics and how he argued, when living in Italy, with "Hobart and Schneeman," two characters who have appeared in his poems before, "that what's outside / The picture is more important than what's in." He admits, "They didn't agree . . ."; it sometimes appears that Wright has devoted his poetry to showing that this assertion is true. To this poem he brings "The Cherokee's mystic Nation," "ended for all time," "*with streams of blood every way*"—a powerful and successful expression of the metaphysics of absence. In this case, a people remembered on an obscure plaque as "Wolf Clan, Blue Clan, Deer Clan, Paint Clan, Wild Potato Clan, Long Hair Clan, Bird Clan" is the paradigm of that important absence. These, the remaining clans of the Cherokee nation in eastern Tennessee, are now owners of Long Island of the Holston. Their presence, a set of words on "a rectangular bloc of marble," point to what's gone.

Ending on Christmas day, the poem closes almost on a note of dissatisfaction, asking, "What is a life of contemplation worth in this world?" But in the penultimate journal entry, speaking of using his son's telescope to watch Halley's comet, Wright anticipates his question with this answer:

An ordered and measured affection is virtuous
In its clean cause
                    however it comes close in this life.
Nothing else moves toward us out of the stars,
                    nothing else shines.

This is a discovery for Wright. His strength as a poet is to make his refrains sound like fresh recognitions; he is always "making it new." But this does seem to be a new thing, a faith that an abstraction—"affection"—can be mirrored in the cosmos, that it can be "empirically true." *Zone Journals* ends with four poems—"Light Journal," "Journal of One Significant Landscape," "Chinese Journal," and a second called "Night Journal"—about light, a light that demonstrates a fundamental way of being—"to shine but not to dazzle."

Wright's transformation of the natural world into imagery is a search for transcendence in the face of mere immanence. Thus his final, austere but courageous, tautological resolution: the earth is itself; it refers only to itself—although whatever is absent from it (Wright must take this on faith, like all who create a metaphysics) defines it, is better somehow, and worth our search. Wright's diminished metaphysics is as close as we can come to the integrated cosmology of Dante, resting on Aquinas's *Summa*, or to Milton, buttressed by the Reformation. "Night Journal," the book's last poem, says it again, in answer to the question "What's-Out-There":

I'd say what it says: nothing, with all its verities
Gone to the ground and hiding . . .

Wright's metaphysics is truly inclusive, as paradoxical as that may sound. Inclusion—the proliferation of detail and image—is what he and C. K. Williams and Philip Levine have in common. Wright's use of the pilgrim as persona is to suggest his forays into the world, in order to discover ways to say freshly what he knows:

I long for clear water, the silence
Of risk and deep splendor,
                    the quietness inside the solitude.
I want its drop on my lip, its cold undertaking.

The words "risk" and "undertaking" work against "quietness" and "solitude," indicating Wright's activity, which is to fill the picture in to make what's left out of it manifest.

III

> ... we know nothing, pure
> and simple, beyond our own complexities.

—William Carlos Williams

In many ways, C. K. Williams' *Flesh and Blood* would seem to be the complete antithesis of Charles Wright's *Zone Journals*: where Wright prefers an unpeopled landscape, except in memory, Williams fills his poems with people and keeps them in their urban milieu; where Wright staggers his lines to keep them from overflowing, Williams lets every line run over, doubling back from the margin; where Wright prefers association to narrative (except in the occasional anecdote), Williams seeks drama constantly (and though he does not go on at length as in *Tar* and *With Ignorance*, some of his uses of narrative in *Flesh and Blood* are as masterful as any in those); finally, where Wright seeks the opportunity to make a metaphysical statement, to stand in the flow of his poem and utter his truth, Williams offers definition poems ("Nostalgia," "Repression," "Conscience," to name a few) in which the abstract nature of these conditions is provisional. And yet, within each of these contrasts is the seed of similarity. Both poets are putting as much into the line as possible. Both poets use narrative in the same way (though Wright does less frequently) as a form of meaning without explanation. Both poets seek a unified vision of existence—but here again there is a difference. Where Wright constructs his metaphysics of absence, Williams insists on presence or "elemental presences." Where Wright makes his metaphysical statements often and in still moments in a kind of serenity, Williams erupts from the turmoil of dramatic conflicts with sudden insights into the nature of experience.

Flesh and Blood includes 130 poems, 129 of which are eight lines long, the 130th, "Le Petit Salvié," contains eighteen of these eight-line strophes. Read straight through, the book is as exhausting as it is exhilarating, and includes extraordinary successes along with a few outright failures. What else would one expect from so much? Formally, the poems divide into definitions and portraits or scenes. The best are those poems in which these forms come together and make use of Williams's dramatic gift, his greatest talent. I am going to quote two poems that seem far more interested in human folly and its impact on us than on anything metaphysical. But a fundamental view of reality is at work here, too, and the urge to make this view manifest unites this book as it moves toward its end, the elegy for Paul Zweig. These poems appear together on one page, as a number of other loosely related poems do:

THE MISTRESS

After the drink, after dinner, after the half-hour idiot kid's cartoon special on the TV,
after undressing his daughter, mauling at the miniature buttons on the back of her dress,
the games on the bed—"Look at my pee-pee," she says, pulling her thighs wide, "isn't it pretty?"—
after the bath, pajamas, the song and the kiss and the telling his wife it's her turn now,
out now, at last, out of the house to make the call (out to take a stroll, this evening's lie),
he finds the only public phone booth in the neighborhood's been savaged, receiver torn away,
wires thrust back up the coin slot to its innards, and he stands thee, what else? what now?
and notices he's panting, he's panting like an animal, he's breathing like a bloody beast.

THE LOVER

When she stopped by, just passing, on her way back from picking up the kids at school,
taking them to dance, just happened by the business her husband owned an her lover worked in,
their glances, hers and the lover's, that is, not the husband's, seemed so decorous, so distant,
barely, just barely touching their fiery wings, their clanging she thought so well muffled,
that later, in the filthy women's bathroom, in the stall, she was horrified to hear two typists
coming from the office laughing, about them, all of them, their boss, her husband, "the blind pig,"
one said, and laughed, "and her, the horny bitch," the other said, and they both laughed again,
"and *him*, did you see *him*, that sanctimonious, lying bastard—I thought he was

going to *blush*."

The poems end deliciously, as fables do or like Kafka's compact and perfect "Meditations." They tell us that the universe is curved, sending back scorn for man's illicit desire; Williams is a satirist and like all satirists highly moral. His use of detail is especially telling: the "filthy women's bathroom" in "The Lover" and the callous changing of the guard in "The Mistress"—"telling his wife it's her turn now"—can seem even greater indictments than the larger transgressions.

In a poem called "The Ladder," Williams corroborates Charles Wright's assertion that "God is an abstract noun." Saying "God was an accident of language, a quirk of the unconscious mind," Williams goes on to complain: "but unhappily never of my mind." However, unlike Wright, he derives no metaphysics from this essential absence; against it, in fact, he poses a psychodrama of abstractions, as in "Thinking Thought": "Oh, the furious illusive unities of want, the frail, false fusions and discursive chains of hope." From a vignette he can suggest whole systems of being; overhearing a girl rage at her younger sister in a quick stop market, he concludes in "Kin": "What next? Nothing next . . . / All that limits and defines us: our ancient natures, love and death and terror and original sin." In "Rush Hour," he tells of witnessing an epileptic fit on the Paris Métro and realizing that the victim's girl friend is as shocked and surprised by the seizure as is the crowd. But after a stranger, an Arab businessman speaking not very good French, keeps the boy from swallowing his tongue, Williams observes the girl's act of tenderness and grace as, terrified, she "Lays her cheek lightly" on the boy's brow.

Williams can trust the big abstractions, those words we need to make our metaphysical statements, only when he sees them in action. Much more often what he sees is the destruction of life and hope, to which he responds with anger and the force of his imagination. In section seven of "Le Petit Salvié" he tries to express conceptually the principles that are implicit in other poems:

> Redemption is in life, "beyond" unnecessary; it is radically demeaning to any
>   possible divinity
> to demand that life be solved by yet another life: we're compressed into this
>   single span of opportunity
> for which our gratitude should categorically be presumed; this is what eternity
>   for us consists of,
> praise projected from the soul, as love first floods outward to the other then
>   back into the self . . .

> Yes, yes, I try to bring you to this, too . . . yes and yes, but this without
>   conviction, too.

The abstractions ring hollow and he knows it. What Williams really imagines is his dead friend "rising in the rosy clouds . . . / wandering through my comforting child's heaven, doing what you're supposed to do up there forever." It frustrates him that he cannot square these absurd and childish images of a transcendent reality with his understanding of the body as a vehicle of biology and genetic history—"species consciousness"—and the construction of politics as a way of dealing with and understanding the world.

But this is a fruitful tension; like Wright's dialectic between presence and absence, it forces Williams to consider what exactly is in the picture and what it signifies. The culmination of this pattern is the elegy for Zweig, though in a series of poems preceding it, Williams offers a clear view of what he has been toiling with through the book. In "Vehicle: Absence" he imagines a child going into her dead father's closet and finding herself "enveloped in the heavy emptied odor"; she "breathes it in, that single, mingled gust of hair and sweat and father-flesh and father." This, he realizes, is what we all seek "in love, in absence"; "as though to breathe was itself the end of all," we wish "to hold the fading traces of an actual flesh." In part seventeen of "Le Petit Salvié," Williams finds the phrase for how we remember those absent in "the sweet, normal, stolid matrix of the merely human"; it is "the way an empty house embodies elemental presences, and the way, attentive, we can sense them":

> Breath held, heart held, body stilled, we attend, and they are there, covenant,
>   elemental presence,
> and the voice, the lightest footfall, the eternal wind, leaf and earth, the
>   constant voice.

These words seem very close to the way Wright might have expressed it, though again, the occasion for expression is different from most of Wright's. Williams' insistence on presence is not so much the opposite side of the coin from Wright's metaphysics of absence as its mirror image.

IV

Truth? A pebble of quartz? For once, then, something.

—Robert Frost

Philip Levine has mastered the undeniable statement, the formulation of a fundamental truth about reality. He makes what Ortega y Gasset claims is the only valid response to reality:

> Since there is no way to escape the essential condition of living, and as living is reality, the best and most discreet course is to emphasize it, to underline it with irony . . .

"Picture Postcard from the Other World," the penultimate poem in *A Walk with Tom Jefferson*, ends by describing what might be pictured on the postcard:

> It could be
> another planet just after its birth
> except that at the center the colors
> are earth colors. It could be the cloud
> that formed above the rivers of our blood,
> the one that brought rain to a dry time
> or took wine from a hungry one. It could
> be my way of telling you that I too
> burned and froze by turns and the face I
> came to was more dirt than flame, it
> could be the face I put on everything,
> or it could be my way of saying
> nothing and saying it perfectly.

This passage plays with a conditional list of possibilities, all of which are themes and motifs of Levine's poetry, in this book and in his previous books. Like Williams and Wright, Levine has a clear idea of the transcendent, but a much surer sense of its earthly limitations—that the other planet has at its center "earth colors," that the "face I / came to was more dirt than flame." The play of elemental opposition that has always been important to his poetry is here; the cloud "that formed above the rivers of our blood" brings rain and takes wine; it is possible both to burn and freeze. But the most telling lines are the last two, which underline the entire list with an Ortega-like irony:

> or it could be my way of saying
> nothing and saying it perfectly.

That conditional tense is one aspect of Levine's style that has been imitated over the years, and the imitations suggest why it is appealing; it blankets reality with possibilities. For this to work one must share Levine's conviction, tempered by his inimitable humor, that to say nothing is, in fact, to say something, to deny is the only way to affirm. But only Philip Levine can make this work; it is his poetic signature.

Which leads me to the question of authority. To say "only Levine" might imply "not Wright and not Williams." But that is not my point. I am speaking of a coming into being, a full maturity that is something a poet may or may not seek. To my mind, in their books Wright and Williams are engaged in the process of becoming, reforming their already identifiable styles into new shapes and thus shifting the lines of their own personalities, their authorial presence in the poem. Levine has imagined himself completely in his book; we recognize him and believe him because his imagination of himself equals his imagination of the world; he underlines both with irony when he suggests the possibility of saying nothing and saying it perfectly, because he has also presented a unified and undeniable picture of reality.

Actually, *A Walk with Tom Jefferson* does not make as much use of negation as do Levine's previous books, especially *Sweet Will*. The new volume contains nineteen poems, two of them quite long, "28" and the title poem; the latter makes up all of the fourth and last part of the book. What the book shares with Wright's and Williams' books is an abundance of detail, a proliferation of imagery, a faith in the world. Levine ranges more widely than he ever has before: from autobiographical reminiscences of his early manhood to speculations on the nature of the soul; from fictional suites about imagined characters to a theory of prosody; from a hilarious diatribe against dogs to the extended meditation of the title poem. Based like many of his poems on Wordsworthian concern for the life of another, set in a defeated urban milieu where it is still possible to have a relationship with the earth, "A Walk with Tom Jefferson" probes deeply and comes up with that "something" that Frost thought he glimpsed at the bottom of the well.

Perhaps because of his roots in Detroit and the "succession of stupid jobs" mentioned in his bookjacket biography, but certainly because he has written about factory work, work in which things are often made for purposes obscure to the maker, Levine sees the irreducible thing at the heart of experience or of the human soul. Sometimes it is the soul itself. In "Buying and Selling," the first poem in the book, it is "untouched drive shafts, universal joints / perfect bearings so steeped in Cosmoline":

> They could endure a century and still retain
> their purity of functional design, they
> could outlast everything until like us
> their usefulness became legend and they
> were transformed into sculpture.

In "The Whole Soul" Levine asks of that essential human quality: "Is it long as a noodle / or fat as an egg? Is it / lumpy like a potato or / ringed like an oak or an / onion and like the onion / the same as you go toward the core?" Once he hits on the idea of "the core" he is able to state, in the form of a question, what is fundamentally true about the body's utility as a vehicle for the soul:

> . . . for is it not
> the human core and the rest
> meant either to keep it
> warm or cold depending
> on the season or just who
> you're talking to, the rest
> a means of getting it from
> one place to another, for it
> must go on two legs down
> the stairs and out the front
> door, it must greet the sun . . .

Like C. K. Williams, Levine is most exacerbated by mortality and its fact leads him to some of his strongest statements. In "28" he speaks of "Nothing . . . that waiting blaze / of final cold, a whiteness like no other." In "Bitterness," hearing of the death of "a love of my young manhood," he faces it with the original Levine negation:

> I did not
> go out into the streets to
> walk among the cold, sullen
> poor of Harlem, I did not
> turn toward the filthy window
> to question a distant pale sky.
> I did not do anything.

This is the classical simplicity, the elegance I spoke of in regard to Levine's negations. He has made the undeniable statement about the fundamental nature of reality by refusing to present himself in any sort of romantic or heroic posture toward death. However, the setting of the poem is actually a February morning in his garden in California, where he thinks back to hearing the news in New York; he is digging through clay to plant a fruit tree that "will give flower and fruit longer / than I care to think about." Even this is a response to mortality, this time as a denial or a recognition of denial. But it summons from the reader a long thought, and I would say a distinctly metaphysical thought, in practical American terms, terms of bitterness at the fact of death, the fact that ends all the aspirations that make up the American soul.

There are other defeats for these aspirations besides death, and Levine is one of our most eloquent poets of failure. "A Walk with Tom Jefferson" shares Frost's and Wordsworth's attention to the milieu of other persons, in this case a defeated neighborhood in Detroit, "A little world, with only / three seasons, or so we said— / one to get tired, one to get / old, one to die," a block of seven rundown houses near the baseball stadium, where he walks with Tom Jefferson, namesake of the "father of democracy," an enlightened man like the other, though descended from men the other might have owned. They talk of many things, but mostly what drew men and women like Tom up from the rural south, and how in the "chalky soil" of their gardens they keep that past alive. The poem covers so much it is risky to say what it is "about," but it seems to be a long meditation on the "Amazing earth" and on the fact that in the brutal factories of Detroit, the product was made of earth's raw materials:

> Whatever it was we
> made, we made of earth. Amazing earth,
> amazed perhaps
> by all it's given us . . .

The poem digs through memories elicited by the conversations with Tom Jefferson down to the poet's own past in Detroit, working for "Chevy Gear & Axle," and to the question "What were we making out / of this poor earth good / for so much giving and taking?" If Levine has a faith, it is that the earth gives with exemplary selflessness, because it cannot help but give. Our failure is that what we make of it often does not equal that gift. Looking deeply into the past, Levine discovers, at least possibly, that "we actually made / gears and axles / for the millions of Chevies / long dead or still to die":

> it said that, "Chevrolet
>   Gear & Axle"
> right on the checks they paid
>   us with, so I can
> half-believe that's what we
>   were making way back then.

There is pathos in this, but truth too, the workable truth of a practical vision that cuts through metaphysics and responds with that mixture of humor and sadness that we call irony. Truth is what we make it—gears and axles, ball bearings, fruit trees, the human soul. Through his negations, Levine, in Ortega y Gasset's terms, stops the eye at these immediate evidences and affirms existence.

V

Let us reveal a secret. Life is a secret.

—José Ortega y Gasset

While writing this I have had two quotations from contemporary American poets on my mind, both statements of great power, great feeling, but ones I would like to amend slightly. The first is from Jon Anderson's "The Secret of Poetry" from his book *In Sepia*: "The secret of poetry is cruelty." The other is the last two lines of Frank Bidart's "Confessional" from his book *The Sacrifice*: "*Man needs a metaphysics; / he cannot have one.*" Both these statements are attempts to express an undeniable truth about reality, one that unifies many things. Bidart's comes out of a poem in which, speaking to a confessor or an analyst, the protagonist anguishes over his unresolved relationship with his dead mother, envying that between St. Augustine and *his* mother and learning that "Forgiveness doesn't exist." It appears that the metaphysics man cannot have is the one Kant said he could not have: a sense of transcendence that unites all that exists apart from the empirical world. The poets I have discussed offer a sense of immanence; even Wright, who claims what is most important is what is not present, points constantly to presences. What Wright, Williams, and Levine give us is the fact of finitude, that sense of the nothingness beyond that gives our lives dignity and meaning. It is a paradox that Augustine would not have accepted, but it is rooted in the pragmatic imagination as a workable metaphysics. Which leads me to alter Anderson's line—bracing, honest, exact, and meant in its context to cut through stock responses to death and love. I believe the secret of poetry is that it has a secret but that it must be revealed in undeniable terms.

13

Narrative Beauty

A family loses a child and the mother's grief is expressed through the story of Niobe, whose great pride in *her* children incurred the wrath of Leto, who in turn sent Apollo and Diana (her own children) to murder Niobe's offspring. The myth and the contemporary event interweave, growing to include the suffering of mothers the world over and to make Niobe the archetype of maternal grief.

The poet and musician Sidney Lanier recounts his childhood, his experiences in the Civil War, his failing health after the war, his life with his wife and children, and finally his death. More important to him even than his tuberculosis is the memory of his time as a Confederate infantryman and as a prisoner of war and his long journey home when the war ended. Only death itself can end the persistence of this memory.

Following his first year of college in Montreal in the 1950's, a bookish young Canadian experiments with the Roman Catholic faith for a summer, becoming a communicant, working in a Dorothy Day-style home for transients, living for a time as a guest in a priory, and finally discovering that love and sexual fulfillment answer some questions that piety cannot.

These are summaries, respectively, of Kate Daniels' *The Niobe Poems*[30], Andrew Hudgins' *After the Lost War*[31], and Daryl Hine's *In and Out*[32]. The plot of a book-length poem may not always be the most interesting element of its narrative; indeed, if the poem is a sequence, like the first two, then narrative may not even be the most important issue. In their book *The Modern Poetic Sequence* (1984), M. L. Rosenthal and Sally Gall make this very argument, suggesting that neither extended narrative nor logical reasoning can carry a modern long poem. "The modern sequence," they write,

> is a grouping of mainly lyric poems and passages, rarely uniform in pattern, which tend to interact as an organic whole. It usually includes narrative and dramatic elements, and ratiocinative ones as well, but its structure is finally lyrical.

[30] *The Niobe Poems, by Kate Daniels,* University of Pittsburgh Press, 1989
[31] *After the Lost War,* by Andrew Hudgins, Houghton Mifflin, Co., 1988
[32] *In and Out,* Daryl Hines, Knopf, 1988

Books like this one usually appear long after the impulse they describe has run its course; certainly the modern sequence is what Rosenthal and Gall say it is, but the post-modern sequence is often quite different. For example, Robert Pinsky's *Explanation of America* employs extensive argumentation and thus revives the verse-essay, while George Keithley's *The Donner Party*, by successfully telling a broad story, revitalizes the epic.

Similarly, beauty may be found in other aspects of the poem than just the lyrical. Dylan Thomas for one considered all poetry to be essentially narrative (in fact, it is not unusual for a reader to seek a narrative spine in a short or medium-length lyric poem), and the element of narrative can be beautiful too, just as lyricism can. But while the notion of beauty lies at the heart of any definition of the lyric (in *The Princeton Encyclopedia of Poetry and Poetics*, James William Johnson says: "The irreducible denominator of all lyric poetry must . . . be those elements which it shares with the musical forms that produced it"), this is not the case with definitions of narrative. Unfortunately, when narrative poetry is defined, the "irreducible denominator" is that is must tell a story, and normally we do not think of stories as inherently beautiful. And yet they can be. I would define narrative beauty in a poem as arising both from the shape of the story and from the apprehension of it—the reader's awareness that a story is being told, sometimes implicitly, working like a clue in and out of the fabric of the verse. When the story is overt, nothing is more obvious in its execution than a narrative poem; one hardly thinks, "What am I reading?" The specific narrativity, the telling as it adheres to the verse (whether formal or free), its very unfolding, can have beauty. That is, it can give pleasure; it can please or exalt the mind or senses. That may sound like a pretentious definition of beauty, but it is straight from Webster's.

Narrativity *per se* in poetry and prose has little or nothing to do with linearity, that Euclidean byword used to beat narrative like a stick. To answer the accusation, we might consider the question we do ask of anything we read: "What is it about?" As Erich Auerbach shows in *Mimesis*, narrative is a representation of reality, and in Western literature reality is variously represented as foregrounded or backgrounded, simultaneous or sequential, hierarchical or egalitarian; narrative is the literary mode that serves reality best. The lyric pivots on its pin. Lyric poets might protest—as Heather McHugh has done— that their poems are not "about," but narrative poets invite us to consider what their poems *are* about, i.e. "What do they encompass?" A line may go in many directions, even a circle. And if narrative must be linear, it need not lead to annihilation or any other reductive conclusion. If there is a story to be told in a poem, narrative is the river it rides on. As lyric beauty is in the singing, narrative beauty is in the telling.

Kate Daniels' *The Niobe Poems* comes with a good bit of apparatus to assist the reader. Although she begins with an epigraph from Adrienne Rich's "Diving into the Wreck" ("the thing I came for: / the wreck and not the story of the wreck / the thing itself and not the myth"), Daniels' project is both to adapt and to transform the Niobe myth and not, as in Rich's case, to get to the bottom of the story, to some ur-place before myths began. Following this epigraph, Daniels gives us a series of complicated introductory sections, the first of which is her own brief, prose retelling of the story of Niobe. This is followed in turn by a) Ovid's version from *The Metamorphosis*, b) Homer's from *The Iliad*, c) an allusion by Dante in The Purgatorio, and d) statements on the myth by Edith Hamilton and Robert Graves. While Hamilton and Graves show no sympathy for Niobe—whose arrogance in the face of divine wrath was foolish—the pictures Ovid, Homer, and Dante paint of her grief resonate with an ancient power. After several more introductory passages (including feminist statements from *The Woman's Encyclopedia of Myths and Secrets* and *Essays on a Science of Mythology* and a Dramatis Personae covering the characters that appear in the poem), Daniels gets to the most interesting of her introductions—a poem called "Mother and Child" by David Ignatow, which Daniels entitles "A Niobe Poem by David Ignatow." Not only does it point the reader ahead into the sequence of poems, as it describes how a mother holds her accidentally-drowned baby, but it also represents a style of writing Daniels herself uses. It is the style of early and middle Williams, long ago mastered by Ignatow, in which the free verse line never extends more than about four stresses and tends to be no longer than two, stanzas may or may not follow a consistent pattern, and the writing suffices unselfconsciously—quickly, provisionally working for an imagistic or dramatic effect. This style is well suited for narrative at a short stretch and for this kind of poetic sequence.

Daniels' sequence itself is divided into four sections and these are given titles that guide the reader and establish the narrative order of the book. Section one is called "The Gods / The Myth / The Accident"; section two, "Before the Accident / A Family Romance"; section three, "After the Accident / The Funeral"; section four, "The End of the Story / A New

Narration / A New Niobe." We note that time is not handled in a straight, linear fashion—Daniels moves fluidly between myth and personal event, from section to section or within a section, and then—in the last section—moves out into the world, where she sees both the myth and the personal tragedy repeated at large. It must also be noted that what I am calling "the personal tragedy"—which appears to be the death of a child who drowned in a river near his house—is never explicitly told. The reader must figure out this story and find a way among allusions to other parallel events (especially in section four) that tend to make it ambiguous. The beauty of this narrative arises from the reader's growing and unsettling awareness of it and its place in the larger world. What I offer here is the version I have been able to infer.

Rage is the tone of this book, sometimes muted by irony, sometimes exploding in obscene assault—rage and a numbing grief that must be endured and overcome. Here, as in the Niobe myth, the gods are the villains. In the first poem, "The Little King," they regard their victim, a loved and pampered little boy: "that's the one / we want, the one / we get to have / because we're strong enough / to take him." In "The Gods Are Optional," they sit in the trees above the fatal river and allow the death to occur, lingering over "a last coffee, / coffee with a shot of rum." But the stricken mother does not accuse the gods—those forces beyond our control that we can't help but think of as gods—she accuses the official embodiment of consolation, after the funeral, "in (his) preacher's frock": "You were the one / she looked in the face / and told to fuck off."

Having established in section two the relationship between the death of the Niobids and the death of the "Little King," Daniels begins a series of lyrics about birth, early childhood and motherhood, and family life. An especially disturbing feature is the parallel that she draws between the father figure here and Narcissus (not Amphion, Niobe's husband, who took his own life in despair). I call these lyrics because, in terms of the larger narrative, they mark time. "Tenderness" describes the birth of a boy to a woman who feared men; "Jeunes Mères," titled after some sculptures by Rodin, depicts two young mothers trapped by motherhood; "Perfect" and "Child Abuse" pinpoint violence, potential in the child and the mother respectively; "Thief" describes a woman trying to nurse a child who is not hers and his angry response; "Ménage à Trois" looks at the source of the Oedipal complex. In "Family Life" the gods of the Niobe story and the father's point of view intersect. Shielding himself from the demands of mother and son, the father contemplates the gods: "*how much we need them, / how much we hate them / for their silence and their distance.*" From this moment on in this section, the father's self-absorption becomes an implicit factor in the singularity and loneliness of the mother's grief. How could she share her feelings with one who, after sex, always bathes his genitals in the sink and whose beauty is "cruel" ("Bathing") and who during sex looks into her face as Narcissus looked into his pool: "how can he hear her / at all, so taken is he / with his own delight?" ("Precious").

A male reader might wish to close the book here, but he would be making a mistake. These are the characters who will experience catastrophe. They are husband and wife, mother and father, Niobe and Amphion. In section three, grief has exhausted them. In "'I Was Afraid of Him'" the woman says about the dead child: "'He wouldn't say anything / back to us though we wailed / over him a day and a night, / wouldn't tell us why or how / the accident happened, / . . . We wept, we wept, we wept.'" The female speaker says also, in "After the Funeral": "'After awhile, / we went upstairs. / I took a pill. / He took a pill. / We took off our shoes / and lay down beside each other / on the double bed. / First, we lay face to face. / Then we turned away . . .'" The loss of the child has shattered their attitudes toward experience and one another. Their former condition will return, if at all, utterly transformed; but now it seems trivial.

Transformation is what Daniels hopes to achieve in her fourth and final section, "The End of the Story / A New Narration / A New Niobe." The contrast between before and after is at the heart of her narrative. Section four includes the various embodiments of Niobe that Daniels sees in history and throughout the world. She includes an Ethiopian woman watching children die of starvation ("Ethiopia") and Rosa Parks ("Bus Ride"); Niobe may be a nun immolating herself ("The Fire Mystery") or a woman looking at a picture of someone else's suffering ("Ars Poetica"); Niobe's children include all those represented by the famous picture of the Vietnamese girl, burned by napalm, running naked down the road toward the camera ("War Photograph"). The Phoenix, from the Dramatis Personae, displays the full effect of this powerful sequence, when her poem, "The New Niobe," ends: "She is hard / as the hardest diamond now. / She can say, *It happened. / He died. / I live.*" Daniels' elemental style and her colloquial language allow her these simple statements. The thing itself that she seeks is to change Niobe from a myth of suffering to "a woman at last." The book ends on a note of surprising grace as the poet watches from a distance the figure she has been studying. As the woman leaves, Daniels notices that "From her hands and skirts / as she walks away, gifts are falling, / glistening and trembling in the wet, dark grass." Niobe's children were replaced by tears, flowing eternally. The poet thanks her for them because they have become poems, these poems. The fullness of the moment, emotionally and poetically, comes from the tale the sequence has completed. It is a telling moment, a told moment, and the best response is to read the poem, the book, again.

Where Kate Daniels achieves narrative beauty by creating a relationship between a particular event and its universal significance, Andrew Hudgins achieves it—in *After the Lost War*—by superimposing his own contemporary life upon that of a long-dead other. Hudgins' preface suggesting how he will use the nineteenth-century Southern poet Sidney Lanier as a persona is worth quoting in full:

> This sequence of poems is based on the life of the Georgia-born poet and musician Sidney Lanier. Though the poems are all spoken by a character I call Sidney Lanier, the voice of these poems will be unfamiliar to anyone who knows the writings of this historical figure. Despite his having been dead for over a hundred years now, I'd like to thank Lanier for allowing me to use the facts of his life—more or less—to see how I might have lived it if it had been mine. And, in too many ways, I suppose it has.

How *has* Hudgins lived Lanier's life? Certainly Lanier's experience of the Civil War and of terminal disease must be imagined by the poet; his sense of the sudden claustrophobic violence of warfare, where a man can lose his hand to shrapnel while drinking coffee at his campfire, rivals any writing I know about combat. And in the final poems of the book, Hudgins details Lanier's growing debility with startling exactitude, at one point describing his prostrate helplessness when his wife mounts him on his death bed. But when Hudgins as Lanier describes his forays into the natural world, especially the sea marshes Lanier himself wrote about, stylistic differences weaken the illusion of exact identity. Hudgins' writing here bears little similarity to the way Lanier wrote himself—in "The Wide Sea Marshes of Glynn," for example—and thus seems to cause a shift from the life of the "historical figure" to a more modern presence. Lanier was a pious Victorian whose sense of language was derivative, as was the case for most American poets of his time. Hudgins writes, as in these lines from "A Child on the Marsh," from the opposite end of over a hundred years of American poetry:

I'd worked my way from fresh water to salt,
and I was lost. Sawgrass waved, swayed,
and swung above my head. Pushed down,
it sprang back. Slashed at, it slashed back.
All I could see was sawgrass. Where was
the sea, where land? With every step,
the mud sucked at my feet with gasps
and sobs that came so close to speech
I sang in harmony with them.
My footprints filled with brine as I
walked on, still fascinated with
the sweat bees, hornets, burrow bees;
and, God forgive me, I was not afraid
of anything. Lost in sawgrass,
I knew for sure just *up* and *down*.
Almost enough. Since then, they are
the only things I've had much faith in.

The book is divided into four sections, each of which begins with a brief prose foreword. That for Part I, "The Macon Volunteers," summarizes Lanier's experiences with his brother Clifford in the Civil War, his time as a prisoner of war, and his marriage after the war. The foreword to Part II, "After the Lost War," notes briefly his post-war activities, including his attempt to recover from tuberculosis in Texas, living for nine months apart from his family. In Part III, "Flauto Primo," the foreword tells of Lanier's days with the Peabody Orchestra in Baltimore and his return to Macon, Georgia to live with his family. Part IV, "Under Canvas," begins with a paragraph explaining that by 1881, Lanier's health had "failed utterly" and so he moved his family to North Carolina and set up a camp in the mountains in a last attempt to prolong his life. These prose additions, unlike those in Daniels' book, do not state themes and attitudes; they do not indicate that the memories of the war will be intercut with poems about the present. Nor do they suggest the extraordinary character Hudgins will create with his Sidney Lanier, a man who hears the earth at his feet as a "lovely sucking sound," knowing that he owes it a death— the death he escaped during the war—and that he will settle that account soon. What the prose forewords do is reinforce the historical fact of Sidney Lanier and the span of his life as the narrative template for this book.

Hudgins' method in the first part of *After the Lost War* is to jump from a

182 ~ Mark Jarman

childhood memory, like that in "A Child on the Marsh," to a grisly account of the war, like that in "Burial Detail," in which the young Lanier describes filling a mass grave:

> Between each layer of tattered, broken flesh
> we spread, like frosting, a layer of lime,
> and then we spread it extra thick on top
> as though we were building a giant torte.

In subsequent sections, Lanier's adult life alternates with memories of the war. In post-war Montgomery, watching how buzzards, everpresent during the war years, are trapped on the river banks by "drunken sailors," doused with kerosene, set on fire, and launched into the evening sky, Lanier observes (in what is the title poem):

> ... perhaps you know,
> with the younger generation of the South
> after the lost war, pretty much
> the whole of life has been not dying.
> And that is why, I think, for me
> it is a comfort just to see
> the death bird fly so prettily.

In those delicate yet stilted rhymes ("me" / "see" / "prettily") Hudgins pays direct homage to Lanier's poetry; it is one of the moments in the book when the poet and his creation seem to be wearing one another's masks.

Hudgins creates at least two personality traits in his Lanier that seem as if they must be original. One is a sense of humor, often vulgar but always ready to deflate pretentiousness, especially in religious matters. Accosted—in the poem "The House of the Lord Forever"—by a "jack-leg preacher," who he recognizes by his outfit must have been "one of those bastards" who rode with Civil War outlaws like Mosby or Quantrill, Lanier answers the scoundrel's pious question, *"Don't you trust in the world beyond / these shadows?"*:

> "Well, Preacher," I said,
> "you've heard about the blind skunk that
> fell in love with a fart?"

The other trait is harder to describe, but seems to be a sense of wonder at the physical world's capacity for beauty at the moment of destruction. Hudgins' Lanier describes how, sitting out one summer dusk with his wife, "we saw":

> a martin hit a dragonfly so hard
> it snapped the body from between the wings.
> They flickered slowly to the ground,
> caught light, and flashed like airborne mica.
> Mary walked over, found the wings,
> and shut them in her locket. I'm not sure why.
> But I had also wanted them.

And in the poem about setting the vultures on fire, he notes, "they fall, like burnt-out stars / . . . One night preoccupied with work, / I think I made a wish on one." As this character develops—through the alternating use of memory and present circumstance, through his observations and his actions—it becomes less and less important that he is the historical figure Sidney Lanier and more and more evident that he is a fictional creation of fascinating complexity, illustrating the kind of beauty narrative is capable of.

In "The Hereafter," the book's last poem, the dying Lanier says:

> For so long I have thought of us as nails
> God drives into the oak floor of this world,
> it's hard to comprehend the hammer turned
> to claw me out.

By becoming Sidney Lanier and by turning Sidney Lanier into himself, Hudgins enacts the intimate relationship between life and death. He does this more forcefully in the poems set in the marsh, which appear in nearly every section of the book and in which we see an increasingly complex character. At first he believes the marsh is "God's mind." Older, he sees it as a place where violence might still be enacted, as when he kills a marsh turtle to make soup, exposing its guts "like the workings of a watch." Near death, he says: "I still probe the salt marsh / as priests three thousand years ago / searched entrails for a sign." Finally he observes how a hawk falls on its quarry and hopes: "God keeps his eye on everyone / and snatches those who flee his grace." *After the Lost War* is a powerful book enacting a fusion of identities and voices; it is a narrative sequence of unique beauty.

Daryl Hine's *In and Out* offers the most traditional approach to narrative of any of these book-length poems, being not a sequence but a series of episodes that culminates in a climactic event wherein we see a changed protagonist. The action is presented, as Hine explains, in "an unbroken, continuous ribbon / of verse from beginning to end" made up of anapestic trimeter lines. *In and Out* is almost a novel in verse—a realistic novel in verse—and thus must both keep the meter and tell the story without growing hackneyed in either; it must present believably deep situations and characters in memorable lines of poetry. Hine meets these demands successfully and, like Daniels and Hudgins, shows that narrative has a beauty that poetry can benefit from and enhance.

Subtitled "A Confessional Poem," *In and Out* tells the story of an auto-biographical protagonist named Daryl. Readers who know Hine's previous book, *Academic Festival Overtures*, have met Daryl before: intellectual, priggish, supercilious, and intensely vulnerable, he is also wry, articulate, given to puns, and remarkably adept at disarming unpleasant remarks. For example, when someone says, "Somebody told / me you were. Homosexual," Daryl refuses to be just one of the guys:

> "That
> is the clinical label, a hybrid
> construction like tele-" I lectured
> him, "-vision. I'm sure that your friends
> at the bar would say *queer*, and I guess
> they are right in my case if they mean
> individualistic, peculiar—
> who isn't?"

A boy of letters who will become a man of letters, Daryl searches in both these books for people like himself—unsuccessfully in *Academic Festival Overtures*, which covers his earliest teenage years, and successfully in *In and Out*, which recounts his first year of college in Montreal, the summer after, and the following fall.

In and Out is divided into four sections—"Presbyterian College," "Lazarus House," "Sweet Saviour Priory," and "Astra Castra." A "Proem" outlines the way much of the volume will be narrated. Hine translates the book's epigraph from Horace, "*Naturam furca expelles, tamen usque recurret*," as "Although / you may drive away nature by means / of a pitchfork, she never the less / will return all the way," then gives another version as epigraph for the first section: "A man may a while / Nature beguile / By doctrine & lore, / Yet at the end / Will Nature home wend / There she was before." Daryl feels no guilt about his homosexuality, but sexual desire has led him into some quandaries, including encounters with heterosexuals whose confusion frustrates him. In "Proem" he says that, as Horace has stated, his attempt to sublimate his feelings will fail; nature will out. Once he finds love, there is no longer any reason to suppress his sexuality.

The goal of *In and Out* is to consider the difference between sacred and profane love. Daryl goes to bed with an unintellectual classmate, after they attempt to trade stories one night on winter vacation together. His friend tells personal anecdotes; Daryl, whose experience is almost entirely from books, retells one of the tales from *The Arabian Nights*:

> I've forgotten the drift of my story
> except that it drifted. Too often
> in retrospect I am unable
> myself to distinguish the fable
> I read or made up from the fabulous
> nonsense that actually happened.

The nonsense that follows is that the boy Daryl sleeps with spurns him for an older woman, a graduate student at their university; she simultaneously tries to seduce Daryl. Ultimately, he feels he must withdraw from this welter of libido and consoles himself with baptism into the Roman Catholic church (his upbringing is Presbyterian) and a summer stint in a home for transients. At Lazarus House, he comes under the supervision of one Alan Waterman, a spartan, "unquestioning Catholic" who sets Daryl to sorting "clothing donated / by well-wishers." "My reward? / Room and board here below, and a similar / set-up hereafter above."

From there, it is by invitation to Sweet Saviour Priory, down in Vermont, where Daryl encounters the monk in charge, Dom Dagobert, in his plush little cell; Abbé Willibrord, an Abbé in name only; and the mysterious Abbé Clément, whose title is a residual honor from years in France Abbé Clément presents Daryl with the riddle posed by Titian's famous painting, *Sacred and Profane Love* (which graces the cover of the book): which of the two women—the clothed or the naked—lounging at the well that looks like a coffin, is sacred love and which profane? Daryl guesses what most people would—that the clothed woman is sacred love. The Abbé responds gleefully:

> "You have wrong! For the sacred is naked
> like truth, which not only has nothing
> to hide but possesses such beauty
> no person that sees may resist."

There follows a theological repartee about the Doukhobors, a sect in Daryl's native British Columbia, and their preference for nakedness. A lot of the pleasures of this book have to do with such exchanges, along with interwoven Latin phrases from the liturgy elegantly translated by Hine. The beauty of the telling is, in part, Hine's eloquence as a translator.

From Sweet Saviour Priory, it is back to school and Daryl's meeting with Hyacinth Star, son of a converted Jew. Daryl has experienced a period of abstinence and meditation; after he and Hyacinth attend a production of "The Messiah" ("this cosy Arminian masterpiece"), the two become lovers. Their exchange before bed is touching. Daryl observes: "'*Totus / in armis et nudus est amor*,' / I garbled a tag from the *Vigil / of Venus*, 'But Love, even naked, / is armed head to toe.'" Hyacinth complains: "'It's like going / to bed with a blooming anthology!'" But Daryl says: "In Hyacinth's arms / I was coming to grasp what was meant / by the mystical body, at last." In Hyacinth's arms, Daryl learns that truth is, indeed, naked.

In and Out adds a tale to the stock of the *bildungsroman*; I kept thinking of J. D. Salinger's precocious Glass children and Knowles's New England schoolboys. Hine's twist is to recount events in a frankly autobiographical way. Thus he brings the authority of the lyric to the narrative by stating that *In and Out* is a confessional poem and by giving the protagonist his own name. An elegiac dimension is added as well when one realizes that the book is dedicated in part to the memory of Anthony Stern, whose name is both a loose anagram of Hyacinth (Anthony rearranged) and a translation of Stern (the German for star). Anthony Stern, apparently, is the star Daryl falls for in "Astra Castra," as well as the star who falls for Daryl.

If the narrative beauty of these three books has a common denominator, it has to reside in the voice used by the poets—the voice of the narrator, the witness, the one who knows and must tell. It is in Daniels' voice as she retells the Niobe myth, Hudgins' as he remakes a character whose history might have been his own, and Hine's—punning, elaborating, confessing—telling the story of his life. We listen to these poets not only because they have a story to tell, but because they have to tell a story.

14

The Grammar of Glamour:
The Poetry of Jorie Graham

"The serpent beguiled me, and I did eat." Eve's famous excuse suggests that she has not only been tricked but charmed. To use an old Scottish word, a *glamour* has been thrown over her eyes, in her case, the allurement of knowledge. For Jorie Graham, the beguiling serpent is time; its succession and linearity give birth to history. Her poetry seeks to break the spell that holds us in time, requiring that history have a beginning, middle, and end, and that art, especially literature and particularly poetry, be mimetic and made up of similitude, metaphor, and narrative or "storyline," as she calls it. Her response to these conventions is to cast a counter spell, to throw one glamour over another, or so it has been in her third book, *The End of Beauty* Ecco[33], and her fourth, *Region of Unlikeness*[34].

There is another sort of glamour that might be associated with her poetry and it is the one we usually think of as allurement and fascinating personal attractiveness, which are both exciting and romantic, but may be illusory. This glamour is rooted in the material she uses from her own life, setting poems in Italy, for example, where she grew up in proximity to works of art that had their own sheen of definite beauty. As she implies in her poem "I Was Taught Three" from her first book, *Hybrids of Plants and of Ghosts*[35], she grew up knowing three names, in English, French, and Italian, for the chestnut tree. She had, as Nabokov once remarked about his own life, a perfectly normal trilingual childhood. The matter of such a life is innately attractive. Glamourous, if you will. In a grosser sense, the very packaging of her books, including their glossy cover art and the striking photographs of the author, proffer glamour.

But I am interested in the other kind of glamour, which is associated with enchantment and is also a form of the word *grammar*. Jorie Graham's recent poetry, with its special vocabulary or lexicon, with its spellbinding repetition,

---

[33] *The End of Beauty*, by Jorie Graham, Ecco Press, 1987
[34] *Region of Unlikeness*, by Jorie Graham, Ecco Press, 1991
[35] *Hybrids of Plants and of Ghosts*, by JorieGraham, Princeton, 1980

with its passionate energy, not to say urgency, reads like a near frenzied search for the magic words, the open-sesame, that will allow entrance to a world before time, a world which may be paradise. Its glamour has a grammar, which is to say it has a structure. Perhaps her most impressive achievement in a decade of writing is to create a new style. No mean feat.

She certainly did not spring fully formed from her own mind equipped with her now identifiable way of writing. Her change of manner has included a change of heart. Her present concerns are similar to those in her first book, but her attitude towards them has altered one hundred and eighty degrees. "The Way Things Work" and "A Feather for Voltaire," the poems that respectively begin and end *Hybrids of Plants and of Ghosts*, tell us much, now, in retrospect. The poet who wrote that " the way things work / is by solution" and that she believed "forever in the hooks," who averred,

> The way things work
> is that eventually
> something catches ...

now regards that catching to be the sort of closure that ends possibility and locks us into history. She has become apocalyptic with this knowledge; for her the world ends not with a bang or a whimper but with a *click*. Still, in "A Feather for Voltaire" she acknowledges that reality inheres in language: "The bird is an alphabet." Graham's poetry has usually been about language and often about her own poetic composition. Her recent epiphany has been to discover that language itself, "the key to the kingdom" in "A Feather for Voltaire," is also a prison. The double-bind may be to make poetry out of what, in her *New Republic* essay on Graham's work, Bonnie Costello calls "the failures of poetry." Yet I do not think Costello has quite grasped Graham's project. It is even more ambitious than that.

Graham wants to make poetry out of the moment before poetry is made. To do this requires that she acknowledge the failures of poetry. At the same time, what she manages to affix to the page identifies her aim, even if it does not accomplish it. *Erosion*, Graham's second, book[36], contains many fine things that have been accomplished because doubt, the catalyst for her change, has not yet taken hold and made her feel bound by an evil spell. In "I Watched a Snake," the image that symbolizes linear succession in her recent poetry here represents an admirable quality. She associates the snake's hunting with work,

[36] *Erosion*, by Jorie GrahamPrinceton, 1983

and work, like the making of art, is related to desire and passion. Graham has always shown a gift for moving facilely among large abstractions, defining them in almost believable ways or in ways we might wish to believe. Having taken her moral lesson from the snake, she writes, "Passion is work . . ."

> It makes a pattern of us,
>   it fastens us
> to sturdier stuff
>   no doubt.

But *Erosion* concludes with "The Sense of an Ending," an artful look ahead to her future methods and a skeptical examination of that "sturdier stuff." Graham imagines human souls "in a frenzy / to be born" pressing into her "human frame." She imagines they feel it would be better to enter "this skin, this line / all the way round and sealed into the jagged island // form, the delicate / ending, better, even for an instant, even if never brought / further than term . . ." And though another poem in *Erosion* is called "Wanting a Child" and one of the most moving poems of the book describes Luca Signorelli dissecting the body of his dead son, Graham comes in "The Sense of an Ending" to suspect the urge, "the procreant urge of the world" as Whitman called it, because it initiates the trap, the spell, the glamour she abjures: history with its beginning, middle, and end.

The End of Beauty, her third book and her most original along with being one of the most important books of the 1980's, seems to be by another poet altogether. Her execution is as close to success as we might expect for one who wishes to capture an instant that is almost ontologically impossible to grasp: the moment before form is born and sealed into its fate with a click.

As it is represented in these poems, beauty is not an instrument of utility or an aim, because the end or ends to which beauty might be employed are not given. The title must be read as it first announces itself: this book will show the destruction of beauty and, by analogy, hint at the end of the world. The reason for this reading, and the one ambiguity we can entertain, is that in Graham's lexicon *end* and *beauty* are synonymous. Both occur in time, and time is what she would be free of. The title phrase occurs in the poem called "The Lovers."

> Here it is, *here*, the end of beauty, the present.
> What the vista fed into. What it wants to grow out of, creeping, succulent. . . .
> No says the voice pinpointing the heart of these narrows.

Here is the heart of her dialectic, her spell against the spell of time, glamour versus glamour. The poem tries to hold a moment of decision, when the lovers commit themselves to one another and time continues. Time, "the vista," is said to be "creeping, succulent," and you can hear the serpentine suggestiveness of both those words. In other poems the verb *hiss* is given as the voice of form, beauty, time, etc.

A number of poems in *The End of Beauty* depict fatal moments in myth: the eating of the apple, Orpheus losing Eurydice, Demeter losing Persephone, Apollo losing Daphne. Some of them, like "Self-Portrait as Apollo and Daphne," draw attention to the controlling hand of the poet. At the instant before the god Apollo can capture her and before she will be transformed into a laurel tree, Daphne is described by Graham in a kind of suspension.

> She stopped she turned,
> she would not be the end towards which he was ceaselessly tending,
> she would not give shape to his hurry by being its destination,
> it was wrong this progress . . .

Here Graham shows the moral authority of her vision. The end of beauty or when beauty is the end is "wrong" because it is a product of "progress."

The beauty brought to an end in these poems is the conventional one that exists in time. Mimetic, finished, it is the sort of beauty we can hold and contemplate, much as Erich Auerbach holds the works of literature he describes with such relish in *Mimesis*. Graham's desire to locate beauty not in the finished product but in the process of composition, which includes the nervous and at times anxious mind in the act of finding not only what will suffice, in Wallace Stevens's terms, but what it will create. The most exact expression of this desire in *The End of Beauty* is "Pollock and Canvas." Here she depicts the abstract expressionist painter leaning over his canvas as God leaned over the earth in the act of creation.

> When he leaned over
>   the undefeated soil
> to make it end somewhere,
>   to make it beautiful . . .
>
> what he chose
>   through the see-no-evil, through the eye for
> the eye,

> choosing to no longer let the brushtip touch,
> at any point,
>   the still ground,
> was to not be trans-
>   formed but to linger
> in the hollow, the about-to-be . . .

She chooses this, too—not to be transformed and thus finished, but to "linger in the hollow." The hook she loved for the way it caught in "The Way Things Work" and that she describes in the poem "Reading Plato" in *Erosion* as part of a lure made of deer hair evoking the graceful deer in its transformation, now she admires as if it were a drop of Pollock's flung paint not yet adhering to the canvas.

3

here is the hook before it has landed, before it's deep in the current

4

the hovering—keeping the hands off—the gap alive,

5

the body of talk between the start and beauty

Graham's use of numbers to separate single lines both suggests sequence and allows her to interrupt sequence with *non sequitur*. The numbers are part of the spell, the glamour thrown over our eyes. But they are beguiling, too, alluring, so that it hardly matters if they are illusory, part of a slippery veil of meaninglessness.

Graham's new aesthetics are exciting. And in so far as she expresses them in poem after poem in *The End of Beauty*, I wonder facetiously if the book could also be thought of as *The Beauty of Beauty*. Yet she is not satisfied to be merely the purveyor of a new way to look at language and poetry. There is a moral dimension to her realization about the trap of time and it has given her a vision of history, too. "What the End Is For" is her most apocalyptical poem and, in its structure, resembles many of the poems in *Region of Unlikeness*. The poet narrates a personal event, in this case being shown in Grand Forks, North Dakota, SAC bombers on alert on a runway. She juxtaposes this with a small domestic drama in which she and a "you" have trouble communicating in a darkening kitchen. She concludes the poem by alluding to the slaughter of Orpheus by the Maenads. We know that the SAC bombers, had they ever gone into action, would have brought our world to an end. The kitchen drama Graham relates also seems to represent an ending—the "you" will not hold the speaker. And though Orpheus's head went on singing after his dismemberment, Graham imagines it floating out into the dissolving noise of the ocean, a noise very like the sound of B-52's on the runway. This vision is based on a belief that time as it has been understood in Western culture has led us to the brink of thermonuclear holocaust. It is a powerful vision, or was a powerful vision. The end of the Cold War seems to suggest that if time, or Western time, has an end, it will not be what any of us, least of all Jorie Graham, expected. I am reminded of Sandra McPherson's poem "Eschatology," which states:

> I am glad when doom fails. Inept apocalypse
> is a specialty of the times . . .

The End of Beauty may be the last major book of poetry to show the influence of the Cold War.

Graham seems to know this, too, for none of the many stories told in *Region of Unlikeness* has quite the eschatological flavor of poems in *The End of Beauty*. This is not to say they do not have historical contexts. They do, indeed, and each has the sense that at this moment in the poet's life she has understood what history is all about. Most of them are like the last poem in *The End of Beauty*, "Imperialism," in that a title claiming an enormous amount, usually in historical or political or mythical terms, is attached to an anecdote, often an event from the speaker's life. Before going on to *Region of Unlikeness*, it might be helpful to look at what happens in "Imperialism."

The poem relates a story from the speaker's childhood. It is being told for some reason not only to the reader but to a "you" with whom the speaker appears to have reached an impasse similar to the one in "What the End Is For." The story is about a nine year old child in India with her mother who takes her to the banks of the Ganges. Mother exposes the child to various life-enriching scenes there, like the cremation pyres whose grilles "covered with ash and cartilage" are rinsed off in the river. The daughter is forced to immerse herself in the filthy water and experiences a vision of the void, the other bank, which appears "utterly blank," as "a line drawn simply to finish

// the river." This vision makes her ill and hysterical. The poem ends with an awful memory of Mother comforting her. And with it a variable of Graham's aesthetic equation is completed.

> And as for her body . . .
>   it became nothing to me after that or something less,
>   because I saw what it was, her body, you see—a line
>   brought round, all the way round, reader, a plot, a
>   shape, one of the finished things, one of the
>
> *beauties*, (hear it click shut?) a thing
> completely narrowed down to love—all arms, all arms
>   extended in the
>   pulsing sticky heat, fan on, overhead on, all
> arms no face at all dear god, all arms—

I fail to see what this has to do with imperialism, unless we really stretch the situation to some understanding of post-colonial India being analogous to the relationship between the mother and the child. But I do see what this has to do with Graham's poetry and her historical vision. This image of Mother as an oppressive presence, even as she comforts, is equated with form, beauty, and the clicking shut of possibility. The vision Graham presents to us is deeply rooted, like all visions, in a personal obsession. This personal obsession, murky, dynamic, and finally elusive, is the catalyst for poem after poem in *Region of Unlikeness*. But the stories she tells are overwhelmed by a style or grammar not really suited for them. The spell is broken. The glamour falls from the eyes.

The most successful thing in *Region of Unlikeness* is the Foreword. It is a masterful compilation of related passages from Augustine, Heidegger, Isaiah, John of Patmos, and Melville, recapitulating the project Graham completed in *The End of Beauty*. Separation from God is the theme that links them, especially in this timebound world with its inadequate mimetic forms. Augustine certainly felt this separation. Heidegger was aware of the ontological barrier to connection with the transcendent. Isaiah, in the passage Graham quotes, offers God's typical Old Testament demurral to being embodied in language or the flesh. In the lengthy passage Graham quotes from *Revelation*, John of Patmos describes his vision of Israel giving birth to Christ; this may be Graham's Yeatsian acknowledgment that modern history begins with Christ's birth. But the final quote from *Moby Dick* offers the most telling, most accurate analogue for Graham's ambition: "'Swim away from me, do ye?' murmured Ahab." Indeed, Graham's ambitions are great.

But her project, as I said, was finished in *The End of Beauty*. *Region of Unlikeness*, if not a false step, is certainly an over-extension, especially since the form she has done so much to demonize—storyline or narrative—is central to these poems. However, if a new idea has been introduced in this book, and I am not sure it has been, it is that in this world, this region of unlikeness, where metaphor is unworkable even provisionally, the only way to represent human experience is through story. I think there is a good argument for this idea, but I do not think Graham is making it. Still, she employs the very poetic conventions she condemns—narrative, metaphor, mimesis. They separate her poetry from the dreary linguistic bits of the Language Poets with whom she has been compared. There is a further thing, too, not to be underestimated, that separates her from poets like John Ashbery and Michael Palmer with whom she has also been grouped. And that is her passion. Their poetry is marked by world-weary knowingness, a cool that is terminally hip. Graham may be cynical at times, with her representation of convention in variables—the x, the y, the —particularly when she realizes she is once again in the grip of storyline, that snake. But the strength of her feeling cannot be doubted and at times it is actually possible to feel it, too, despite the mannerisms which convey it.

When she embodies her idea in the mythic moments of *The End of Beauty* or even in a scene fraught with Cold War anxiety, she not only makes a point, but her grammar works toward its proper end; the anxious repetition, the search for a way out or in or a way of holding this instant in place before time starts again and brings about the end, her glamour, her very act of spell-casting, are tragic. But when in the first poem of *Region of Unlikeness* she tells us where she was when she heard the news that Kennedy had been shot, the same portentousness does not apply. In fact, it is sentimental to believe that if Kennedy had lived, the last 25 years of history would have been different. And it is very hard not to be sentimental when recreating the moment one first heard the news of his assassination. Everyone of Graham's generation or older knows where he or she was when the news broke and just how it felt. The speaker of "Fission" was watching a matinee showing of "Lolita." How the title, the movie, and the horrible news go together, except in their surreal inexplicability, is as puzzling as anything in this book, where many similar juxtapositions occur. But was Kennedy's assassination on the order of atomic fission? Was the lust of Humbert Humbert, depicted gigantically on the screen, part of it? A motif reintroduced from *The End of Beauty* is the veil, "the layers of the / real," here shown as the movie screen, the interruption of its light by the houselights, then daylight, and the man down front who is frantically announcing the event to the crowd. Graham manages to end the poem on the passionate wish that the news not be true, that the inevitable can be forestalled:

> what is, what also is, what might be that is,
> what could have been that is, what
>   might have been that is, what I say that is,
> what the words say that is,
>   what you imagine the words say that is—Don't move, don't
>
> wreck the shroud, don't move—

"Fission" sprawls over half a dozen pages; a number of the 24 poems in the book are as long or longer. The Shroud of Turin itself is introduced in a later poem, one of more modest scope and hearkening back to *Erosion*. I think the problem with "Fission" is that for an experience so many of us share, Graham has claimed too much.

"Fission" and the other poems like it are monumentally ambitious, but they are rather like hearing a Wagnerian soprano singing a Mozart aria about the end of the day. "Manifest Destiny" is another example of a poem whose title is disproportionate to its subject matter. The poem includes a moving portrait of a friend, apparently a drug addict, who has died; the feelings are elegiac. But the central event is a day in Rome when the speaker and her friend pause outside of Rebbibia, which a note tells us "is the name of the women's jail in Rome." The two watch and listen to the women calling and gesturing from their barred windows. The poem ends with an exhortation of humanity.

> Oh why are you here on this earth, you—*you*—swarming, swirling,
>   carrying valises, standing on line,
> ready to change your name if need be—?

If questions are remarks, as Wallace Stevens said they were, then this one suggests that humanity's existence is outweighed by the friend's death. As intense as that feeling is, it does not convey the intenser tragedy that the friend's death is insignificant.

"From the New World" comes closer to justifying its claims, although once again, a personal matter is juxtaposed with a larger historical one. The trial

196 ~ Mark Jarman

of John Demanjuk, the so-called Ivan the Terrible of Treblinka, is recounted along with a story of two elderly grandparents being put into separate nursing homes. Presumably, "the New World" has meant a kind of incarceration for both Demanjuk and the grandparents. But there is a third element in the poem and that is the anecdote of a child in a German death camp who, instead of remaining in a gas chamber, somehow got out and was found looking for her mother. This sort of moment, this suspension of the inevitable, now bears Graham's signature. She is at her best, responding to it in her reflexive mode, at once identifying her motivation and casting her spell.

> God knows I too want the poem to continue,
> want the silky swerve into shapeliness
> and then the click shut
> and then the issue of sincerity, the glossy diamond-backed
> skin—

Nothing she can do can change the facts or save the particular child she has in mind. It is a curious consequence of Graham's aesthetic vision that she should blame the tragedy she describes on a poem's "shapeliness" rather than on Nazi Germany.

That metonymic reference to the snake of storyline ("the glossy diamond-backed / skin") comes again later in "Who Watches from the Dark Porch," one of the book's most interesting poems and most moving. The poet produces an event: she is sitting in a rocking chair on her porch in the evening and hears a cry, perhaps the cry of a child, coming from her neighbor's house. "Now I will make a sound for you to hear," she writes and goes on to describe the sound, which is the beginning of a speculative story, as "a shriek? no? a laugh?— // lung-stuff, flinty, diamond-backed, floating through / the layer of flesh, the layer of house ..." She suggests that there are all sorts of ways to mask such a sound, a sound that may require a response. One way is to turn on the TV and channel surf. The passage in which she describes the surreal montage of changing channels is dazzling and illuminating, as well. Is it possible that TV itself is the mimetic source of these poems? Whereas the numbering and repetition of the poems in *The End of Beauty* were ways to bind a spell and stop time, in *Region of Unlikeness*, the excess verbiage and the onslaught of stimuli form a kind of word-noise, not unlike the imagery and sound that emanate from the TV, the reality of which is, as she says, "dots, dots / roiling up under the golden voice—"

Now: connect the dots, connect the dots,
connect the dots, connect the dots,
      connect the dots, connect the dots,
connect the dots, connect the dots—

Feeling okay?

Graham is never funny, but here one is inclined to give a small, exhausted, but real laugh. We *have* learned to make reality into an infinitely variable fiction through the medium of television. But is language itself the culprit? Are the conventions of poetry to blame? Well, questions *are* remarks, and so are mine. I don't think so.

There are two passages in *Region of Unlikeness* that are more moving as poetry than any others in the book. Both occur in the book's best poem, "The Phase After History." They seem to occur almost in spite of Graham's usual grammar, but as part of poetry's capacity for metaphor and for making everyday speech into poetry. The poem, which is 11 pages long and occupies its own section in the book, concerns in part the attempt of a young man, a student, to cut off his own face. His parents must be notified and their child committed to a mental institution. The poet reports a remark of the student's mother:

We called him the little twinkler
      says his mother at the commitment hearing,

because he was the happiest.

This is as unadorned as anything we might find in the recent poetry of Louis Simpson. Later, Graham describes the young man:

His wrists tied down to the sides of the bed.
And the face on that shouldn't come off.
      The face on that mustn't come off.
Scars all round it along the hairline under the chin.
Later he had to take the whole body off
to get the face.

And that is a moment of insight, conveyed metaphorically ("take the whole body off // to get the face"), as penetrating as anything in poetry or literature.

Except for the repetition that charts her progress toward enlightenment, it is also an exceptional passage in this poet's recent poetry.

"The Phase After History" also includes some portentous and inappropriate language that overinflates many of the other poems. Trying to locate a bird trapped in her house, the poet asks, "Which America is it in? / Which America are we in here?" Those hardly seem to be the questions to ask. And yet woven into the poem are also allusions to *Macbeth*. In reference to Stuart, the young man who tries to cut off his face, she writes, "Who would have imagined a face / could be so full of blood." And to encourage herself to go on with her anecdote, she says wittily, "Oh screw thy story to the / sticking place." But the clincher comes when she tries to put the anecdote of the trapped bird, the story of the suicide, and the tragedy of *Macbeth* together: "Lady M. is the intermediary phase. / God help us." Somehow Lady Macbeth's attempt to wash the blood from her hands is another image, for Graham, of the deadliness of form, story, shape, what you will, all that destroys innocence or, as she says, "the free." But that's just a guess.

The last poem in the book, "Soul Says," is subtitled "(Afterword)." A note says it is spoken by Prospero. Aside from the presumption of speaking as Prospero, Graham does appear to say something about all of this.

(This is a form of matter of matter she sang)

(Where the hurry is stopped) (and held) (but not extinguished) (no)

(So listen, listen, this will soothe you) (if that is what you want)

Though Graham's poetry, at its best, is an imitation of stopped or held "hurry," the speed of the mind trying to find its place, it does not soothe me. But soothing is not what I want. I want a poetry in which the subject matter and the means of conveying it are equal to each other. When that occurs in Jorie Graham's poetry, the grammar of glamour turns invisible with its exactitude. It does so in *The End of Beauty*, but not in *Region of Unlikeness*.

15

The Curse of Discursiveness

C. G. Jung discovered that as much of a patient's unconscious could be revealed by having him freely associate with letters from the Cyrillic alphabet as
by the more traditional psychoanalytic method of working from the patient's
dreams. My own experience reading John Ashbery's new book-length poem[37]
proves Jung correct. Time and again I found what Ashbery himself refers to
as the "appealing nonsense" of the poem a stimulus for the associations of my
own mind. Or better yet, I recalled the protagonist's dilemma in Ashbery's
"The Instruction Manual," from his first book, *Some Trees*. He admits that he
wishes he "did not have to write the instruction manual on the uses of a new
metal" and finds himself, instead, dreaming of Guadalajara. I knew exactly
how that dreamer felt each time I guided myself back into *Flow Chart*. The
poem is more flow than chart. Its discursiveness is more a ramble from topic
to topic—if topic is the right word—than a coherent argument from point to
point.

The only time I thought I knew where I was was during passages of self-ref-
erence, when the poet acknowledged my presence as a reader:

> And if I told you
> this was your life, not some short story for a contest, how would you react?
> Chances are you'd tell me to buzzoff and continue writing ...

Ashbery has always displayed a droll wit. Here it has given him a canny sense
of what must be going through an honest reader's mind as he make his way
through what the poet calls his "wrenched narrative" as it "drips on, decays."
I say honest reader, because Ashbery has many dishonest readers. They are his
admirers. They include anyone who claims that a poem like *Flow Chart* is not
boring, not devoid of any subject except its own composition, and not finally
unrereadable. By unrereadable, I mean that, having read it once, I hope never
to read it again. How can a poem do this to a reader, except by being bad?
I can't think of a single poem I have read and admired, of whatever length,
that I would not willingly read again. By the time I reached page 201 of *Flow
Chart*, fifteen pages from the end, and read "there is / always the possibility

[37] *Flow Chart*, by John Ashbery, Knopf, 1991

something may come of something, and that is our / fondest wish though it says here I'm not supposed to say so," I felt as if Ashbery and I had formed one of those bizarre intimacies kidnappers and hostages form. I had tried to cooperate and he knew it. Also on page 201, he writes:

> Excuse me while I fart. There, that's better. I actually feel relieved.

This is the only declaration in the poem not shaded into evasive circumlocution. Still, it reflects the poem's existence as a running commentary on the poet at his typewriter. The poem makes a kind of musical noise, something like the easy listening jazz of the Windham Hill productions. But why is it in chapters? Why sections? Why even numbered pages? They must be part of the joke. I think that, unlike his admirers, Emperor Ashbery knows he is naked.

Robert Creeley's new volume of selected poems[38] shows that he has written some of the finest lyrics in American poetry, most of which he published in the 1960's. He was at the peak of his powers in that decade. Since then he has written only two or three poems to equal his best. Still, in the Age of Ashbery, one wishes more attention were paid to a poet, like Creeley, who weighs not only every word but often every syllable.

> I approach with such
> a careful tremor, always
> I feel the finally foolish
>
> question of how it is,
> then, supposed to be felt,
> and by whom.

So begins one of Creeley's most moving poems, "Something," from his best book, *Words*. He remembers a time with a lover that anyone who has read the poem must have indelibly printed in memory, along with its ending: "What / love might learn from such a sight." Creeley is a love poet. Love is the subject of his most memorable poems, like "Something," "The Rain," and "The Moon." Yet in his early work there are others that also justify his rank as a major poet. They include "After Lorca," "I Know a Man," "The Flower," "A Wicker Basket," and the superb longer poem—longer for Creeley—"Anger," in which his minimalism is used to its greatest effect.

---

[38] *Selected Poems*, by Robert Creeley, University of California Press, 1991

During the 1970's there is a falling off in Creeley's work, mostly because of his indulgence in his own notebook doodling and also an Ashberyesque discursiveness. "Desultory Days" is typical, beginning:

> Desultory days,
> time's wandering
> impermanences—
>
> like, *what's for lunch*,
> Mabel?

In the 1980's Creeley recovers some of the excitement, the drama of an active syntax that animated his early work. It is present in these stanzas from "The Edge":

> I take the world and lose it,
> miss it, misplace it,
> put it back or try to, can't
>
> find it, fool it, even feel it.
> The snow from a high sky,
> grey, floats down to me softly.

Poems like "Self-Portrait," a bitter examination to put beside any of Philip Larkin's, and the heartrending "Mother's Voice," the best of his elegies for his mother, have the old dynamism. "Age," too, is a late masterpiece, ending on a sense of "imploding / *self.*" But Creeley's style does not bear up through many poems. At times banal, conventional, even clichéd statement is laid down over his unique lineation but not transformed. He is still best when he dramatizes or speaks to a lover, as in "The Rain":

> Love, if you love me,
> lie next to me.
> Be for me, like rain,
> the getting out
>
> of the tiredness, the fatuousness, the semi-
> lust of intentional indifference.
> Be wet
> with a decent happiness.

James Tate has also published a selected poems[39] and it is good to have it. He has edited himself well, but he, too, sometimes shows the consequences of emulating Ashbery. Luckily his other influences—from Roethke, Berryman, Justice, and Plath—are so strong and so healthy, he remains largely untainted. His is a poetry of connections, from first to last. Its means and the surreal menagerie of his imagination may be irksome, but in the end it conveys the emotions of a profoundly lonely individual who is trying to reach out, as he says in "Dear Reader," "to pry open your casket / with this burning snowflake."

Like Creeley, Tate is a lyric poet, but his are mainly songs of alienation. *The Lost Pilot*, his first book, is still a wonderful read and one can tell why it excited people when it appeared 25 years ago. Its zest and good humor are hard not to like, even as the poet reveals his baffling sense of loneliness. The story the book tells characterizes Tate's generation, as well. The absence of Tate's father, the lost pilot of the title, symbolizes the gulf between generations during that vivid decade. Poems like "For Mother on Father's Day" and the title poem move through short lines, in tercets, in a deft way reminiscent both of Sylvia Plath's charged-up, compressed imagery and Donald Justice's elegant exactitude. Tate's comic but accessible surrealism continues throughout *The Oblivion Ha Ha*. It contains the splendid "Shadowboxing," probably the key poem of his work, and the fine, but atypical, "Failed Tribute to the Stonemason of Tor House, Robinson Jeffers." "It's Not the Heat So Much as the Humidity" is representative of the Tate who loves to send up his own poetic posturing with a comic image that still resonates:

> When Autumn comes, O when Fall arrives
> in her chemise of zillion colors,
> I will sigh noisily, as if an old and
> disgusting leg had finally dropped off.

Hints to Pilgrims contains a curious foray into the territory Ashbery was exploring at the same time, in poems like his "Fragment." That Tate calls his asyntactical nightmare, "Amnesia People," shows he can match Ashbery's wit. *Absences* is the last book, published before Tate was 30, that contains more strong poems than weak ones. "Contagion" is Tate at his melancholy finest and "The Distant Orgasm" is still splendid—funny, vital, ironic, with a youthful appeal we find in Keats, Rimbaud, and Dylan Thomas. But in this book are also the long sequences, like "Absences" and "Cycle of Dust," whose

---

[39] *Selected Poems*, by James Tate, Wesleyan/University Press of New England, 1991

hermeticism characterizes so much of the later work. In the subsequent books, *Viper Jazz*, *Riven Doggeries*, *Constant Defender*, and *Reckoner*, selected from here, there are good poems, but not so many as in the earlier books. "Read the Great Poets" in *Viper Jazz* has some of the knowing self-satire of "The Distant Orgasm" but with an admixture of desperation. "Tell Them Was Here" in *Constant Defender* is also first rate, one of Tate's best ever. Stood up at an appointment, the speaker leaves a note to his "Unreliable ancestors!"

> Green was here, I scrawled
> on a scrap of paper, and stuck it
> inside the screen. Started to leave,
>
> turned, scratched out my name—
> then wrote it back again.

Tate observes the conventions of narrative, argument, even discursiveness, yet still aims to avoid all predictability. Most of the time we are treated to surreal parables and self-revelations in a style that, in the 1960's and early 1970's, spawned more imitators per little magazine page than any before in America, and that now exists solely in the master's hand.

I'll bet the poems in Ann Lauterbach's fourth book[40] sound pretty interesting when read aloud, as a sort of word-jazz, again of the Windham Hill variety. Like so many of Ashbery's ephebes, she cops his riffs without his sense of humor. *Clamor* is a book of noise punctuated by embarrassing howlers. In "Mountain Roads," the poet says, "It we say often, and it is always the same it." The poems in this book are constantly proposing an *it*—that thing poets must try to define—and never telling us what the poet has in mind, except to offer unforgettable, ingenuous hermetica, as in "Forgetting the Lake": "Everything I am thinking of rhymes with *spires*." All one can say in response is "Surely not *everything*." When Lauterbach does attempt a metaphor, it is also subject to the reader's skepticism. In "Day," she claims, "The sky I say is an adulating glass." Yeah? Well, I say it isn't. And in the title poem, she slings abstractions around in a void, stating, "Affection is merciless." One can try to imagine a context for that statement. This is doubtlessly her aim as a poet—to make the reader imagine a context. But this reader can only question in which contexts affection *would* be merciless. I like her best when she spouts something ridiculous as if it were a profound truth. In "Further Thematics" she avers, "The

---

[40] *Clamor*, by Ann Lauterbach, Viking, 1991

salad bar attests to basic freedoms." Julia Child or M.F.K. Fisher might say that, with a wink, but Ann Lauterbach is tediously solemn and sententious. In "Boy Sleeping," when she asks, "Should I tell him his face mirrors the lost?," I want to intervene and say, "Let him sleep!"

I read this book with a growing sense of irritation, relieved only by the hilarity of so much silly writing. The poet continually begs the question, veering away, because she has nothing to impart. Unlike the missing portions of Italian Renaissance frescoes, in which paint has come loose from its anchor of plaster, the lacunae in her poems represent only failures of imagination. Imagine bringing Piero della Francesca back to Arezzo and persuading him that his pictures, in their advanced state of deterioration, were still beautiful. Imagine wishing to emulate such sad losses, in poetry. But let the poet speak herself. In "Annotation," she says,

> To say sky in the face of sky
> Is a failure of duration;
> The sky escapes.

W. H. Auden in "In Praise of Limestone" says that the poet is "admired for his earnest habit of calling / the sun the sun." But apparently, for Ann Lauterbach, even to name a thing is to betray it with the mystification of language, all of which is metaphor. Thus, her own idiom is made up of inapposite images and variable, unfixed abstractions. The one poem in *Clamor* that achieves something like a sustained artistic effect is "Prom in Toledo Night." It is reminiscent of James Tate's "Amnesia People." But the only speck of humor in it is the epigraph from Michael Palmer: "La—la—la is the germ of sadness / said the speaker in sneakers." Without the wit to see that a poetry of non-representation is in itself absurd, Ann Lauterbach cannot be tolerated for long without a laugh, either at her invitation or her expense.

There is a handful of successful poems in Thylias Moss's fourth book[41]. One of them, "Poem for My Mothers and Other Makers of Asafetida," which contains the phrase that is the book's title, is first rate. These poems succeed for many of the same reasons that the others fail. Moss constructs an elaborate syntax, often discursive, yet seeking always to make distant connections and to illuminate them by the flame of her insight and imagination. When she succeeds, the results are breathtaking:

---

[41] *Rainbow Remnants in Rock Bottom Ghetto Sky*, by Thylias Moss, Persea, 1991

> Live to the fullest and just
> have more to lose to death but Grandma said, Mama says, now
> I say: *maybe possible to have so much*
> *death can't take it all*; asafetida still on the shelf, oil in the puddle
> still ghetto stained glass, still rainbow remnants in rock
> bottom ghetto sky like a promise of no more tears, asafetida
> bottle floating there, some kind of Moses, some kind of deliverer,
> there's always a way.

But often Moss does not find her way. Though every poem contains something brought to radiance, many poems begin nebulously and grope their way to an almost crystallized argument-in-an-image; or, after a clear start, the poem ends in murk. Sometimes the murk is opaque syntax; sometimes it is changing subject in midstream. "Birmingham Brown's Turn" has examples of both, plus some unfortunate cultural stereotyping:

> You can bet that Charlie can take you
> to the cleaners; isn't he Chinese?
> Don't they boil the clothes and the
> rice in the same woks? . . .
>
> I still dream of it, digging to China,
> going through the center of the earth's
> meaning to earn passage there.

Moss's large and expansive poems many times seem like exercises in association. She gives us everything she's thought of without pruning. I'm ambivalent about the necessity of all the verbiage in her poems, but recognize that she is trying to manipulate a narrative syntax that poets like Norman Dubie and Roger Weingarten have often worked with successfully. The difference between those poets and Moss is that she isn't narrative at all. Charles Simic, who chose her book for the National Poetry Series, calls her a "visionary storyteller," but she tells no stories. She pirouettes in place, flinging sparks and cinders. The book is quite a performance. Curiously one of the best poems is "Interpretation of a Poem by Frost." It deserves a place in future anthologies and ends movingly with an echo of Frost's most famous poem:

> She has promises to keep . . .
> And miles to go, more than the distance from Africa to Andover
> more than the distance from black to white . . .

I wish I liked all the poems more than I do, but while I admire their ambition, I find that Moss shows a kind of complacence in assuming that putting
one thing on one side of an equals sign and one on another is imagination.
Consider her image of a bible in "Congregations."

> His bible warms his hands, never
> leaves them, a dialysis, transfusion that keeps him alive . . .

A dialysis is not a transfusion. In "Time for Praise," extending a metaphor
of a car as a whale that has swallowed Jonah and his family, she is led to call
a Toyota, "a whale with a door." Finally, this is the first poet I have encoun-
tered who, in the poem "News," actually has used the word *hopefully* as it is
currently employed, which is to say incorrectly. Moss's errors appear to be the
result of hurried composition. Often they are part of her poetry's dazzling
improvisatory effects, but just as often they are not.

Lynda Hull's second book[42] is full of poems in which history, narrative
complexity, symbolism, and the lyricism of a passionate voice all work together. Her narrative technique is cinematic, often striving for simultaneity, and
fuguelike. "Shore Leave," one of her best poems, is like a filmed memory of
the poet's rakish father, set with New York City in the background, in an illusory present-tense piece-of-time. The character of the father in "Shore Leave"
is a model for other male characters, preserved in the poet's memory, who
descend into and rise from the underworld or the demimonde. Hull writes
like Persephone back from hell. Behind her are drug addiction and the seduc-
tive charm of life on the margins. Hers is not an imagination that yokes any
old things together, but one disciplined by intelligence into making magic
equations. Here, in "The Real Movie, with Stars," is an unforgettable moment
typical of much in this book:

> I took the kiss full on the mouth, sweet fruit, miraculous
> chemistry of salts and water that keeps the flesh, that swells
>
> and spills and feels so like weeping.

I would like to say something about every poem in this book, because the
whole collection is so compelling, but I will stick to a few standouts. "Gate-

---

[42] *Star Ledger*, by Lynda Hull, University of Iowa Press, 1991

way to Manhattan" seems one of the best contemporary poems about New York City. Examining her sympathy for a woman who has attempted suicide in a public toilet, the poets says to herself:

> She'd have nothing but contempt for you, guilty and standing here
> long past the last train, waiting for the police sweep,
> waiting for the clamp on the wrist, concrete sweating against your forehead.
> It's almost time for the sirens to begin, the shaking,
> a trembling from within.

Hull is impassioned about the doomed and about doomed men in particular. The most moving and forceful instance in her poems comes in her "Lost Fugue for Chet," an imagined narrative of the jazz trumpeter Chet Baker's last day in Amsterdam. Although the following passage might seem to glamorize the condition of being lost, I think it shows off a style that is just about unique in our poetry today:

> After surviving, what arrives? So what's the point
> when there are so many women, creamy callas with single
> furled petals turning in & in upon themselves
> like variations, nights when the horn's coming
>
> genius riffs, metal & spit, that rich consuming rush
> of good dope, a brief languor burnishing
> the groin, better than any sex. Fuck Death.

Lynda Hull knows something about life and death and in her poetry she tells us what they are like. She does not hide her knowledge or lack of it in ruptured syntax or aimless discursiveness. She seeks and finds the connections and makes them with the experience of one who has returned from the underworld with a fire inside. When she says, "Fuck Death," I say, "Amen."

16

Shifting Sands:

The Columbia History of American Poetry

In the mid-1600's, as the Massachusetts colonist Anne Bradstreet was writing the poems that would be published in London in 1650 as *The Tenth Muse Lately sprung up in America*, the oral tradition of Native American poetry was uniting use and beauty inextricably, though in ways unknown and even ignored, until Henry Wadsworth Longfellow, two hundred years later, tried to capture them in *Hiawatha*. And in the early 1700's, the nonconformist minister and colonist Edward Taylor wrote the last of his "Preparatory meditations" some twenty years before Lucy Terry, a slave, also in Massachusetts, wrote "Bars Flight" about an Indian massacre, the first formal poem known to be written by an African American. As this useful new reference book[43] makes clear, all sorts of Americans have been composing poetry, from the first American colonies, and before, until the present day. Some have enjoyed celebrity in their day, others have not and have waited to be retrieved at different times. Bradstreet was known as a poet during her lifetime, but Taylor had to wait to be rediscovered in the 1930's by that invaluable editor Thomas H. Johnson, who also labored long and fruitfully to give us the poetry of Emily Dickinson. As for poetry by African Americans, its history is lengthy, but made up of even more piecemeal retrievals, until the 19th century and the Harlem Renaissance, and even today major figures like Gwendolyn Brooks and Robert Hayden are subsumed by categories of African American literature where they do not exactly fit. Native American poetry, on the other hand, has only recently developed a tradition of written texts. Otherwise Native American poets have had to look, like most other American poets, to Anglo-American and European traditions, a vexing issue for its practitioners.

What is happening to canon formation elsewhere in American literature is at work in American poetry, and this book is a reflection. It's the sand dune effect. Prominent features of the landscape are being effaced by the sands of reaction, reformation, and forgetfulness, as others are revealed. William Pritchard writing about T. S. Eliot assumes "there does not exist a younger

---

[43] *The Columbia History of American Poetry*, edited by Jay Parini, Columbia University Press, 1993

nonacademic reading public for Eliot's writings." The poet who for Pritchard is "the major poet-critic of the century" lives on only where such designations matter—in the academy. Whereas Ann Charters in her contribution, "Beat Poetry and the San Francisco Renaissance," states confidently that Ginsberg and his associates are "some of the most widely read American poets of the last half-century." The difference between Pritchard's approach and Charters' is that as a good practical critic Pritchard tries to determine which of Eliot's poems still deserve even academic interest ("Prufrock" does, but "Gerontion" may not). He leaves it up to future generations to hear the personal note in Eliot that Randall Jarrell first detected. Charters, on the other hand, seems to think there's very little difference between a landmark work like Ginsberg's "Howl" and the puerile, drugged mumbling of Michael McClure. This lack of practical discernment characterizes a number of the book's entries, especially in those areas where the writer is trying to sweep away the dune and reveal forgotten glories. Writing about poets Amy Lowell, Sara Teasdale, Elinor Wylie, Edna St. Vincent Millay, and Louise Bogan, Jeanne Larsen reminds us just how modernism à la Pound and Eliot served to squelch these poets because of its aversion not only to their elegant, at times brittle, lyricism, but, she argues, because of an aversion to women's love poetry. But when she tries to make a case for Amy Lowell as a writer of memorable lesbian erotica, it just doesn't wash. Lowell was a terrible poet, and the other four were good, particularly Louise Bogan.

The sand dune effect all but buries Robinson Jeffers in Lynn Keller's "The Twentieth Century Long Poem." After mentioning his name in regard to the long narrative poem, she pays no more attention to him or to the form. Her interest is in the modern sequence, as defined by M. L. Rosenthal and Sally Gall in their book on the subject. Though Keller understands that recent interest in the long poem is a response to the exhaustion of the lyric, she ends her essay with an obtuse statement about how nondiscursive patterns "point to a language in which women and colonized people might achieve liberty and self-portraiture." In fact, traditional narrative serves much more ably than the disjunctive techniques she refers to. How would Rita Dove's *Thomas and Beulah* or Garrett Hongo's "Stepchild" hold together without the binding of narrative? This is a vital point she also misses in her reference to Gwendolyn Brooks' "The Anniad" or Marilyn Hacker's *Love, Death, and the Changing of the Seasons*. Her refusal to see the importance of narrative in the long poem may be why she won't touch Jeffers or mention a major achievement in the form like George Keithley's *The Donner Party*.

As valuable as a book like this is in unearthing what we might otherwise forget, when most of its contributors accept the ongoing sweep of modernism—and over twenty of its thirty-one entries deal with modern American poetry—many things will remain ignored or buried even deeper. The most interesting example of the conflict created by the sand dune effect and the conventional wisdom that modernism is an advance can be seen in the contrast between John McWilliams' "The Epic in the Nineteenth Century" and Dana Gioia's "Longfellow in the Aftermath of Modernism." McWilliams takes the view that James Fenimore Cooper was an epic poet, that *Moby Dick* was an epic poem (he even includes a politically correct nod to the racial balance aboard the Pequod), and that Whitman's "Song of Myself" displaces the traditional epic hero with the self. None of this is news, at least from the modern perspective. McWilliams dismisses *Hiawatha* along with some justly forgotten attempts at the epic, like Barlow's *The Columbiad* and a number of other "iads" (*The Coloniad, The Judead*). About *Hiawatha*, McWilliams writes:

> . . . when Longfellow raided Schoolcraft's research into Winnebago customs, fitted them into an overlay of Iroquois mythology, blithely transformed the whole into the tripping meter of the Finnish *Kalevala*, and then offered *Hiawatha* as a coherent series of North American Indian legends, the result could only be poetic make-up of the most transparent kind.

Such a history should probably record conventional wisdom like this somewhere in its voluminous pages. But how much more interesting it is to learn the following contradictory, fresh, and much more thoughtful assessment from Dana Gioia:

> The stylistic objections to *Hiawatha* . . . are largely based on misconceptions of Longfellow's intentions. The most frequent criticism is of the poem's meter . . . which has seemed too artificial and formulaic to some readers. The chief advantage of this measure, however, is that it isn't naturalistic. It was an overt distancing device, as was the incorporation of dozens of Ojibway words. These devices continuously remind the listener that *Hiawatha*'s mythic universe is not our world. . . . Although more often ridiculed than understood, the style of *Hiawatha* is in its own way as original as that of Pound's *Cantos*.

Gioia's entry asks us to think again about Longfellow, whose poetry is still part of the culture at large and whose occupation as a "poet professor" foreshadows the role most American poets play in the academy today. He is the antecedent of Eliot and Pound, a father they had to dispose of. Gioia makes the point at least three times that Pound was Longfellow's grandnephew. He also makes a case for the great variety of the poet's work, for his major narratives, *Hiawatha* and *Evangeline*, and for his many lyrics, which include a range of tone and subject no other American poet has equalled. And Longfellow has at least one modern heir who did not disown him—Robert Frost. Still, I am afraid that when I read Longfellow's poems beside Whitman's or Dickinson's or even an English contemporary like Browning, there is always that aura of the Genteel Tradition about his language that makes me reluctant to endorse him as Gioia has done.

The sand dune effect isn't all bad. It also allows an enterprising and discerning critic to clarify an issue that was ambiguous, with a good deal of sweeping and polishing in one area. Two entries that give us a definitive outline of what we might only have guessed at are J. T. Barbarese's "Ezra Pound's Imagist Aesthetics: 'Lustra' to "Mauberly'" and "Hart Crane's Difficult Passage." A third is W. S. di Piero's "Public Music."

Barbarese argues that Pound was an imagist and never ceased to be one and that the visual dimension of his poetry, especially in the *Cantos*, was as important as the linguistic one. He also provides an accurate and serviceable definition of Imagism. It is "essentially an elliptical approach to poetic design, substituting juxtapositional for connected meanings." That more or less defines Pound's method and, furthermore, it characterizes those descendants of Pound who usually have only that elliptical approach in common with him. Barbarese is probably the most idiosyncratic of the writers assembled, given to obscure gems like "chthonian," "ouranian," "fideism," and my favorite, "pococurantism," a synonym for indifference. In his essay on Hart Crane he asserts that Crane was never a "vernacularist." Neither is Professor Barbarese. But he has an excellent sense of what makes modern poetry, and this also comes out in an observation comparing Pound and Crane. He finds Crane difficult often because there is no source, no allusive echo, for his difficult passages, whereas the echo is an essential ingredient for Pound. In Pound's elliptical poetry "the inherent wisdom (and moral purpose) . . . is never to leave the scene of the crime." This seems brilliantly simple as a description of Pound's modernism.

W. S. di Piero's "Public Music" may be the most interesting and challenging entry, because he takes as his subject the problematic issue of American poetry and politics. He finds Pound a useful figure as well and contrasts him with George Oppen. In both poets he examines the difficulty of bringing public speech into poetry and in making poetry public. Pound fails, di Piero claims, because "he lost his way by becoming snared in the very confusion his poem presents as a matrix for renewals." George Oppen, whose political activism served to silence his own poetry for twenty years, found that "the political lay in writing truthfully one's perceptions, not arguing one's beliefs." I am not sure if this issue will ever be settled when there are so many political avenues, each with its own lingo, inviting the poet to feel engaged. But di Piero makes sense. "Poets," he writes, "cannot finesse idiosyncrasy so that it seems populist or communal." This may be the very reason that, as Auden wrote, "poetry makes nothing happen."

One reads a reference book like *The Columbia History of American Poetry* expecting information and good sense. If one is lucky, there will also be entries that offer fresh perspectives that cut through accepted opinion, like Dana Gioia's on Longfellow. And there will be only one or two that are so conventional in their restatement of the status quo, like McWilliams on the 19th century epic poem, that one wonders why the author bothered and the editor did not. Most of the entries reflect the current topography of American poetry with a clear sense of why the sands lie as they now do. Cynthia Griffin writes about Emily Dickinson and Donald Pease about Walt Whitman both with an up-to-date understanding of their status in modern American poetry, to wit, as foremother and forefather. Pease reminds us that the Saturday Club, of which Longfellow was a member, rejected Whitman's application for membership. There is that strain of gentility to hold against Longfellow, though why one of the roughs would want to join the Saturday Club is worth wondering about. Margaret Dickie in "Women Poets and the Emergence of Modernism" asserts that Gertrude Stein, H. D., and Marianne Moore were "a century ahead" of their time because they were "not limited by the misogyny, reactionary politics, and conservative impulse that held back their male counterparts." Insofar as gender and other political issues have come to play a central role in literary criticism, Dickie's assertion has merit. Jay Parini states right off the bat in "Robert Frost and the Poetry of Survival" that Frost "was among the great poets of this century—or any century." It's good to hear that said, even though it is Stevens, as Helen Vendler describes him in her entry, who reigns supreme among Frost's male counterparts at the end of the century. Arnold Rampersad contributes a helpful entry on the Harlem Renaissance, touching on the conflicting attitudes of Countee Cullen and Langston Hughes about the degree of blackness their poetry should display. William W. Cook in his entry on the Black Arts Movement emphasizes the strengths of Amiri Baraka, Don Lee, and Sonia Sanchez as performers of their poetry, and also casts a dubious look at the work of Nikki Giovanni, characterized by some as "a black Rod McKuen." It is a pity that the most gifted African American poets of the century, Gwendolyn Brooks and Robert Hayden, do not have an entry to themselves. Instead they are merely referred to in the two entries on African American poetry and not in great detail. The most troubling entry is on Native American poetry. Not because there is an entry, but because it is clear that there is very little to say about a written tradition of poetry by Native Americans. There is no entry on Hispanic American or Asian American poetry and these genres, though also relatively new, are much more advanced. The problem for all of these ethnic genres is the one tacitly admitted in the entry on Native American poetry. Lacking a tradition, will future Native American poets have only the current generation, poets like Louise Erdrich, Leslie Silko, and Joy Harjo, to look back to? The sand dune effect swallows the fact that these accomplished writers were nurtured by a more extensive tradition.

As the history approaches the present day, it's easy to find fault with the representations. The editor, Jay Parini, is himself apologetic in his introduction that he has set aside no single chapter for Adrienne Rich or, perhaps, Adrienne Rich and a contemporary, as he has for John Ashbery and James Merrill, Philip Levine and Charles Wright who are subjects of the last two entries. John Shoptaw uses Merrill and Ashbery to represent divisions in contemporary poetry between formalism and language-oriented poetry. Yet his actual analysis of the two poets is based on their long poems. He detects a strain of elitism in Merrill's *The Changing Light at Sandover*, but he manages to suggest that in *Three Poems*, for example, Ashbery is actually comprehensible. Edward Hirsch refers to the poetics of Philip Levine and Charles Wright as "visionary" and states that Levine "has created a memorializing poetics of human separation and connections" and Wright "has defined a radiant metaphysics of absence and aspiration, of the longed-for presence of the divine." He traces the development of both poets (something Shoptaw does not try to do), but in the meantime makes these living masters sound posthumous, a necessary side-effect, I suppose, of a book like this.

Finally, *History* comes with surprises pleasant and unpleasant. The unpleasant surprise might better be called bizarre. It is Gregory Orr's "The Postconfessional Lyric" in which he vacillates among the terms lyric and dramatic lyric and postconfessional lyric in order to describe a kind of contemporary autobiographical poem and invokes Whitman and Keats at various stages as precursors. Mainly what the writers of the p-c lyric have in common, according to Orr, is a traumatized childhood, like Orr's own (his book *Gathering the Bones Together* is based on his accidental killing of his brother when they were children), which they also write about, like Orr. He creates a genealogy of poets that includes Jarrell, Kunitz, Bishop, James Wright, Levine, Rich, Bidart, Orr himself, Glück, and Olds. While acknowledging that the Confessional Poets broke the ground he is describing, he concludes:

> Perhaps one of the most inadvertent gifts of the confessionals was to blur the distinction between art and life. Such a blurring can have destructive and self-destructive consequences but can also have salutary effects: what can't be resolved in life can be brought over into art, where it is again engaged, again encountered by a self struggling to extract sustaining meaning from experience.

I'm sorry, but this makes poetry sound like therapy. Orr adds a series of strategies that the p-c poets employ to set them apart from the confessional poets. One of these is "the proportionate ego." According to Orr the p-c poet does not indulge, for example, in Robert Lowell's excesses of appropriation. The kinder, gentler poet that Orr describes sounds as if he or she were made up by a committee of human potential experts.

The pleasant surprise is Claude J. Summers' "American Auden." Summers charts what he calls "the metamorphosis of the enfant terrible of English poetry into the religious Horation ruminator of American poetry" and considers each of Auden's major long poems with a good deal of understanding and gives us some of the life Auden was living as an American when he wrote them. It is a pleasure to see this great poet treated to his own entry, to consider the sand dune effect working to his favor, as it mantles over some of Auden's most damaging and persistent critics. Summers ends his entry with the aptest lines anyone wrote about Auden after his death, these from Richard Howard's elegy:

> After you, because of you,
> all songs are possible.

There is not a poet writing in the English-speaking world that does not owe Auden something, usually a vital debt.

I imagine in another generation aspects of this book will look quaint, especially as it tries to map the current terrain. The future may look back and wonder why Robert Lowell had become only one of a number of poets treated in the entry on Confessional Poetry and why Elizabeth Bishop had to share an entry with Marianne Moore. It may look back and wonder why a unique master like Louis Simpson is nowhere mentioned. He actually would have provided an excellent contrast to Merrill or Ashbery, Levine or Wright. And when the future does look back, perhaps it will see an edition in which the numerous typos and misspellings are corrected and the index is adjusted for accuracy. Meanwhile, we can be grateful for this history which tries to reveal more than it conceals, to retrieve and preserve more than it discards and dismisses, before the sands shift again.

17

Solving for X:

The Poetry and Prose of Wallace Stevens

I heard a young literary critic say recently that Edgar Allan Poe was beyond criticism. I'm not sure if she meant that Poe was not worth writing about anymore or if he was beyond reproach. Perhaps, she meant both. And perhaps that is what it means to be canonized, if being included in the Library of America series, as Poe has been, means canonization. The Library of America has also added Wallace Stevens to its pantheon[44]. Does that mean Stevens is beyond criticism? Is the poor opinion of Randall Jarrell about his late work, for example, no longer relevant? There are good reasons for thinking of Stevens as beyond criticism, even as for many contemporary critics of poetry, he remains predominant, "man number one" among the "man-poets," as he called them, of Modernism. Of course, I am aware that the problem with thinking this way, as if the work of any major literary figure were of interest only to literary critics, is limited. Presumably, now that Stevens' poetry, most of his prose, and some of his letters are available in a single volume, he will be more accessible to the general reading public, as he deserves to be. It is clear from reading his collected poetry and prose that among modern American poets his project, though it is hard to describe, is the richest, most sustained, most highly developed, and finally, most relevant to our time or to what his biographer Joan Richardson has called "a century of disbelief." But because his project is hard to describe, the question remains whether or not the bulk of his work is of interest only to literary critics.

Most of the poems for which Stevens is famous come from his first book, *Harmonium*, published in 1923 when he was 44. It reads as freshly and strangely and beautifully today as it must have read then. In *Harmonium* life on earth appears as fantastic as life on another planet. If Stevens had never written another poem, or published another book, he would still be read as the author of "In the Carolinas," "Domination of Black," "The Snow Man," "Le Monocle de Mon Oncle," "Nuances of a Theme by Williams,"

---

[44] *Collected Poetry and Prose*, selected by Frank Kermode and Joan Richardson, The library of America, 1997

"The Comedian as the Letter C," "Valley Candle," "Anecdote of the Prince of Peacocks," "A High-Toned Old Christian Woman," "The Emperor of Ice-Cream," "Disillusionment of Ten O'Clock," "Sunday Morning," "Anecdote of the Jar," "Gubbinal," "To the One of Fictive Music," "Peter Quince at the Clavier," "Thirteen Ways of Looking at a Blackbird," and, though it was added later, "Sea Surface Full of Clouds." I have listed only the poems I believe are best known and most often found in anthologies. For some of these, in that single book, there are other gems of equal worth, and I can imagine another reader's list might include them. It was at the end of his negative review of Stevens' 1950 collection, *The Auroras of Autumn*, that Randall Jarrell made his famous comment about a poet being great if he has been struck by lightning a dozen times. The electrifying poet of *Harmonium* meets that quota.

Whatever it was and is that makes these poems so appealing, a couple of things allow us to look at Stevens' first book with a more retrospective awareness. First, the developing aesthetic project of the subsequent books affects the way we read the longest poem in *Harmonium*, "The Comedian as the Letter C," and some of the others, like "Sunday Morning," of course, but also "Palace of the Babies" and "Architecture." Second, thanks to Stevens' own criticism and to his biographer, we can identify the effects of what he was reading and what he had read. The influence of at least two of Stevens' fellow poets in the Library of America series can be detected in *Harmonium*. The gnomic fables of Stephen Crane's poetry are echoed throughout, from the first poem, "Earthy Anecdote," to the last, "To the Roaring Wind." (Stevens attended Crane's funeral in New York in 1900, the year he turned 21, and admired and briefly tried to emulate Crane's career.) The other poet who echoes through Stevens' work, both early and late, is—you thought I was going to say Walt Whitman. In fact, Stevens had little use for Whitman, except for a couple of marvelous images, most notably in "Like Decorations in a Nigger Cemetery" ("In the far South the sun of autumn is passing / Like Walt Whitman walking along a ruddy shore"). The other American poet we actually hear in Stevens' poetry is Edgar Allan Poe, whose sound effects and tintinnabulation appear in poems throughout Stevens' career, polished to suavity, but still audible in "the turbulent tinges" that "undulate" in "The Bird with the Coppery, Keen Claws," and in the late poem "Of Mere Being," in which a bird's "fire-fangled feathers dangle down." It is not Poe's sound alone which seems to have influenced Stevens, but also his taste for the exotic, the imagined land where he had never been, the very sort of thing that attracted Baudelaire and Mallarmé, who were in turn favorites of Stevens, so that it is possible the younger American imbibed the older American as he was distilled in the French Symbolists.

The Library of America edition allows us to follow the development of Stevens' poetry and his thought, especially his thought. For after *Harmonium*, Stevens' ambition is to work out a very large idea: to find a substitute for the absence punched through heaven by Darwin and Freud. Helen Vendler in her book on Stevens' long poems correctly relates this ambition to his constant aim to write a long poem. Time and again, it seems that either Stevens has succeeded in writing a long poem or he has fallen short. As with the memorable poems in *Harmonium*, we can list the long poems that attempt to work out his great idea. Besides "The Comedian as the Letter C," they include "Owl's Clover," "The Man with the Blue Guitar," "Extracts from Addresses to the Academy of Fine Ideas," "Examination of the Hero in a Time of War," "Chocorua to Its Neighbor," "Esthétique du Mal," "Description Without Place," "Credences of Summer," "Notes Toward a Supreme Fiction," "The Auroras of Autumn," "An Ordinary Evening in New Haven," and "Things of August." Many of the shorter poems that appear with these seem to be corollary or adjunct versions of the longer disquisitions.

Stevens' prose, especially in *The Necessary Angel*, illuminates and confirms, sometimes even clarifies, what he seems to be talking about in his long poems. In "The Noble Rider and the Sound of Words" he informs us that "the soul no longer exists" but that "art sets out to express the human soul" and the poet's role "is to help people live their lives." The consolation the poet offers is imagination, of which art and especially poetry are incarnations. As he says succinctly in his collection of aphorisms, *Adagia*, "After one has abandoned a belief in god, poetry is that essence which takes its place as life's redemption." In his 1949 essay "Imagination as Value" he comes up against the crux of his thought and resolves it in the person of George Santayana, his friend and mentor at Harvard, but at that time living in retirement in a convent in Rome.

> . . . the function of the imagination is so varied that it is not well-defined as it is in arts and letters. In life one hesitates when one speaks of the value of the imagination. Its value in arts and letters is aesthetic. Most men's lives are thrust upon them. The existence of aesthetic value in lives that are forced on those that live them is an improbable sort of thing. There can be lives, never-

theless, which exist by the deliberate choice of those that live them. To use a single illustration: it may be assumed that the life of Professor Santayana is a life in which the function of the imagination has had a function similar to its function in any deliberate work of art or letters. We have only to think of this present phase of it, in which, in his old age, he dwells in the head of the world, in the company of devoted women, in their convent, and in the company of familiar saints, whose presence does so much to make any convent an appropriate refuge for a generous and human philosopher.

Clearly Stevens believed that there need be no choice between perfecting the life or perfecting the work, if one were allowed to treat both as products of the imagination. A mark of his generation of Modernists, perhaps because of their exposure to philosophers like Santayana and William James, was that belief itself, belief in *something*, was imperative.

Stevens' prose constantly sends us back to his poetry, so we can be grateful for the generous selection of it in this volume. The short piece, only three paragraphs long, with which he concludes his 1942 collection *Parts of a World* is one of his most helpful essays, and especially in the following passage:

> The poetry of the work of the imagination constantly illustrates the fundamental and endless struggle with fact. It goes on everywhere, even in the periods that we call peace. . . .Nothing will ever appease this desire except a consciousness of fact as everyone is at least satisfied to have it be.

An echo of William James, another of Stevens' teachers at Harvard, can be heard in the phrase "consciousness of fact," but "the work of the imagination" is purely Stevens. That this work might be endless and unappeasable and yet might ultimately satisfy everyone tells us something about Stevens' poetry after *Harmonium*. It is one long struggle with a non-fact: the existence of God. He must create a theology from scratch, "as if," as he says in "The Rock," "nothingness contained a métier." That theology or philosophy or aesthetic (or all three) must be based on the recognition that between the human eye and reality, myths are constantly imposing their old forms. The imagination has played a part in creating these myths, and it must be trained to strip them away, even while inevitably it creates new ones. As Professor Eucalyptus says in "An Ordinary Evening in New Haven," "'The search / For reality is as momentous as / The search for god.'" Yet the mind reels at these lines from "Credences of Summer."

The physical pine, the metaphysical pine.
Let's see the very thing and nothing else.
Let's see it with the hottest fire of sight.
Burn everything not part of it to ash.

Trace the gold sun about the whitened sky
Without evasion by a single metaphor.

Since language itself is metaphor, these imperatives are impossible to satisfy. Robert Frost believed that the attempt of poetry to say matter in terms of spirit and spirit in terms of matter was a great attempt that ultimately failed, because every metaphor eventually broke down. Frost seemed to be satisfied with that knowledge. Stevens is not, and that is why his poetry after *Harmonium* remains important but hard to read.

By hard to read, I do not mean only difficult, requiring the hermeneutic intelligence of a critic, but I mean hard to *keep* reading. Jarrell said bluntly that Stevens' philosophizing was "monotonous." My own opinion is that reading Stevens after *Harmonium*, especially his long poems, is an acquired taste. And yet, having said that, I can go through the later work and find as many wonderful poems as there are in the first book: "The Idea of Order at Key West," "The American Sublime," "A Postcard from the Volcano," "The Men That Are Falling," "The Man on the Dump," "A Rabbit as King of the Ghosts," "Loneliness in Jersey City," "The Sense of the Sleight-of-Hand Man," "Martial Cadenza," "Of Modern Poetry," "The House Was Quiet and the World Was Calm," "Large Red Man Reading," "An Old Man Asleep," "Final Soliloquy of the Interior Paramour," "The Planet on the Table," and "Of Mere Being." Others will have different lists, but I think most readers would agree that after *Harmonium* Stevens never returned to the wildness and mystery of, say, "Domination of Black" with its peacocks, whose remembered but unstated cry is "Help!" There are no more encounters with the likes of "Berserk" ("Oh, sharp he was / As the sleepless!") and Chieftain Iffucan of Azcan ("Fat! Fat! Fat! Fat! I am the personal."). Even the delectable shorter poems of his later work wear the complexion of his larger endeavor. He always knows what he is after. One way or another, as he tells us in "Mere Being," it is "The palm at the end of the mind, / Beyond the last thought . . ."

That Stevens became enveloped in his philosophy, as surely as Dante was in his cosmology, is a principal reason that we think of him among what are called the High Modernists. Certainly, the poets we place him among, Yeats,

Frost, Eliot, and Pound, all recognized the same problem and all had a plan or vision that tried to resolve it. The way each of their careers ends may reflect the efficacy and validity of their visions. Pound ends in incoherence and apology, Eliot in high church Christianity, and Frost in self-congratulation. But Stevens continues to extend the possibilities. There is nothing in the last poems that makes us sorry, as there is in Frost. We may feel that we have heard it before, but not as if we are reading self-parody. There is a serenity to Stevens' attempts to keep finding variables for the imagination, to keep solving for X. He unfolds the endless pleasure of metaphor, of saying "It is" or "It is like," as if all experience could be found to have endless resemblances ("The weather is like a waiter with a tray"; "The moon follows the sun like a French / Translation of a Russian poet"; "The whole race is a poet that writes down / The eccentric propositions of its fate"), and all the while he keeps the placid equanimity of a photograph of Lake Geneva in the summertime. The serenity of late Stevens has an excellence that equals the passion of late Yeats. And that serenity has a music as unique as we find in any of Stevens' contemporaries. We can hear its cool gravity in the opening lines of "The Rock."

> It is an illusion that we were ever alive,
> Lived in the houses of mothers, arranged ourselves,
> By our own motions in a freedom of air.
>
> Regard the freedom of seventy years ago.
> It is no longer air. The houses still stand,
> Though they are rigid in rigid emptiness.
>
> Even our shadows, their shadows, no longer remain.
> The lives these lived in the mind are at an end.
> They never were . . .

A poet friend of mine recently quoted these lines to one of our teachers, himself one of the masters of the older generation, who responded, "Tell me about it."

The publication of a volume in the Library of America series stimulates a desire to grasp an entire career, to understand the whole work once and for all, while at the same time recognizing that the ultimate value of a literary creation, like Stevens' poetry, will never and should never be understood once and for all. Nevertheless, our responses may differ. Poe may be beyond criticism, but the publication of Robert Frost's work by the Library of America has signaled a reassessment of that great but misunderstood poet. The publication of Stevens' collected poetry and prose, made possible by support from the late James Merrill, is further sign of Stevens' eminence at the end of the century, in no small part as the most pervasive influence on contemporary American poetry. Theodore Roethke was simply stating the facts forty years ago when he imagined young poets singing, in "A Rouse for Stevens," "Wallace Stevens—are we *for* him? / Brother, he's our father!" But he was also being prophetic.

And yet a question remains about Wallace Stevens' own parentage. Even though critics have amply supplied lines of descent, especially from the English Romantics, and his biographer, Joan Richardson, has speculated extensively on the influence of French and German poetry on Stevens, as I read from *Harmonium* through his uncollected poems and compare the imagination of the poetry with the exposition of the prose, I hear the voice of one who may be more predecessor than parent, another American poet whose project most resembles Stevens' attempt to create a new faith in poetry. Gender politics has obscured the lines of descent for now, but there is definitely a link, if not a lineage, between Emily Dickinson and Wallace Stevens. Her epic for the age of disbelief—nearly 1800 poems and innumerable letters—anticipates all the moderns who were Stevens' contemporaries, and her conclusion is most like Stevens' own. Fifty years before the publication of his first book, she wrote:

> Those—dying then,
> Knew where they went—
> They went to God's Right Hand—
> That Hand is amputated now
> And God cannot be found—
>
> The abdication of Belief
> Makes the Behavior small—
> Better an ignis fatuus
> Than no illume at all—

"Better an ignis fatuus / Than no illume at all": these lines could have been plucked right out of *Harmonium*. With them Dickinson not only anticipates Stevens' coinages ("illume"), but his sentiments. He pays her homage, perhaps unwittingly, with the following lines from a late poem, "Final Soliloquy of the Interior Paramour."

We say God and the imagination are one . . .
How high that highest candle lights the dark.

At this remove, their visions do seem much the same, and hers seems even more daring and radical because of when and how it occurred. Recent critical theory sees only daughters for Emily, but Wallace has to look like a son or at least a nephew. Incidentally, she has yet to be included in the Library of America series. It must be about time.

BIOGRAPHICAL NOTE

Mark Jarman is the author of many books of poetry, including *The Black Riviera*, winner of the 1991 Poets' Prize, and *Questions for Ecclesiastes*, winner of the 1998 Lenore Marshall Poetry Prize. He has received fellowships from the National Endowment for the Arts and the John Simon Guggenheim Memorial Foundation. He is Centennial Professor of English, Emeritus, at Vanderbilt University in Nashville, Tennessee.

Printed in the USA
CPSIA information can be obtained
at www.ICGtesting.com
JSHW022329140824
68134JS00019B/1378